BUILDING
EVALUATION
TECHNIQUES

Eval

Centre for Building Performance Research
Victoria University of Wellington

George Baird, John Gray, Nigel Isaacs,
David Kernohan, Graeme McIndoe

Victoria University of Wellington, New Zealand

Building
uation
Techniques

McGraw-Hill

New York San Francisco Washington, D.C. Auckland Bogotá
Caracas Lisbon London Madrid Mexico City Milan
Montreal New Delhi San Juan Singapore
Sydney Tokyo Toronto

Library of Congress Cataloging-in-Publication Data

Building evaluation techniques / Centre for Building Performance Research, Victoria University of Wellington : George Baird...[et at.]
        p.   cm.
Includes bibliographical references.
ISBN 0-07-003308-0
1. Buildings—Performance. I. Baird, George. II. Victoria University of Wellington. Centre for Building Performance Research.
TH453.B864   1995
690'.22—dc20   95-24810
                                                 CIP

McGraw-Hill
    A Division of The McGraw-Hill Companies

1 2 3 4 5 6 7 8 9 0 KGP/KGP 9 0 0 9 8 7 6 5

ISBN 0-07-003308-0

The sponsoring editor of this book was Wendy Lochner, the editing supervisor was Penny Linskey, and the production supervisor was Suzanne Rapcavage. Interior design and composition: Silvers Design.

Reprinted by arrangement with The McGraw-Hill Companies, Inc.

McGraw-Hill books are available at special quantity discounts to use as premiums and sales promotions, or for use in corporate training programs. For more information, please write to the Director of Special Sales, McGraw-Hill, 11 West 19th Street, New York, NY 10011. Or contact your local bookstore.

Contents

Preface

Buildings affect our health, our work, our leisure, our thoughts and emotions, our sense of place and belonging. If buildings work well, they enhance our lives, our communities, and our culture.

Each of us wants the buildings we use to support our individual needs. If organizational objectives are to be met as well, it is vital that we understand how these diverse requirements can be matched to the performance of our buildings. Organizations should be able to design or select the building that best meets their requirements. Building performance evaluation enables this to happen.

The objective of building evaluation is to gain knowledge about our buildings and the way we use them. The challenge for owners, occupants, and building producers is to develop cost-effective techniques that best meet this objective. Following evaluation, the imperative is to learn from and apply the knowledge gained in order to realize the tangible benefits that evaluation can bring. Systematic evaluation works to the benefit of all who use buildings or are otherwise involved in their creation and operation.

The techniques described in this book will help you understand how buildings work and how they can be made to work better. They will assist you to select, develop, or modify buildings so that they satisfy the demands of a competitive and continually changing environment where responsiveness to user needs, productivity, and cost-effectiveness are paramount concerns.

The scope, persuasiveness, and international currency of the ideas in this book, will raise the insight and expectations of building users and help those who supply buildings to be responsive to that demand. The possibility for all of us will be a better environment.

George Baird, John Gray,
Nigel Isaacs, David Kernohan,
Graeme McIndoe
January 1996

Acknowledgments

The genesis of this book was the appropriately named IDEA conference held in Wellington, New Zealand, in October 1985. The acronym stands for "Investment and Design, their Effect on your Assets." Following this gathering, the conference committee funded the production of a Building Evaluation Techniques Resource Guide for Building Users. The task was taken up by the Centre for Building Performance Research (CBPR) based at Victoria University of Wellington. A Resource Guide (Baird, Bruhns, and Kernohan, 1990) was duly disseminated to delegates. Our first thanks, therefore, go to the members of the IDEA 1985 Conference Committee for their foresight and initiative.

Given the limited circulation and scope of the original document, the CBPR team subsequently proposed to develop it for a broader and more international audience. Funding was obtained from the Internal Grants Committee of the Victoria University of Wellington and from the Lottery Grants Board of New Zealand (Te Paori Rota), which enabled us to undertake this development. We are grateful to both these bodies for their support.

Ideas and funding are essential components of a project such as this; gaining the interest of a publisher is another. We are most appreciative of Senior Editor Joel Stein's faith in our concept and McGraw-Hill's support throughout its development and production.

It will be evident already that very many people have had a hand in the creation of Building Evaluation Techniques, and we thank them all. However, we especially acknowledge and applaud our 25 contributors, who not only drafted lucid text but also provided it in time to meet our deadlines. We have worked or corresponded with them over the last decade or more and feel privileged that they not only accepted the invitation to join with us in this endeavor but also embraced the whole concept with enthusiasm. It was heartening to find, even in the current environment of competition and user-pays that the spirit of cooperation and free exchange of information is still very much alive.

We should like to single out Harry Bruhns for special mention. While a research fellow at the CBPR, he made a substantial contribution to the structure and the content of the 1990 Resource Guide on which this book has been based. We are delighted to have his continued contribution.

Last, but by no means least, we have pleasure in recording our tremendous debt of gratitude to all the staff at the Victoria University School of Architecture who have assisted us in this endeavor, with particular thanks to Tania Henare for wordprocessing and David Eyles for graphics.

Authors

George Baird received his engineering education at Glasgow University and the National College for Heating, Ventilating, Refrigeration and Fan Engineering, London. He spent 6 years at the Building Services Research Unit, Glasgow, and then a further 6 at the Scott Sutherland School of Architecture, Aberdeen. He joined the Victoria University of Wellington School of Architecture in 1975, teaching environmental design and establishing a research program on the energy performance of buildings, one of the outcomes of which was *Energy Performance of Buildings* published by CRC Press in 1984. Dr. Baird served as Dean of the Faculty of Architecture from 1986 to 1988, and in 1989 became the foundation director of the Centre for Building Performance Research. He is active in professional circles, being a member of CIBSE, ASHRAE, and IPENZ, and is currently Associate Dean (Research) of the Faculty.

John Gray has practiced architecture in Melbourne and London, specializing in office design and interior architecture. While teaching communication and management at the VUW School of Architecture, he has also maintained links with architectural practice. Following his participation in the design team that won the international ideas competition for the Wellington waterfront, he is now urban design consultant to Lambton Harbour Management, Ltd., who are implementing the outcomes of this competition. In 1990–1991 he spent 14 months at the International Centre for Facilities in Ottawa, where he worked with a small team of consultants to develop serviceability scales for office facilities owned by the Government of Canada. He continues as a senior advisor to the International Centre for Facilities. He provides programming and design services as a consultant to a number of design and management organizations and recently completed a major post-occupancy evaluation for the head office of the New Zealand Ministry of Health. He was a coauthor of *User Participation in Building Design and Management,* published by Butterworth Architecture in 1992.

Nigel Isaacs is a building scientist specializing in the development and application of building assessment methodology. He has degrees in electrical engineering and building science and a diploma in business administration. He has over 16 years of research experience and since 1986 has worked at the School of Architecture developing tools for evaluation and management of building energy use, building codes, and building evaluation. He was a major contributor to the development of the Building Quality Assessment (BQA) methodology for office and, more recently, retail buildings. He has experience within New Zealand in a wide range of commercial buildings, including offices, banks, and schools. During 1989, working with the University of Strathclyde Department of Architecture and Building Science and the Lanarkshire Health Board, he undertook the first major application of the Estatecode methodology to the functional suitability of hospitals. He is also active in education and training, conducting seminars throughout New Zealand in specialist areas. He is the manager of the Centre for Building Performance Research.

David Kernohan is an architect who has been involved with building evaluation for 20 years. He worked with the ABACUS computer unit at the University of Strathclyde on computer-aided building appraisal and while there acted as consultant to the Building Performance Research Unit (BPRU). He then joined the Scottish Health Services Building Division, where he was project architect for a district general hospital and other health building projects. Since 1977 he has lectured at the VUW School of Architecture and is currently Dean of the Faculty. He is a member of the Architecture Research Group (ARG), which has developed a generic method for negotiating design quality using participatory building evaluations, and is coauthor of *User Participation in Building Design and Management* (Butterworth Architecture, 1992), which describes the application of the ARG's generic building evaluation methods. *He is author of Wellington's Old Buildings and Wellington's New Buildings,* which were published by Victoria University Press in 1994 and 1989, respectively.

Graeme McIndoe is an architect and urban designer and lectures at the Victoria University of Wellington School of Architecture. Following completion in 1986 of urban design studies at the Joint Centre for Urban Design, Oxford Polytechnic, he worked on new-build architecture at DEGW London before returning to practice in New Zealand. While gaining experience as designer of a great variety of projects, he was responsible for the design and project delivery of high-rise office buildings and large-scale office interiors for both governmental and corporate clients. Since 1992 he has lectured in architecture and urban design while continuing as principal of his own consultancy practice. His recent work has included authorship of a series of local authority design guides, including guides on multi-unit housing, public space in residential areas, and crime prevention through environmental design.

CBPR may be reached by contacting
Centre for Building Performance Research
Victoria University of Wellington
P.O. Box 600
Wellington, New Zealand
Tel: +64 4 802 6200
Fax: +64 4 802 6204
E-mail: cbpr@vuw.ac.nz

Contributors

Franklin Becker, Ph.D., is a Professor in Facility Planning and Management and Human/Environment Relations in the College of Human Ecology. He is also the Director of the International Workplace Studies Program (IWSP) and coleader of the Industrial Development Research Council (IDRC) CRE 2000 research program. Both research programs focus on the changing workplace and its effects on individuals, organizations, and communities. In particular, the research has looked at new ways of working involving home-based telework, telework centers, nonterritorial offices, and team and collaborative environments. Professor Becker has written a number of books, including *Workspace: Creating Environments in Organizations* and *The Total Workplace: Facilities Management and the Elastic Organization*. A new book coauthored with Fritz Steele is titled *Workplace By Design: Mapping the High Performance Workscape* (Jossey-Bass, 1995).

International Workplace Studies Program
Cornell University
NYS College of Human Ecology
E213 MVR Hall
Ithaca, NY 14853
USA
Telephone: +1 607 255-3145
Fax: +1 607 225-3542

Harry Bruhns joined the Open University in 1990, where he began working on the development of a national database of the nondomestic building stock, designed to aid energy research and policy development in the United Kingdom. Previous to that he worked in New Zealand at the School of Architecture, Victoria University of Wellington, in a variety of research areas encompassing commercial and institutional building energy use, database development, and building performance analysis.

Centre for Configurational Studies
Faculty of Technology
The Open University
Walton Hall
Milton Keynes
MK7 6AA
United Kingdom
Telephone: +44 908 653-554
Fax: +44 908 654-052

Gerald Davis, F.A.S.M., C.F.M., A.I.A., is President/CEO of the International Centre for Facilities and President of TEAG-GEHM, Inc., and TEAG, Inc. (The Environmental Analysis Group). Davis is Chair of the ASTM Subcommittee E06.25 on Whole Buildings and Facilities, Second Vice Chairman of the ASTM Committee E6 on Performance of Buildings, USA voting delegate to ISO Technical Committee 59 on Building Construction and to its Subcommittee 3 on Functional/User Requirements and Performance in Building Construction, and Chair of the IFMA

Standards Committee. Davis is an internationally recognized expert and teacher in user needs analysis and strategic planning, facility programming, evaluation, and standards. He is one of the pioneers in this field, having founded TEAG—the Environmental Analysis Group—in 1965 and the International Centre for Facilities (ICF) in 1987. Throughout his career, Davis has been an advocate for and leader in analyzing and specifying the needs of building occupants and other stakeholders.

International Centre for Facilities
440 Laurier Avenue West 200, Ottawa, Ontario, Canada K1R 7X6
Telephone: +1 613 727-1788
Fax: +1 613 723-9167

Hans de Jonge is a Professor of Real Estate and Development at Delft University of Technology, a position held since 1991, and is currently on the executive board of a major consultancy firm in the Netherlands. This follows his nearly 10 years at the Rijksgebouwendienst, the public agency responsible for all central government buildings in the Netherlands comprising a portfolio of some 4500 buildings with 6 million square meters gross of floor area. From 1987 to 1995 he was Director for Research and Development at the Rijksgebouwendienst, responsible for a program that covered topics such as property and facility management, building economics, quality assurance, building physics, environmental issues, and post-occupancy evaluation. In addition to consultancy activity, he has published and lectured on various research topics in Europe, North America, and Asia.

Delft University of Technology
Postbus 5043
2600 GA Delft
The Netherlands
Telephone: +31 15 784-159
Fax: +31 15 783-171

Michael Donn is a Senior Lecturer in the School of Architecture at Victoria University. He has been involved in building science research for 18 years. He has authored over 70 papers and has coauthored three books, one on energy performance and two on solar design. For 10 years he has been on the IEA Solar Program Executive Committee. His particular interest is in the interface between building environmental systems and their users and improvement of the application of scientific information in design. In his consulting activities, he has had a major influence on the aerodynamics of the City of Wellington, assisting in the writing of the ordinances for pedestrian safety and comfort and auditing wind reports for the council. He has also worked in the energy analysis team for an award winning low energy commercial building.

School of Architecture
Victoria University of Wellington
PO Box 600
Wellington
New Zealand
Telephone: +64 4 802-6221
Fax: +64 4 802-6204

Dr. Francis Duffy is immediate past President of the Royal Insti-tute of British Architects (RIBA) and Chairman of DEGW, the leading European designers of the working environment, with offices in Amersfoort, Berlin, Glasgow, London, Madrid, Milan, and Paris. His architectural education was in London at the Architectural Association and in the United States at Berkeley and Princeton. Dr. Duffy is the author of The *Orbit* studies, of *Planning Office Space, The Changing City,* and *The Changing Workplace.* His latest book on the futures of office work and office design is *The Responsible Workplace.*

DEGW International Limited
Porters North
8 Crinan Street
London N1 9SQ
United Kingdom
Telephone: +44 171 239-7777
Fax: +44 171 278-4125

Jay Farbstein, Ph.D., A.I.A., is President of Jay Farbstein and Associates, San Luis Obispo,

California, specializing in facility programming and postoccupancy evaluation. Recent projects include large office settings, criminal justice facilities, and post offices. Jay is the author of books on urban planning, correctional facility planning, and behavior in the environment. Jay was educated at Harvard's GSD and the Bartlett School of Architecture in London. He has won three *Progressive Architecture* awards in applied research and twice served on that jury.

Jay Farbstein and Associates, Inc.
1411 Marsh Street, Suite 204
San Luis Obispo, CA 93401-2921
USA
Telephone: +1 805 541-4940
Fax: +1 805 541-0612
E-mail: 74627.2711@CompuServe.Com

Iain Hair, M.B.A., B.A. (hons.), M.H.S.M., Dip., H.S.M., graduated in 1980 (Social Sciences, Sociological Theory) and entered the Scottish National Health Service (NHS) Graduate Management Training Scheme. Subsequent NHS posts provided a wide range of experience in a range of health care environments including acute and long stay hospitals, community and primary care, capital planning and area (560,000 population), strategic planning for acute maternity and primary care services. He has significant experience in health care estate evaluation, capital planning, investment appraisal and estate disposal, and facilities management and recent experience in health care contract monitoring and evaluation and the development of primary care services.

Assistant Director of Planning and Contracts
Lanarkshire Health Board
14 Beckford Street
Hamilton
ML3 OTA
Scotland
Telephone: +44 698 281313
Fax: +44 698 423134

Alan Hedge, Ph.D., is a tenured professor in the Department of Design and Environmental Analysis, Cornell University, where he directs the Human Factors and Ergonomics Program. He conducts research on office design topics, especially indoor air quality, computer workstation ergonomics, and lighting for computerized offices. Recent projects include the effects of indirect and direct lighting on VDT users, effects of breathing-zone filtration technology on office worker comfort, health, and productivity, reactions of facility managers and officer workers to underfloor task-air ventilation, effects of smoking policy on indoor air quality, comfort, and sick building syndrome, and ergonomic designs that protect against repetitive motion disorders. He chairs the Ecological Ergonomics Technical Subcommittee of the International Ergonomics Association, the Work Environment Subcommittee of the Human Factors and Ergonomics Society ANSI/HFES 100 VDT Standard Revision Committee, and the American Standards for Testing and Materials (ASTM) Task Group on the Development of Behavioral Tools for Assessing the Performance of Facilities. He is a founding member of the International Society for Indoor Air Quality and Climate. He was President of the Division of Environmental Psychology of the International Association of Applied Psychology from 1982 to 1986.

Department of Design and Environmental Analysis
Cornell University
NYS College of Human Ecology
MVR Hall
Ithaca, NY 14853-4401
Telephone: +1 607 255-1957
Fax: +1 607 266-0785

Duncan Joiner, B.Arch., Ph.D. (London), was Assistant Government Architect (Design) in the former N.Z. Ministry of Works and Development. He was responsible for the design of a number of major government buildings. His interest in building evaluation and participation in design stems from his doctoral work, which investigated spatial behavior in offices and from his experiences running New Zealand's largest architectural practice. As Chief Architect of the recently formed Works Corporation, his concern was that the organization provided responsive, efficient, and effective design and management services to its clients. He is now the head of the Wellington Polytechnic School of Design.

School of Design
Wellington Polytechnic
Private Box 756
Wellington
New Zealand
Telephone: +64 4 801-5799
Fax: +64 4 801-2799

Min Kantrowitz has had almost 25 years of professional experience in evaluation research. Her experience includes projects for public and private clients, large and small. Min Kantrowitz is President of Min Kantrowitz and Associates, Inc., a multidisciplinary applied research and consulting firm specializing in behavioral aspects of planning and building design. She is a member of the American Institute of Certified Planners. She has received three applied research awards from *Progressive Architecture* magazine.

Min Kantrowitz and Associates, Inc.
P.O. Box 792
Albuquerque, NM 87103
USA
Telephone: +1 505 842-5660
Fax: +1 505 842-5804
E-mail: MINKANTR@UNM.EDU

Professor Walter M. Kroner serves as distinguished Professor of Architecture at Rensselaer Polytechnic Institute. He has been Director of Rensselaer's Center for Architectural Research from 1977 to 1994. He is also the principal of WMK Associates, a private architectural, planning, and research firm. His major research interests include advanced architectural technologies, intelligent architecture, the relationship between architecture and productivity, and advanced housing systems. Professor Kroner is a member of the American Institute of Architects, the World Futures Studies Federation, and a Trustee of the Intelligent Building Institute Foundation.

School of Architecture
Rennsselaer
Troy, NY 12180
USA
Telephone: +1 518 276-6461
Fax: +1 518 276-2999
E-mail: kronew@rpi.edu

Adrian Leaman B.A., F.R.G.S., F.R.S.A, is Director of Research at the Institute of Advanced Architectural Studies, University of York and Managing Director of Building Use Studies, Ltd. In 1971, following study in social science specializing in spatial analysis and 2 years in the Science Policy Research Unit at the University of Sussex, he joined the RIBA's research unit. At this time he edited the *Journal of Architectural Research* and began teaching and researching at the Bartlett School of Architecture and the Unit for Architectural Studies at University College, London, where he helped to found the Space Syntax research program. With Building Use Studies since 1986 and managing director since 1987, he was appointed Director of Research of the Institute of Advanced Architectural Studies in 1993. He has over 100 publications and is a regular speaker at international conferences. His current research interests are in decision making in building and in the consequences of complexity.

Institute of Advanced Architectural Studies
University of York
90 Boothham York Y03 7DG
United Kingdom
Telephone: +44 1904 671 280
Fax: +44 1904 611 338
email: AL18@YORK.AC.UK

Building Use Studies
42–44 Newman Street
London W1P 3PA
United Kingdom
Telephone: +44 171 580 8848
Fax: +44 171 580 2749

Wolfgang F. E. Preiser is an international building consultant and Professor of Architecture at the University of Cincinnati School of Architecture and

Interior Design. He holds a Ph.D. in man-environment relations from Pennsylvania State University and Masters degrees in Architecture from Virginia Polytechnic Institute and State University and the University of Karlsruhe, Germany. He has accumulated over 20 years of experience in consulting, research, and teaching, with special emphasis on evaluation and programming of environments, health care facilities, design for special populations, and design research in general. He has had visiting lectureships at more than 30 universities in the United States and over 35 universities overseas. Dr. Preiser was cofounder of Architectural Research Consultants, Inc., and Planning Research Institute, Inc., both in Albuquerque, New Mexico. He has edited and written numerous books, including *Post-Occupancy Evaluation, Design Intervention: Toward a More Humane Architecture, Pueblo Style and Regional Architecture, Programming the Built Environment, Building Evaluation, Professional Practice in Facility Programming,* and *Design Review.*

University of Cincinnati
College of Design, Architecture, Art and Planning
Cincinnati, Ohio 45221.0016
USA
Telephone: Office +1 513 556-6743
Messages: +1 513 556-6426
Fax: +1 513 556-3288

Kristen Quinn, M.S., is the research coordinator for the International Workplace Studies Program (IWSP) at Cornell University. The IWSP is an international research consortium studying new workplace strategies, their implementation, and their impact on organizations. She holds a Bachelor of Industrial Engineering and an M.S. in Health Systems Engineering from the Georgia Institute of Technology. She has coauthored various research publications on such topics as workplace strategy implementation, new workplace practices, telework centers, and team environments.

International Workplace Studies Program
Cornell University
NYS College of Human Ecology
E213 MVR Hall
Ithaca, NY 14853
USA
Telephone: +1 607 255-3145
Fax: +1 607 255-3542

Henry Sanoff, A.I.A., is Professor of Architecture in the School of Design at North Carolina State University. He has won numerous awards for his designs, research, and achievements as an educator and several *Progressive Architecture* design awards. He is one of the founders of the Environmental Design Research Association (EDRA) and a recent recipient of a Distinguished Fulbright award to Korea. Mr. Sanoff has directed projects throughout the United States and served as a visiting lecturer at schools all over the world. He is also the author of *Visual Research Methods in Design* and *School Design.*

School of Design
North Carolina State University
Raleigh, NC 27695-7701
USA
Telephone: +1 919 515-2205
Fax: +1 919 515-7330

Robert Shibley and Lynda Schneekloth are partners in the design and management consulting firm, The Caucus Partnership: Consultants on Environmental and Organizational Change, based in Buffalo, New York. The partners have worked over the past two decades on over 22 institutional building evaluation programs in several countries specifically engaging over 200 individual buildings. Their recent book, *Placemaking: The Art and Science of Building Communities,* published by John Wiley and Sons offers a critical analysis of their practice. The partners are currently employed by the State University of New York at Buffalo, New York, where:

Robert G. Shibley, A.I.A., A.I.C.P., is a Professor of Architecture and Planning, a licensed architect, and a certified planner. He is the former Chairman of the Department of Architecture and currently serves as Director of Urban Design. He is a coauthor of the book *Urban Excellence,* published by Van Nostrand

Reinhold, which describes the evaluation of five urban places being considered for the prestigious Rudy Bruner Award for Excellence in the Urban Environment.

Lynda H. Schneekloth, A.S.L.A., is an Associate Professor of Architecture and a Landscape Architect teaching at the State University of New York at Buffalo. She is a coeditor of the book *Changing Places: Remaking Institutional Buildings,* published by White Pine Press, and of the recent *Ordering Space: Types in Architecture and Design,* published by Van Nostrand Reinhold.

University of Buffalo
State University of New York
Department of Architecture
School of Architecture and Planning
112 Hayes Hall
3435 Main Street
Buffalo, NY 14214-3087
Telephone: +1 716 829-3483
Fax: +1 716 829-3256

William Sims, Ph.D., is Professor of Facility Planning and Management and Chairman of the Department of Design and Environmental Analysis at Cornell University. He is a member of the International Workplace Studies Program, the Building and Properties Committee of the Cornell Trustees, the Education and Certification Committees of the International Facility Management Association. Professor Sims, the author of many scholarly and professional publications, has consulted, conducted research, and lectured widely in North America, Europe, and Japan.

Department of Design and Environmental Analysis
Cornell University
Ithaca, NY 14853-4401
USA
Telephone: +1 607 255-1954
Fax: +1 607 255-0305

Donald Sinclair, Sinclair and Naito Architects, has practiced as a principal in an architectural firm for 45 years. With expertise developed, in building science and quality control of construction, he specializes in building condition audits of public buildings. Mr. Sinclair is senior Advisor to the International Centre for Facilities, developing serviceability ratings for office buildings, and ASTM task group chair, standardizing Serviceability ratings of office buildings.

Sinclair and Naito Architects Limited
4212-98 Street
Edmonton, Alberta, Canada T6E 6A1
Telephone: +1 403 463-6207
Fax: +1 403 463-6965

Ms. Jean Anne Stark-Martin is currently Research Architect at Burt Hill Kosar Rittelmann Associates. She is an architectural intern with special expertise in the relationship of architecture to the workplace and productivity. Her research includes productivity studies, analysis of advanced building enclosure technologies, and the design of affordable housing and advanced housing systems.

Burt Hill Kosar Rittelmann Associates
1056 Thomas Jefferson Street, N.W.
Washington, DC 20007-3813
USA
Telephone: +1 202 333-2711
Fax: +1 202 333-3159

Françoise Szigeti is Vice-President, TEAG-GEMH, Inc., and TEAG, Inc. (Environmental Analysis Group), and Vice-President, International Centre for Facilities (ICF). Szigeti is Vice-Chair of the ASTM Subcommittee E06.25 on Whole Buildings and Facilities, Chair of the ISO Technical Committee 59/Subcommittee 2 on Terminology and Harmonization of Language and a member of the IFMA Standards Committee. She is a former member of the boards of EDRA (Environmental Design Research Association) and IAPS (International Association for the Study of People and their surroundings). She joined TEAG in 1970 and has 25 years of experience as a facility programmer, facility analyst, and manager of information resources and technology.

TEAG-The Environmental Analysis Group
440 Laurier Avenue West 200, Ottawa, Ontario,
Canada K1R 7X6
Telephone: +1 613 727-1788
Fax: +1 613 723-9167

Ross Thorne is an Associate Professor in the Department of Architecture at the University of Sydney. His main research interest is environment behavior studies. Since 1970, when with psychologist colleagues he set up an architectural psychology research unit, his research has included studies on recreation activities and facilities and office buildings. Recently, as director of a housing research center he has completed a major and long-term study of attitudes and preferences for housing types.

Department of Architecture
University of Sydney
NSW 2006
Australia
Telephone: +61 2 351-2826
Fax: +61 2 351-3855

Helen Tippett is a Senior Professor in Architecture at Victoria University of Wellington, New Zealand, with a concurrent appointment at Deakin University, Australia. Her teaching and research in both universities is focused on management education for the building professions to improve not only the process of producing architecture but the performance of the product. After 15 years in practice as an architect and project manager in Australia and the Middle East, she began her career as an educationalist in 1970 at Melbourne University. In New Zealand her research on the economic impact of building regulations led to reforms and a performance-based national building code in 1992. President of the N.Z. Institute of Architects 1989–1990, she is active in professional development education in both countries and has received a number of industry awards and national honors for service to architecture and the building industry.

School of Architecture
Victoria University of Wellington
PO Box 600, Wellington, New Zealand
Telephone: +61 4 802-6230
Fax: +64 4 802-6204
E-mail: tippett@vuw.ac.nz or
tippett@deakin.edu.au

Professor Thomas R. Willemain is Associate Professor, Department of Decisions Sciences and Engineering Systems, Rensselaer Polytechnic Institute. He received the B.S.E. from Princeton University and the S.M. and Ph.D. from Massachusetts Institute of Technology. His research focuses on time-series analysis and modeling. He is a member of the American Statistical Association, the International Institute of Forecasters, and the Institute for Operations Research and the Management Sciences.

Department of Decision Sciences and Engineering Systems
Cll 5207
Rensselaer
Troy, NY 12180
USA
Telephone: +1 518 276-6622
Fax: +1 518 276-8227
E-mail: willet@rpi.edu

Introduction

Building evaluation is the systematic assessment of building performance relative to defined objectives and requirements. The assessment process is a means of getting buildings right for the people who own, manage, and occupy them. In a world characterized by intense commercial competition, rapidly developing information technology, changing user expectations, and increasing need for ecologic sustainability, it is critical that we individually and collectively make the right decisions about our buildings. Building evaluation allows us to do just that.

A well-conceived and well-directed evaluation program can be extraordinarily effective in delivering real benefits to building owners, managers, and occupants. These benefits can be as significant and diverse as

- Better matching of demand and supply
- Improved productivity within the workplace
- Minimization of occupancy costs
- Increased user satisfaction
- Certainty of management and design decision making
- Higher returns on investment in buildings and people

Building evaluation is well established as a concept. Most of the techniques described in this book have reached their current level of sophistication through a process of development and refinement over the last two decades. The main opportunity for further innovation lies in their application. Through evalua-

tion, people get commercial, organizational, operational, and design intelligence and make confident, successful decisions about buildings and operations within buildings. Few, if any, other tools offer such potential for radical improvement in the way we manage, design, and use individual buildings.

Evaluation Success Stories

A few examples will indicate some of the benefits of evaluation:

- Due to restructuring, a national bank was left with half its regional headquarters building empty. In a soft market, the bank was worried that it would be unable to find tenants willing to lease this prestigious space at a high enough rent. The Serviceability Tools and Methods (STM) scales were used to rate the building, and to compare its serviceability profile to the requirement profiles of potential tenants. It soon became obvious that there were indeed office users in that locality with a matching profile of requirements. Once the market niche was identified, it was easy for a broker to approach prospective tenants, using the serviceability profile to demonstrate how the space would meet their requirements. The space was rented very quickly.
- The installation of Environmentally Responsive Workstations (ERWs) in a large corporate office

provided the opportunity to measure the extent to which individual control over environmental conditions affected worker productivity, absenteeism, and response to environmental qualities. The evaluation established a positive link between office productivity and aspects of design. Specifically, it was found that ERWs with individual controls led to increased worker productivity. After adjusting for other variables, a 3 percent increase in productivity was achieved, representing a major gain for a company with a payroll of $10 million annually. The company reported that their investment in the new system was paid back within 2 years, and the number of occupants satisfied with their workplace rose nearly sixfold to in excess of 75 percent.

- Architects designing a new city library engaged an energy research group to provide design analysis services. A study of local weather data and of heating, lighting, and ventilation needs challenged client perceptions and design assumptions. Opening windows were selected in preference to air conditioning after it was shown that the risk of overheating was slight compared with the benefit of individual control over air quality. The reductions in system cost were used mostly to provide additional features such as clerestory windows and an internal courtyard that enhanced both natural ventilation and lighting. In addition to significant immediate capital cost savings and what was recognized by occupants as an improved environment, the building won a national energy efficiency award for its low energy use and low operating costs.

- Recognizing that the quality of student life and the quality of education are directly affected by the quality of the school environment, a participatory process was chosen for the design of an elementary school. The school was to be responsive to variations in styles and types of learning, accommodate the learning objectives and aspirations of users, and meet the requirements of the funding government department. A process involving walkthrough evaluations of the existing building, interviews, and workshops, followed by post-occupancy evaluations, resulted in a building that met objectives and has been received with enthusiasm by all involved,

including the funding authority. The participatory process enabled people to understand decision making and become aware of the opportunities and constraints in the use of their buildings. The sense of "ownership" arising from participation has had positive and far-reaching social effects.

- A health service provider had a portfolio of diverse hospital buildings. It was faced with the difficult task of making decisions about the management of facilities for which it lacked data and a systematic framework of analysis. An audit was carried out, focusing on functional suitability. This provided an overview of the facilities' capabilities in this specific area. On the basis of the comprehensive and objective information obtained, informed management decisions were made and justified. A program of site development and sale was put in place, with full confidence that it would meet organizational and operational requirements.

- A major institutional property investor carried out a Building Quality Assessment (BQA) on a building in its portfolio that was untenanted and failing to meet investment expectations. The BQA revealed building services and energy efficiency as two areas where the building quality was substantially below that of its competitors. These areas were addressed by substantial refurbishment work. The outcome was that the quality of the building came to meet the expectations of its target market, and building operating costs were substantially reduced. The work undertaken had a payback period of a small fraction of the life of the refurbishment, and the building became fully tenanted.

These examples illustrate some of the significant benefits of evaluation that may be gained by specific groups or institutions. But what, if any, are the wider benefits that evaluation can bring? Why is acquiring and sharing knowledge about building performance of fundamental importance?

Investment in Building

Buildings are a significant investment in the economy of any country. In the United States, for example, the current building stock represents around a quarter of the national corporate balance sheet. Over recent decades it is typical for a developed country to have spent around 10 percent of GDP per annum on building. About half this is non-residential construction, the majority of which is office building. The evidence suggests that a similar proportion of the resources in the commercial sector as a whole goes into building. Effectively, some 5 to 10 percent of the operating costs of the commercial sector can be attributed to the procurement, leasing, and operation of buildings.

The value of this substantial global investment in built resources underscores the importance of informed decision making about its utilization and control. But investment value alone does not adequately indicate the enormous influence that buildings have on us. As large as the capital and ongoing rental and maintenance investments in buildings may be, they do not reflect the enormous investment by organizations in the people who use buildings. A measure used to compare major costs over the lifetime of a building is the 1:10:100 rule. That is, operating costs (energy, maintenance, and taxes) are approximately one-tenth the total combined capital and rental costs of a building, which are in turn one-tenth the total salaries paid to employees over the life of that building.

The People Cost

Salary is the single major cost associated with commercial buildings. Over the life of a building, salaries outweigh rent or purchase costs and far outweigh energy and maintenance costs. There is growing evidence of a significant connection between job performance and various physical attributes of the workplace. The costs to organizations are considerable if employees are performing below their full potential because their workplace does not fully meet their needs.

Buildings are the settings for people's lives, and while many of the costs of a user-environment mismatch may be intangible, the financial implications of the salary bill are real. This is a compelling reason for finding out more about the performance of buildings.

Is There a Knowledge Gap?

How can performance be measured, and in whose terms? Our knowledge about how buildings respond to corporate, organizational and individual goals is sadly (and we believe expensively) lacking. There is a dearth of information on these matters. Even among professional building managers, conventional practice rarely includes the systematic performance evaluation of previous designs. Buildings are usually created for short-term gain without clearly defined medium- or long-term goals.

Sufficient consideration is rarely given to the life-cycle costs of maintaining and operating buildings, the benefits of adaptability, and the means of coping with growth and change. Rarely is there adequate consultation with tenants, users, and occupiers, either before a building is designed or during its lifetime. The process of building, as presently structured, takes little account of the full costs and, in focusing primarily on the supply of buildings, does not take advantage of the substantial benefits that understanding and catering for occupier demand can offer.

This is why building performance, in the broadest sense, should be of great concern to the building industry and all its clients.

Better Building Performance

The aim of this book is to assist people to achieve better building performance. It is written for building industry clients: all those who work in or otherwise have an interest in improving the performance of buildings, including investors, owners, tenants, managers, and the building occupiers and users themselves. Ultimately, it is the latter who set the standard of performance, whether concerned with briefing for new accommodations, selecting from among alternative designs, choosing between existing buildings, or specifying fit-out or refurbishment.

Scope

This book deals with all aspects of effective building performance evaluation. It presents basic principles and theory, explaining how to design and direct an evaluation to meet specific objectives. It gives guidance on specialist evaluation methods and their application, bringing together the work of leading theorists and practitioners to summarize international thinking on building performance evaluation. It provides evaluation resource data to assist in the planning of evaluations and in the selection of techniques. It gives an example in checklist form of a practical, conceptually simple framework for performance evaluation. Comprehensive references to additional relevant information complete the picture.

The techniques described here focus on office building and the workplace but are generally applicable to all building and facility types. In any event, the principles of evaluation have universal application, and the best results are likely when an evaluation process is designed to focus on specific objectives in a unique situation. We show here how this may be done.

This book has been structured in three parts, considering evaluation processes, practices, and resources in turn. Part 1, "Evaluation Processes," explores the practical and theoretical issues of planning and undertaking evaluations. Recognizing that an effective evaluation is tailored to the specific demands of each particular situation, this part of the book focuses on refining the approach to evaluation and provides guidance on designing and managing evaluations.

Part 2, "Evaluation Practices," is a sample of the success stories as told by expert evaluation practitioners from around the world. Each contributor describes a key evaluation procedure or technique and its application in practice. These demonstrate the benefits that result from evaluation and establish its universal applicability. At the same time as giving detailed guidance on a specific technique, these contributions place evaluation in context, giving the flavor of what is involved in their practical application.

The final part of this book, "Evaluation Resources," is a reference source of detailed information. It begins with the "CBPR Checklist," which provides a framework for comprehensive building evaluation. While designed for office buildings, this checklist nevertheless provides the base structure for more generalized applications. The "CBPR List of Techniques" that follows is a resource of around 120 concepts, tools, and techniques that may be used in evaluation. "Definitions" are included to clarify the language of evaluation. A "Bibliography" and list of "contributors" complete this section.

Taken separately or together, the three parts of this book represent a comprehensive resource that we believe will inspire everyone involved with buildings to grasp the opportunies that evaluation offers and to reap the benefits of better building performance that will certainly follow.

BUILDING
EVALUATION
TECHNIQUES

evaluation processes

CHAPTER 1

How to Plan and Conduct Evaluations

John Gray and George Baird
VUW Centre for Building Performance Research, New Zealand

There are many ways to plan and conduct a building evaluation. The examples discussed in this book reveal a world of possibilities for using evaluation as a tool in the pursuit of both better buildings and more workable relations between building users and providers. The diversity of methods that is revealed in the work of the contributing authors is a consequence of the complexity of modern buildings and the unique requirements of different user groups. Buildings, organizations, and the relationships between the organizations and the buildings they inhabit are increasingly complex and increasingly subject to change. Among the qualities that distinguish a good building from a bad one is the good building's capability to provide for different demands by owner and occupant groups and to respond quickly to the changing demands of its occupants and owners. These complexities, and the many permutations of demand and supply that can occur between users and buildings, help explain the profusion of techniques that have been invented to evaluate buildings.

People ask, "How do we do an evaluation?" Often, behind this question is the presumption that there is a single or "best" way to do an evaluation. We caution against the view that there is, or should be, a single formula for evaluation. This would be like saying that there is a single best way to cook a meal. Each manager (or cook) may have a preferred way, but this is not the same as saying there is a best way or an only way. Since we cannot know the spe-

cific circumstances and context in which you and your organization operate, we cannot nominate a best or most appropriate way to evaluate your buildings or facilities. Instead, we can be your partners in finding or developing an evaluation process that best serves your specific needs.

We start this chapter with a generic process (or universal recipe) for building evaluation, distinguishing the main roles, phases, and tasks in that process. Then we discuss basic strategies that have been adopted regularly in practice to assist you in selecting or devising a framework (at the broadest level you will need) for the more detailed planning that follows. Next, we go to the most detailed level of discussion in this chapter, posing a series of questions that focus on the main options and critical choices that typically you would face in planning, conducting, and using an evaluation. Through all this advice and discussion, our aim is to enable you to plan and manage an evaluation. Alternatively, if your choice is to call on outside experts to help plan and conduct your evaluation, our aim is to help you specify what you want to achieve through the evaluation and arm you with ideas and information needed for a fruitful collaboration with experts.

Roles in an Evaluation Process

In any evaluation process (as with all social processes), we can distinguish two fundamental roles for the people involved: *managing* what is to be done and *doing* what is to be done. Broadly speaking, managing an evaluation means deciding what is to be done, setting up the conditions for doing it, and then making sure that it is done. When people talk of "doing an evaluation," they often mean, loosely, all the activities from inception to completion, including the management functions. More rigorously speaking, however, the "doing" role in a building evaluation involves executing tasks that ultimately produce new knowledge about a specific building or new knowledge about some general aspect of all or most buildings of a certain type.

A typical sequence of "doing" activities includes collecting data, analyzing the data to make sense of them, deriving new knowledge from the information gained, and presenting the new knowledge as output that enables people to take appropriate action. Another possible "doing" sequence (motivated more by socially oriented concerns than the product-oriented approach just mentioned) is to gather different bodies of opinion about a facility, identify issues that show up, and facilitate a process of negotiation to reach consensus on what to do about the issues identified.

The key role of management underpins the whole process of evaluation, whatever motivation may have prompted it and however it is executed. This chapter, and indeed this book as a whole, is intended for people who take on (or are assigned) responsibility for managing evaluations. We recognize that there will be occasions when the distinction between managing and doing is somewhat blurred, particularly when an individual or group accepts responsibility for both.

Thus far we have discussed roles in terms of *types of jobs to be done,* leaving open to question the *types of people for the job.* This is a very important issue because at any point in the evaluation process where judgment is called for (and there are many, even in the most systematic and rigorous evaluation programs), each person's past (experience, training, point of view, etc.) and present circumstances are a frame through which everything becomes an interpretation to some degree, ultimately influencing the conclusions reached in an evaluation. To take a very

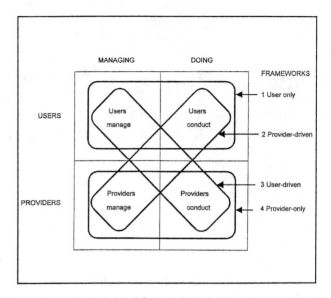

Figure 1.1 Four role-based frameworks for building evaluation.

simple example, a person asked to assess the quality of a meal will interpret the same criterion, say, quality of presentation, differently depending on whether he or she is replete, mildly hungry, very hungry, or actually starving. And in any one of these circumstances, the cook is likely to provide yet another interpretation of presentation quality. In plain language, the answer you get depends on who you ask.

In the building industry, we can identify many types of people (or groups) with a specific interest in buildings, including owners, occupants, professional designers, real estate agents, manufacturers, builders, and so on. However, at the broadest level of classification, we distinguish two types of people: *providers* of buildings and *users.* Figure 1.1 displays these two "work life" roles and two evaluation roles. Since it is assumed that managing and doing are indispensable evaluation roles, there are four possible role-based structures for the design of an evaluation:

1. *User-only evaluation,* in which user groups manage and do the evaluation, e.g., for operational reasons, or to develop more effective use of buildings, or to determine requirements for future construction or leasing.

2. *Provider-driven evaluation,* in which providers plan and manage the evaluation and draw on user

Phase	Task	Role
		managing . . . . . . doing
INITIATE	- Receive or make a request	managing . . . .
	- Identify purpose and motivation	managing . . . .
	- Authorize the evaluation, subject to plan	managing . . . .
PLAN	- Identify the key problem, issue or question	managing . . . .
	- Identify the key opportunity or benefit	managing . . . .
	- Identify main sources and kinds of knowledge	managing and doing
	- Decide who will take part in the evaluation	managing and doing
	- Decide on the scope of the enquiry	managing and doing
	- Decide on the method/process of enquiry	managing and doing
	- Identify any constraints of time and cost	managing . . . .
	- Organize resources to execute and use	managing and doing
	- Approve the plan, and direct next operations	managing . . . .
EXECUTE	- Select appropriate techniques and tools	managing and doing
	- Gather and analyze data	. . . . doing
	- Extract information and new knowledge	. . . . doing
	- Check validity, reliability and workability	managing and doing
	- Add, redo, or rework if necessary	. . . . doing
	- Arrange to communicate the results	managing and doing
USE	- Discuss the results, especially any issues	managing and doing
	- Negotiate meaning and actions as needed	managing . . . .
	- Decide and authorize appropriate action	managing . . . .

Figure 1.2 Basic phases, tasks, and roles in building evaluation.

knowledge and experience, e.g., to test the acceptance and usability of a technical solution or product.

3. *User-driven evaluation,* in which users plan and manage the evaluation and employ provider groups as experts to conduct the evaluation, e.g., to fix physical deficiencies in the building that are affecting its use or the health and well-being of occupants.

4. *Provider-only evaluation,* in which provider groups manage and do the evaluation, e.g., for technical reasons, or to develop more efficient processes, or as a part of "basic" research in a research institution.

Basic Phases and Tasks in an Evaluation

We distinguish four phases in building evaluation: *initiate, plan, execute,* and *use* the evaluation. Figure 1.2 displays these four phases and the main tasks associated with each, plus the likely allocation of tasks between people, whether with a "managing" or "doing" role or on a joint basis.

Alternative Strategies in Building Evaluation

Inevitably, it is necessary to plan each evaluation, because each context for an evaluation is unique. No two organizations and no two buildings are precisely the same. One useful way to view the process of planning an evaluation is to see it as an enquiry into the match between people and the buildings they use. Obviously, the opportunities (or problems) in matching buildings and people are potentially very numerous. As a consequence, there are potentially many permutations for the detailed planning of an evaluation. For simplicity, we can identify two broad approaches: *empirical* and *theoretical*.

Some managers, particularly those with experience in facility management or a similar field, prefer to use an empirical approach to planning an evaluation. A workable way to do this is to scan the examples in this book and adapt one or more that seem applicable. Our experience of such empirical planning suggests that it is useful to conduct a trial or test evaluation to start with, developing what works and reworking or discarding what does not work so well in practice. For example, some facility managers experiment for a while with evaluation methods before they create winning formulas that suit a particular organization or work well in a particular set of circumstances. Similarly, most practitioners who offer evaluation services regularly use one or a few particular methods and adapt them to suit the particular needs of different client groups. Some corporations and companies have tailored to their own needs a program of evaluations designed to routinely provide answers to recurring questions such as "How do the buildings in our portfolio compare with others available in the market?"

An equally sure-footed, but different, way to plan an evaluation is to work from first principles. This approach starts from a theoretical framework and proceeds along traditional scientific lines, or at least

adopts a method that is rigorous, systematic, and stands up to tests of validity and reliability.

Both approaches, empirical and theoretical, have their distinct advantages and both are legitimate ways to work, but it is not necessary or essential to choose between them. Our point is that there is at least one middle ground in which ideas, views, and actions take shape in language that shifts back and forth between theory and practice. This is close to what Bob Shibley and Lynda Schneekloth refer to as "dialogic practice." (See Chap. 2 for an outline. For more depth on this topic, refer Schneekloth and Shibley, 1990). In this chapter we head for the middle ground between theory and empiricism, focusing on the theoretical underpinnings of evaluation work while being orientated toward the practice of evaluation. Our intention is to give guidance on how to plan an evaluation that is soundly based on established theories of management and evaluation *and* offers direct, pragmatic advice.

Another strategic dimension to consider in planning an evaluation is the extent to which the knowledge gained from the evaluation can be generalized. The distinction here is between "This we take to be true for all office buildings" and "This we take to be true for this specific office building in these specific circumstances." Again, in Chap. 2, Shibley and Schneekloth make a similar distinction, referring to motivations for evaluation as either "internal" or "external" to the organization doing the evaluation. An internal evaluation is characterized by a desire to have the answers *now* as distinct from *later* to assist with decisions that are context-specific and have to be reached quickly, say, in hours or days. External evaluation is directed to knowledge that can be applied generally to many buildings and assists with decisions about buildings other than those used to derive the knowledge. As with empirical and theoretical thinking, there is a middle ground possible between internal and external, in which the information from an evaluation provides for both dimensions.

If we consider the *internal-external* and *empirical-theoretical* dimensions together (Fig. 1.3), it is possible to conceptualize up to nine strategies for evaluation of buildings. For example, at one extreme we have

	INTERNAL = Immediate answers Context specific Inside the organization	HYBRID = Some of both	EXTERNAL = Generalized knowledge Widely applicable Outside the organization
EMPIRICAL = Experiential knowledge Trial and error	'Works for us' 'Quick and dirty' 'Here and now' 'Try it and see'	'Our experience, and some others experience'	'Works for most/all' 'Different groups, same experience' 'Generally understood'
DIALOGICAL = Moving between empirical and theoretical	'What works and is true for our group, supported by our experience and internal research'	' What we and others have found from experience, compared with theories derived by us and some others'	'Widespread experience of different groups, compared with widely held theory'
THEORETICAL = Systematized knowledge, Logically deduced	'True for us' 'Our data, our analysis' 'What the theory says for situations like ours'	'Our theoretical knowledge, and some others theoretical knowledge'	' Scientifically rigorous' 'True for many/most/all' 'Now, and in the future' 'Externally reliable and valid'

Figure 1.3 A framework of evaluation strategies.

"quick and dirty" evaluations, and at the other we have "rigorous basic research." This framework provides a broad perspective on some workable strategic options in evaluation work. Obviously, the conduct of the work necessarily differs, appropriate to each strategy. Next, we take a closer look at detailed aspects of evaluation work.

Key Questions in the Detailed Planning of an Evaluation

The latter part of the chapter is structured as a set of questions and a further set of issues/options that need to be addressed in planning and managing an evaluation.

We begin with the questions. The idea behind posing questions (and issues/options) is that they are a convenient and natural way to enquire into the details that must be thought about before an evaluation plan can be finalized. We also use the list of questions as a suitable structure within which to provide further advice. If you are working in a team, the questions and options will provide a convenient agenda for your planning meetings. The questions are in a sequence corresponding to the phases and tasks already outlined in Fig. 1.2. We suggest that the questions be used as a basis for planning a specific evaluation or, if required, a program of evaluations. The point is that the *answers* to the questions and the key options that follow *become* your plan.

1. Request

Who initiated the idea for an evaluation or a program of evaluations?

Has there been a request to do an evaluation, and if so, from whom?

Have others (individuals or groups) been enrolled in the possibility of an evaluation?

In most organizations, it is acceptable for anyone to suggest an evaluation, but equally, position and authority can and usually do count for a lot in how readily an idea is accepted by the group. Socially and politically, it is best if there is a broad constituency wanting an evaluation to be done. Another side to this issue is the rule of thumb that says that no evaluation should begin until it has been requested. A request is a sure foundation for ultimate acceptance of the outcomes in any project. Without a request, and in the absence of a broad constituency, an evaluation is likely to be viewed primarily as a fault-finding exercise.

2. Motivation

What is the main motivation behind the request for an evaluation?

What is the purpose of the proposed evaluation or program of evaluations?

Are there any secondary motivations?

Is there any serious conflict or issue with respect to (say) different motivations?

There is an obvious connection between this question and the preceding one. The person or group that initiated the idea of evaluation will have done so for a reason. What is that reason? In general, motivations fall into one of the following categories: fix something that is wrong with the present facility, decide what is to be done or not done with respect to future accommodation, select or choose between two or more facilities or plans for facilities, persuade someone or some group that change is justified, develop new generalized knowledge about a building type, or develop new knowledge of environment/behavior relations.

3. Authorization

Who needs to authorize the evaluation?

Very broadly, what are the main benefits, what are the likely costs, and who pays?

What other information is required for authorization?

Who will plan and manage the evaluation, assuming it goes ahead?

What would be the consequences of not authorizing the evaluation?

Before authorizing an evaluation, it is usual to enquire into the benefits of the evaluation and the costs. Very broadly, the practical benefits may be economic, environmental, functional, social, or a combination of these aspects of a building and its use. The costs, again very broadly, are financial and (possibly) political or social in nature. At this early stage in planning, it is sufficient to answer these questions at the broadest level—they are the triggers for action and form the starting point of the inquiry. It is sufficient to give authority to someone to develop the proposal. The authorization can be made conditional on there being a suitable plan developed.

The person or people who will plan and manage the evaluation (as distinct from the people who provide the information needed; see question 6) should be decided early because they will need to take part in the early planning tasks.

4. Issue

What is the key issue?

What is the main question to be answered?

If there is a problem to be solved, what is it?

An *issue* is any unresolved problem or disagreement. How do issues manifest themselves in buildings? Complaints are one obvious signal of a possible issue, as is a physical breakdown in the building. Less obvious clues that something could be improved with a facility include rising absenteeism, an increasing incidence of minor illnesses, low morale, and evidence of problems with the use of a building, such as corridors that are cluttered with equipment. Behavioral and cultural issues are even more difficult to notice, and when noticed, people tend to attribute a problem anywhere but to the building. For example, in one case from our experience, senior managers in an organization that was experiencing serious disagreement among staff attributed the problem to cultural disharmony. But the problem (or a major part of the problem) was finally tracked down to the location of toilets close to areas regularly used for intensive, full-day meetings—for one cultural minority, the proximity of the toilets was a highly significant negative aspect of the work environment, deeply but subconsciously affecting how they related to everyone else in the work setting. The organization changed the venue for their large meetings, and the disharmony was very substantially reduced.

The question, "What is the problem?" is deceptively simple, requiring considerable discipline to tease out the "real" problem from the apparent problem. For example, a topic of complaint might be "air quality." The issue might be a disagreement between occupants and technical experts—for example, the occupants could be reporting illnesses that they attribute to poor air quality, but the experts are reporting that the system is working to specification. In this situation, many useful questions are possible. For instance, "What is the precise nature of the complaints and illnesses reported, and where, if anywhere, are the complaints concentrated?" is a question string that would lead into one form of inquiry,

with a view to finding and fixing the problem. Another possible question out of the same circumstances is, "How does this air supply rate in relation to other available accommodations?" and this simply accepts that there is a problem of air quality (regardless of who might be "right" or what is "really true"), leading to a very different type of inquiry, and may be resolve in a very different way, such as by moving to new accommodations.

5. Benefits

What are the anticipated benefits?

Who benefits?

How could the benefits be increased and/or accrue to a wider constituency?

Some of the possible benefits of evaluation are outlined in the Introduction to this book and are described in most of the contributions from practice. The more benefits there are, and the more people or groups stand to benefit from the evaluation, the more likely it is that the evaluation will be considered a success and produce action for change and improvement. Therefore, it is a good idea to communicate the intention to conduct an evaluation. Even if people do not actually take part in the evaluation, it helps to have a broad-based understanding that it is to occur and why. People do not like having evaluations "done to" them without warning.

It may be important to ask whether there is any person or group who stands to be harmed or disadvantaged by the evaluation. For example, designers sometimes perceive that an evaluation of a building will reflect badly on them if serious faults are identified and possibly result in legal action. What works well is to identify, from the outset, the situation with respect to blame for faults. Best, in our experience, is a no-blame policy. Incidentally, we have yet to hear of a case where the designers or anyone else has been sued for negligence for faults found in an evaluation *when the people responsible have taken an active part in the evaluation and have supported it from the outset.*

Generally speaking, benefits may include one or more of the following: increased knowledge of a specific facility, increased knowledge generalized for a group of facilities or a type of building, context-specific improvement to a building, political/social healing such as improved relations between users and providers or between tenants and owners, better information on which to base choices between buildings, and improved understanding of organizational requirements for the qualities of building.

6. Sources

What kind or information is needed?

Who has the information needed?

What form is the information in?

These questions focus on the nature of the information that would be needed to adequately address the question or issue (question 4). The point is to make a very direct connection between the question or issue to be addressed and the information that would provide the answers. When the *kind of information* is determined, then the next question can be asked, "Who has the information needed?" It is not essential at this stage to actually name people or other documented sources of information, only to identify the type needed and, broadly, where to find it.

7. Evaluators

Who (specifically) will conduct/manage the evaluation process?

Who (specifically) will take part in the evaluation as information providers?

In answering these questions, it is essential to distinguish between the tasks of *facilitating* the evaluation process and actually *evaluating*. The evaluators' task is to provide fact, opinion, and judgment, measured against a standard of some kind (it may be their own). Evaluators make judgments about the feature or quality being evaluated, whereas facilitators attend to the process and assist the evaluators in their task. Not all evaluation processes include the role of facilitator, but the principle to keep in mind is avoidance of bias and the separation of the tasks of planning and controlling the *process* from the tasks involved in providing *content*.

8. Scope

What is the required scope of the evaluation?

This question has two sides: the *width* of investigation that is needed and the *depth* of information needed. Wide-ranging investigations match the motivation to have a measure of overall performance of an entire facility. Narrow or focused investigations concentrate on only one or a few topics of concern. Depth is synonymous with the amount of detail that is required or how thoroughly or completely something must be done. Thus one requirement of a checklist is that it cover every known thing or aspect that could be covered in the subject of the checklist. Generally, but not always, evaluations are either narrow and deep or broad and relatively shallow in scope. Exploratory evaluations are of the latter kind, aimed at finding whether there is a problem or opportunity in any part or aspect of a facility but not attempting necessarily to find answers to any problems that are identified. If one issue arises, say, problems of wayfinding around the building, then a detailed or focused investigation into that would encompass every known angle of the subject in depth.

9. Method

What process or method will be used?

Method is probably best thought of as "way of working." This distinguishes it from *technique*, which is a broader term for the entire body of procedures and methods of a science (this book is about technique). Method is also distinct from "tools" (question 13).

This entire chapter is devoted to the question of developing an appropriate and workable method (or plan or design) for an evaluation. Within this chapter, the discussion on strategies in evaluation planning is especially significant in developing an appropriate way of working for an evaluation. The task of developing and deciding on a method is probably best thought of as an iterative exercise—start with a possible method, and return to it from time to time as other tasks are addressed and further ideas occur.

10. Constraints

What constraints are there, including time?

Typical constraints are cost, time, and availability of resources. Others, usually more context-specific, may include limitations on access to certain information that is sensitive (such as wages and salaries) or restricted access to part of a facility (for security reasons). Constraints are best discussed in relation to resources (the next question).

The cost of an evaluation will obviously vary depending on its scope and the method of inquiry. Very broadly, the cost is likely to be less than 1 percent of the annual operating costs (assuming that the facility is one that is occupied by salaried people at the density typical of an office building). The question of who pays, first raised when the evaluation is in the initial phase of planning, may be revisited in discussion of the constraints. Many organizations are now adopting the principle that the user pays, i.e., the person who asked for it pays, or the groups that benefit contribute to the costs of the evaluation.

The time taken to do an evaluation also, like cost, varies with the scope and method of investigation. The two aspects of time to consider are elapsed time for the entire event and time actually spent on the evaluation tasks and activity. Some of the more systematized processes such as STM (Sec. 4.4) require less than 1 day for field work and a further few days for preparation and reporting. Other evaluation processes involving a single building may take a little longer but rarely more that a few weeks elapsed time and 3 to 5 days for the core activities. Evaluations involving a sequence of investigations and many buildings obviously take considerably longer, certainly months (e.g., see Sec. 5.3).

11. Resources

What resources are needed, i.e., who and what must be organized?

In traditional economic language, the categories of resources are labor, land (including facilities, materials, and equipment), and capital (time is not, strictly speaking, a resource, although many people think of it as such). Translating the categories into terms more familiar in the field of building, we have *people's labor; materials and equipment, including the building that is the subject of an evaluation; money; and information (from people, documents, and other sources).*

12. Approval

Is the evaluation plan subject to approval? Who will manage the evaluation process from now on?

If the authorization (question 3) is conditional on there being a suitable plan, final approval will be needed before the execution phase begins. A classic test of suitability is to check that the process will result in an outcome that is *valid, reliable,* and *workable.* To be valid, the evaluation must provide answers to the questions or issues that it set out to; to be reliable, the evaluation, if repeated, should provide the same answers or nearly so; and to be workable, the evaluation process and outcomes need to be acceptable to all groups with a legitimate and close interest in the building and be congruent with the political, social, and economic culture of the group or groups for whom the evaluation is done. Workable evaluations are ones that have been requested. It does not work to have evaluations "done" to people against their wishes or without their knowledge. A further test of workability is that the evaluation can be done within the constraints and with the resources allocated to it.

13. Tools

What types of data are to be collected?
What tools and techniques are appropriate (and available)?
What techniques will be used?

By *tools,* we mean instruments that are employed to gather the data that are required (question 14). The CBPR list of techniques (Sec. 3.3) is an excellent catalog of tools for use in evaluations. Obviously, before tools can be selected intelligently to do a job, it is necessary to know the nature of the job. In evaluation work, tools are needed for *making observations* (e.g., taking time-lapse photographs), *asking questions* (e.g., applying a questionnaire), *making physical measurements* (e.g., measuring air temperature), and *analyzing data* (e.g., using a statistical software package).

Evaluation involves assessment against a value measure. For this to occur, four elements have to be present: *a standard or set of standards* (a planned outcome or level of performance against which actual outcome is to be measured), *a unit of measurement* (quantifiable terms such as dollars or units of production or a numeric scale for subjective opinion), *actual measurements* (collection of data for comparison with the standard), and *judgment* (a decision or choice on whether or not deviation is significant).

In practice, there is a major obstacle to satisfying each of these requirements in the evaluation of buildings: There is *no single unit of measurement* that can be applied to all features and qualities of a building or its use. Some attributes are readily measured using standard units of measure such as meters or feet (for length) or degrees Celsius or Fahrenheit (for temperature), but they cannot be compared unless converted to a common unit such as dollar value. Other attributes, such as "building image" or "cleanliness," have no universally accepted unit of measure. In one-dimensional evaluations this is not a serious problem, but it is a problem where the overall performance of a facility is an issue. One way this problem has been tackled is to adopt a numeric scale for all attributes, relying on *relative numbers* for scoring purposes. Examples include STM (Sec. 4.4), BQA (Sec. 4.3), and REN (Sec. 4.5).

14. Data

What data are needed?

Are the collected data valid and reliable?

How will the data be analyzed?

The standard way to review whether there are sufficient data and whether they are of the right kind is to test the data for validity and reliability (as for question 13), and if statistical material is included, it is also normal to test for significance.

15. Knowledge

What information and new knowledge can be extracted from the analysis of data?

This is the point at which answers to the questions should be made clear.

16. Review

Does the information and new knowledge adequately answer the issue or question (question 4)?

If there is any doubt that the information and new knowledge "do the job," it is a good idea to show the results in draft form to the person or group that initiated the evaluation and those who will benefit from it, if different from the initiators.

17. Rework

Do any parts of the evaluation or analysis need to be reworked?

Our experience is that there are occasions when further investigations are worth the added effort to complete an area of information that is "thin" or to clarify an area of uncertainty or to investigate a part in more detail. It is as well to make a program that has the flexibility to provide for the added cost and time needed to rework parts of the evaluation.

18. Communication

How will the results be communicated?

It is usual to prepare a written report, but other inventive and effective ways to communicate the results include posters, video presentations, discussions (see question 19), prototypes, and trial layouts. Possibly the most direct form of communication following an evaluation is physical change to the building. Less obvious, but also effective, is change in organizational behavior in using the building. In these latter two situations, it is advisable to acknowledge the influence of the evaluation on decisions taken by management. It is very important that people who participated in the evaluation are fully aware of the outcomes and the decisions that result. For some, this is the only reward for their efforts.

19. Discussion

How will the outcomes be discussed—what forum?

What are the main outstanding issues for discussion?

Who takes part?

What agenda and particularly what conditions, such as time, expenditure, and extent of action?

In large communities within which an evaluation has just been completed, uncertainty and misunderstandings can occur easily. We have found that discussion of the outcomes is a very simple and effective way to clarify the outcomes and to raise awareness of the benefits achieved by the evaluation.

20. Negotiation

What is there to be negotiated, if anything?

Who takes part, including who will facilitate or lead the negotiation?

Who will authorize action/use?

A building is an interesting phenomenon, because it both *reduces* the differences between people (all of us have an equal right to and equal need for good-quality air) and *emphasizes* the differences between people (in a crowded setting where space has special value, some people use their power to take the pick of places with better air quality). As social processes, building evaluations tend to throw light onto the way a building is used, as well as on how it works. Some evaluation processes create social situations in which people feel free to state their point of view about the building they occupy or otherwise have some involvement with (see, for example, the contributions in Chap. 5 of this book for more about evaluation processes that enable wider participation).

Evaluation frequently requires different groups of building users to come to a consensus on differing and conflicting requirements. The review meeting stages of a general performance assessment can provide a forum in which different requirements are agreeably settled.

21. Action

What action(s) will be authorized

When?

To bring the process of an evaluation to proper completion, appropriate actions must occur to honor whatever commitments were made to participants and contributors of the process. Failure to do this seriously discredits the process and makes it difficult to gain acceptance if the same people are asked to undertake another evaluation.

Issues and Options in the Planning and Management of Building Evaluations

We conclude the chapter by presenting a set of options and issues that we have found to be useful in planning and managing evaluations. These are strategic and operational concepts introduced earlier in the text but now thrown into sharper contrast by being expressed as opposites.

Exploratory level versus focused level evaluation

Exploratory evaluation is a general level of evaluation. It is characterized by an open-ended discussion about what is important about a specific building, what works, and what does not work so well. Those involved in the evaluation listen to and observe what the issues are rather than gather data on predefined issues. A focused evaluation is an in-depth investigation, usually of one or a few topics of special significance. It has the advantage of gathering more precise information that can support more detailed analysis. Generally, exploratory evaluations precede focused ones, and much wasted effort is likely if an exploratory evaluation is approached with the same resources and techniques as a focused one. For example, expensive instrumental monitoring of thermal conditions is wasted if everyone in the building could tell you that wayfinding is the most pressing issue.

Overall performance as a single score versus overall performance as a profile

This is a debate over the aggregation or separation of scores in evaluation systems that utilize scoring methods. It is appealing intellectually to have one number to symbolize the total value of a building, but the argument against this is that the figure hides more than it reveals about the qualities (plural) of the building. The alternative to a single score is a group of scores for different and interesting aspects of the building. This approach can result in a kind of "personality profile" for the building as a whole.

Qualitative focus versus quantitative focus

Where it is available, quantitative information is preferable because it allows a more precise and specific performance evaluation. For example, it is difficult to analyze the durability of a building without detailed maintenance dates, work done, and costs. However, some factors are not amenable or are less appropriate for quantitative analysis (e.g., ambience, suitability of location), and informed judgment is required. A related issue is objectivity versus subjectivity. Qualitative information tends to be subjective, and quantitative information is commonly taken to be objective. But the distinction is never entirely clear-cut. For example, qualitative factors can be introduced into apparently rigorous measurements by both the choice of what is measured (and not measured) and how measurements are interpreted. Ideally, qualitative and subjective information should be complementary and in agreement with quantitative and objective information. We also would urge that if the two forms of knowledge are in disagreement, then the subjective evaluations be listened to.

Expert evaluation versus user evaluation

A key issue is whose judgments should be sought in an evaluation. Of course, there is no single correct answer to such a question, although there is a tendency for people to regard expert opinion as *always* more reliable and correct. Actually, it is surprising how much documentary evidence there is that tells us the opposite—for example, occupants using their senses to guide them about air quality have been known to "pick" problems that experts previously overlooked or denied. Many issues become obvious when the users are prompted to consider them. Our view is that, in general, evaluation is best seen as an interdisciplinary activity. A full building evaluation may require experts, and there is no doubt that technical issues are best addressed by the people best trained to do so—the professional experts. On the other hand, it is worth bearing in mind that for many aspects of a building the true experts are the people who know most about using it—the users.

Concluding Comment

Having reached the end of this long chapter, you are likely to be in one of three positions: (1) you may be convinced that evaluation is an excellent tool and feel ready to start, (2) you may be equally sure that you will never do an evaluation, but more likely, (3) you are somewhat confused and unsure about whether evaluation is worth the effort.

If the latter applies to you, we invite you to consider doing an evaluation despite your doubts. Preparation and full understanding make an excellent foundation, but taken to extreme, they are a recipe for no action at all. We have noticed that people succeed very well who simply decide to try evaluation and start, however haltingly and tentatively. Most, if not all, the expert contributors to this book have experimented at some time with alternative methods or simply worked from a hunch. What none of them did was wait for the perfect method of evaluating in all circumstances. Our final words of advice are "Just do it!"

CHAPTER 2

Evaluation as Placemaking:
Motivations, Methods, and Knowledges

Robert G. Shibley and Lynda H. Schneekloth
Department of Architecture
State University of New York at Buffalo

Knowledge from building evaluation never tells us what to do, regardless of the rigor of the methods employed or any underlying motivation to improve people's lives. For knowledge to have an influence, it must connect with the political and social context in which placemaking decisions are made. In every evaluation, many kinds of knowledge and experience are brought to and disclosed in the specific place under examination. Because the initiating motivations define the scope and methods of inquiry, the usefulness of the resulting knowledge depends less on how "true" it is than on how that knowledge is *translated* and *situated* in a given context. Moreover, it is often necessary to engage in the construction of specific knowledge in each location—a process by which insights emerge from the experiences and perceptions of the people-in-place and from theoretical knowledge that is not simply "applied" but transformed, refuted, and/or expanded.

Using three case studies from our own practice, we explore the dynamics of motivation, methods or the conduct of work, and the relationship of motivation to the concept of knowledge. We suggest that building evaluation is a process that generates and situates knowledge in the context of institutional and individual motivations. These same evaluation processes contribute to the disciplines and professions that build and manage places, as well as to the broad practice of *placemaking* as it is employed by people every day (refer to Schneekloth and Shibley, 1995).

Motivations, Methods, and Knowledges

Organizations and institutions that have sought most actively to gain value from post-occupancy evaluations are those responsible for the construction, management, and maintenance of large building stocks. Institutions such as Public Works Canada and the U.S. Army Corps of Engineers, for example, seek to be more effective and accountable in their activities and share a focus on long-term institutional learning. Other agencies or large institutions that seek evaluations are often concerned with a specific topic, an example being the U.S. Department of Energy with its work on passive and hybrid solar commercial buildings, a program we will cover in some detail in this chapter.

The structure and conduct of a building evaluation will differ depending on how much of the underlying motivations are internal or external to a specific building/organization. In some evaluation processes, a defined site is studied by a large organization with the primary intention of using the knowledge gained later in the construction of other facilities. At other times, the aim is not only to address future construction but also to influence decisions about changes in existing places to improve their functioning. In each of these situations, the impetus to initiate an evaluation process rests *external* to the place of inquiry, and its goal is usually knowledge. This has a significant impact on many aspects of the evaluation process, such as methods of work, topics to be explored, the scope of legitimate knowledge, range of participation, and decisions regarding any changes on site.

When the motivation for an evaluation is primarily *internal,* attention is most often focused on decision making and place learning, including issues such as occupant competence, productivity, and quality of life. For example, the agenda for the School of Architecture at Florida A&M University in Tallahassee, Florida, in the making of their new facility was to use evaluation, including programming, construction, and post-occupancy evaluation, as an educational vehicle (Farbstein et al., 1986). Its focus was the place/organization within the context of a university setting. One of the case studies we will use is a banking institute, which, like the School of Architecture, is concerned with learning as a goal and creating interpersonal and institutional competency in the ongoing management of their facility. When building evaluations are motivated by internal forces, they are often used as an explicit part of an organizational development agenda.

There are also hybrid evaluation processes that balance motivations from both *inside and outside,* and we will present a series of short examples of this situation. Because the motivations for these kinds of post-occupancy evaluations are diverse and complex, the conduct of work and the methods employed are varied and context-specific. However, because they have been undertaken with discipline and rigor, it is possible to generalize the findings, which in turn creates the possibility for others to "situate" them in different contexts.

The *internal, external,* and *hybrid* labels collectively describe a range of motivations for building evaluations for institutions and organizations that inhabit and maintain buildings. Different again are the professional motivations of those who actually *do* the evaluations—people who view building evaluation as a special form of practice in the field of environmental design research. The practice is differentiated from more general forms of research because the results of the work are intended to be used immediately. This use can be internal to the organization/place that is the site of the inquiry, or it can have a much broader area of application such as research into a building

type, e.g., the evaluation of post office buildings throughout the United States (see Sec. 5.3). Building evaluation is often considered to be on the "applied" side of the broad field of person-environment relations, although the scientific methods developed for basic research are often employed.

The practice of building evaluation has its origins in two divergent traditions: advocacy for the users of the environment[1] to improve their quality of life and the systematic pursuit of knowledge about the relationship between people and environments.[2] The methods of achieving these aims have been competing and at times contradictory. Advocacy calls for a method of work that invites participants to draw from their own understanding of what constitutes legitimate knowledge, often seeking to increase the range of participants included in decision making. This form of environmental design and evaluation is often considered a "nice" thing to do, but some critics believe it is outside the legitimate scope of scientific work, which they define as the systematic pursuit of knowledge. It is often argued that the problem with advocacy interventions that have high degrees of participation is one of validity—how do you know something is "true" or replicable if the rules of evidence are not agreed on, as they are in the practice of science?

Scientifically based evaluations tend to be more exclusive, defining very specific rules for what constitutes knowledge, and are often focused on measurable phenomena. As all researchers know, the practice of science is based on a concise way of working and the employment of particular methods that must be rigorously applied and remain uncontaminated by situational factors. Furthermore, science has two domains—the basic and the applied. Building evaluation has been assigned to the applied side, while the basic research that seeks knowledge about building systems and/or human and environment relations is carried out in more controlled settings.

One of our arguments is that the apparent conflict between these two approaches—advocacy or knowledge—is not a necessary condition of the building evaluation process.[3] Our intention is to demonstrate a way of thinking about building evaluation that allows advocacy and knowledge to coexist.

We present three case studies to describe the ways in which client motivations and professional motivations coexist in evaluation processes. These situations are drawn from over 20 institutional building evaluation programs in which we have participated as part of our professional practice. Each situation was different in terms of motivation and the conduct of work. There was, however, a central motivation in each situation that had the dominant influence over methods selection and results analyses. What follows is a description of the cases and some thoughts on the practice of evaluation when situated in the larger framework of making places. We hope to offer insights into how the basic-applied knowledge dichotomy can be avoided and a more postmodern approach[4] to the evaluation process can be embraced.

Three Case Studies

Knowledge as Motivation: The U.S. Department of Energy Passive and Hybrid Solar Commercial Buildings Program

Where generalizable knowledge is the motivation for building evaluation, the result is *methods-driven* evaluation programs structured around the tools available. Evaluators measure what their tools allow them to measure. There is a detached or objective stance toward the client/occupant organization, and data, empirical fact finding, and external expert opinion generally comprise the central part of the evaluation effort. Service to or advocacy for the occupying or owning organizations is a secondary concern and often restricted by demands for scientifically reliable and valid information.

The U.S. Department of Energy's experimental Passive and Hybrid Solar Commercial Buildings Program is a good example of this approach. Nineteen buildings were assessed in the program in three discreet categories: energy performance, economics, and occupancy. *Energy performance* was assessed in a variety of ways to include end-use measurements of specific energy sources consumed, in addition to total consumption statistics. The buildings in the program used 47 percent less energy than

comparative "base case" buildings that were conventionally designed and constructed.[5] An alternative benchmark for the program was the U.S. Department of Energy Building Energy Performance Standards (BEPS), which were idealized standards. BEPS simply assumed that efficient conservation strategies were inherent in the building design and management process. The buildings in the program performed at a level 10 percent better than the BEPS requirements.

Energy monitoring was only one aspect of the evaluation needed to test the desirability of the solar strategies being examined. *Economic analyses* included a tabulation of actual cost data on 13 of the final projects and a comparison with both standard area cost figures available in industry and the actual costs of base case buildings. The results of this analysis revealed that the passive solar buildings did not necessarily cost more to build than conventional construction. Utility costs added further to the discussion of economics. The evaluators drew on four different data sources to compare monthly utility bills. On average, against all four comparative sources, the program buildings showed a 30 percent improvement over projected utility costs for a nonsolar building. In the best building, there was an 80 percent improvement in utility costs.

An analysis of the circumstances of *occupancy* was the third primary area of concern in the building evaluation program. As part of the end-use energy assessment and utility costs evaluation, the evaluation team compared actual use and costs with those uses and costs which were predicted in the design phase of the project. The discrepancies were used as a point of departure in attempting to improve prediction methods, discover design or construction errors, identify unusual climate variations, and document a variety of occupancy factors that could account for the variations.

Of all the reasons for discrepancy between predicted performance and results, it was clear that occupancy factors were the most influential. This assertion resulted from a research design wherein occupants completed a series of questionnaires, an evaluation team conducted on-site inspections, and architects, building managers, and occupants were interviewed.

According to the evaluation team, "Actual occupancy patterns differed significantly from those predicted in most buildings."[6] The team reported that there were several categories of difference between predicted occupant use of the buildings and actual use, such as time, location, and type of activity. Some of the project occupants reported that the popularity of the project led to increasing hours of operation; modifications in the planned use of space led to changes, such as employing storage space or mezzanines as activity space. Increases in population and the unplanned use of space clearly influenced comfort indicators and energy consumption in the buildings. Other variables included changes in building operations. All these occupancy patterns significantly influenced the buildings' ability to meet predicted energy performance targets.

In evaluation processes where the primary motivation is the search for knowledge, the methods of physical measurement, interview, observation, and questionnaire are employed most commonly. An analysis of the methods-driven evaluation approach employed in the Passive and Hybrid Solar Commercial Buildings Program reveals the following:

1. The client for the research was a large agency, the U.S. Department of Energy (DOE), responsible for a single issue (in this case, energy). The motivation for the evaluation program was to gain knowledge relevant to that issue.

2. The results of the evaluation were not directly relevant to specific building owners or managers. There was no action component tied directly to the building sites where the research was performed.

3. The methods employed were based on available and tested scientific procedures. There were relatively few significant contextual constraints on the methods employed.

4. The program was tightly bounded, with a fixed budget and an absolute endpoint past which it did not continue.

5. The program was driven by expertise *outside* the occupant and management structure of the individual buildings being studied. Occupants and managers were research subjects rather than core-searchers.

6. The DOE intended the information derived from the evaluation to be used by general categories of people, e.g., "the research community," "the design professions," "building owners and managers," and so on.

In short, this program was not developed to influence the decisions and actions of any specific place other than the broad general aspiration to influence the "building industry" and the U.S. Department of Energy research programs. There was no intention to increase the competency of the occupants, their management structure, or the specific building owner or officials responsible for any one individual building. While some of these intentions were fulfilled, they were not the primary motivation of the program.

What did occur was directly related to the original motivation and aim of the evaluation intervention, i.e., the testing of assumptions and practices of energy-efficient design in commercial buildings and the acquisition of new insights into the economics, energy performance, and occupancy behavior of this building type. This goal, generated outside the buildings used as the subjects of the research, was achieved, and many things were learned in the process.

What is interesting, in light of this discussion, is that the variable of "occupant behavior" (i.e., how people actually use the building) was the least predictable and most fertile for future inquiry. However, it is reasonable to question whether this form of knowledge-driven enquiry generated outside the subject organizations would be the most useful in either understanding user behavior or creating the conditions where people learn to use the buildings well. These goals demand a very different approach to evaluation, one in which the purposes, methods, and interpretation of results become subject to negotiation with building occupants, managers, and owners.

Competence and place-learning as motivation: The Banking Institute

Competence and place-learning (the development of individual, interpersonal, and institutional competence) are best served by context-driven evaluation processes. This type of evaluation is place-specific and open to the influences of institutional cultures and interpersonal dynamics. Learning-centered evaluations often seek information on what needs to be done and what can be done, working within the institutional contexts and recognizing prevailing assumptions. These evaluation programs tend to emphasize that it is more important for individuals and institutions to be enabled to act and reflect on action than it is to get the right answer to empirical questions or even to employ the academically correct methods. Therefore, the primary purpose of this kind of evaluation is the incremental development of environmental[7] and social competence within a given institution. Better internal organization is an explicit outcome of the improved decision-making ability that evaluation offers. The ongoing efforts of a large banking institution to monitor their facility management process illustrates this approach.

Building evaluation efforts at the Banking Institute are means by which tough choices on alternative courses of action can be negotiated or through which such alternatives merge into a single "preferred" option. These programs are often designed to help ensure staff or occupant commitment to a decision prior to action and to solicit staff reflections on action as it relates to maintenance or future change. In the type of evaluation that originates within an organization, the goal is ongoing inquiry and incremental adjustment rather than the acquisition of abstract general truths. This does not mean, however, that empirical knowledge is not constructed, tested, and used in the making and management of the place. Nor does it imply that knowledge from sources outside the institution, such as expert knowledge, is excluded from the arena for discussion and evaluation. But it does suggest that the knowledge from outside is not given favored status in the evaluation process, nor is it allowed to be coercive or manipulative.

When organizational development and learning are the objective of evaluation programs, it is acceptable to allow political, status, corporate culture, or social motivations. Such variables influence the aims of evaluation, the methods employed, the interpretation of results, and any decisions for change that may occur. Again, the evaluation program becomes the context where these variables can be made explicit and tested against group experience, as well as against knowledge received from external expert sources.

In all, over 30 separate commissions have been awarded to our firm over the 10 years of our work with the Banking Institute. An analysis of these commissions reveals six consistent themes that run throughout:

1. The goals placed more emphasis on facilitating repair rather than on resisting breakage.[8]
2. Each evaluation sought decisions about future actions from those affected by the decisions, not just "input." Occupants were coresearchers able to influence research design and data analysis construction.
3. Each commission had motives that both included and transcended making competent decisions. The work was always about both technical competence of decisions and organizational development.
4. No single methodology was ever established as the accepted procedure across all jobs.
5. The work modified the problem as presented, through the recurrent displays of conflict between an organization's or individual's "theory in use" contrasted with their "espoused theory."[9]
6. The record of previous work helped establish the context for current work.

Evaluation programs with the primary aim of immediate decision making are characterized by a recognition that knowledge is both "out there" to be discovered through science or quasi-scientific methods and is *constructed* by those who must use it to direct action. In the latter case, neither the knowledge nor the action are seen as ends in themselves but are related to a complex set of individual, institutional, and cultural intentions. Yet programs of building evaluation developed in this category do not exclude the methods and structures of knowledge-based evaluations already described. For example, the Banking Institute uses very general tools in diagnosing problems but allows for a great deal of negotiation among those affected in order to set priorities on problems identified. This interplay between the rigor of evaluation method, the rigor of consensual values clarification, and the rigor of accountable action is facilitated by the building evaluation program itself.

Hybrid evaluation processes

The motivations for this type of evaluation process are diverse and can be both external and internal. Therefore, this category of evaluation is not constrained by either service delivery or method. Typically, programs in this category are *issue- or topic-driven,* and promote critical reflection. The methods employed and conduct of the work respond to the predetermined issues or concerns and are adjusted as evaluation progresses, responding to newly discovered issues.

Building evaluation programs that promote critical reflection are particularly useful in enabling trends to be identified or critical insights to be made through the comparison of a large number of building projects. For example, trends in perception, the use of design strategies, project development procedures, and so on can all be observed and critiqued from different perspectives. Evaluation of this kind is also a very useful source of hypotheses that may be tested further in evaluation programs generated by the other motivations already described.

An example of government use of critical reflection of this type is the U.S. Department of Energy's analysis of the Owens Corning Fiberglas Design Awards Program (Shibley and Weaver, 1982). By looking at 10 years of award-winning buildings, cited by juries for their energy efficiency and their innovation in climate responsive architecture, the research team was able to plot trends in technology and design strategy utilization. This, in turn, helped the DOE fine tune its approach to energy systems development research in the future. The investigation, however, went well beyond the analysis of empirical data by looking into the political and economic circumstances that enabled the award-winning buildings to be built. By showing the complex social negotiations behind each project, the research team challenged the DOE's preconceived models of "technology transfer" that had been a basic part of their long-range planning.

Large institutions often create and maintain hybrid programs that involve many different forms of building evaluation. The U.S. Army Corps of Engineers, for example, has employed broadly based building evaluations in the development of design guides, the establishment of quality-of-life standards, the development of user-based programming procedures, and the development of a new generation of military housing. The program of evaluation did not arise from conscious separation of evaluation activity from the mainstream of decision activity. Rather, it was an integral part of each strategic change in their facility procurement and maintenance process. There was no formal post-occupancy evaluation program, yet there was a tremendous amount of building and program evaluation institutionalized as part of the organization's work.[10]

Common characteristics we experienced in the implementation of more hybrid methodologies include

1. The goals often combine motivations of both knowledge and competence/place learning, leaving room for genuinely critical[11] explorations of the results from both approaches.
2. The results of hybrid programs have the capacity to redefine issues internal to organizations while they concurrently identify the limits of external methods.
3. Hybrid methods have the capacity to question what and who should be included in or excluded from the process.
4. There is no "moral high ground" in the employment of hybrid methodologies. They do not favor knowledge over institutional competence but rather establish the conditions under which knowledge goals and aspirations for organizational development are in dialogue.
5. Hybrid methods tend to focus on relationships and context rather than on single issues. By embracing rather than denying paradigm conflicts, hybrid methodologies place as much emphasis on raising questions as they do on resolving them.

Another example of a hybrid evaluation process is the Rudy Bruner Awards Program (RBA). The Bruner Foundation began with the question, "What is urban excellence?" and decided to set up an awards program honoring places considered excellent. Unlike many awards programs, however, they sought to include large constituencies in the evaluation process. An entry requirement was that places/organizations, ranging from cities to single buildings, perform an evaluation process of their own. Thus, although initiated by an outside motivator (the RBA), each participant set in place an internally organized evaluation process that enabled many people to reflect on their own activities and to recognize their own knowledge and experience in placemaking. And at the same time, the Bruner Foundation, by evaluating many acts of urban placemaking, was able to develop general principles and forms of knowledge about the question of urban excellence.

Evaluation as Placemaking[12]

Building evaluation programs are part of a larger practice of placemaking by which people collectively create, transform, maintain, and renovate the places in which they live and work. The role of professional evaluators can be understood as enabling and facilitating others in the various acts of placemaking while offering specific expertise in planning, design, scientific inquiry, representation, construction, maintenance, and destruction. Redefining the professional work of evaluation within the context of the broader practice of placemaking offers some insights into the issues of motivations, methods, and knowledges.

Motivations

If the motivation of evaluation is to enable placemaking, then the practice will focus on *place* and the *people-in-place* as the basic unit—the frame through which any intervention occurs. The people who inhabit and are affected by the particular place therefore need to be an integral part of the processes of evaluation and/or change. Further, if the goal of the process is placemaking, a paramount concern will be *relationships*—the relationships of people with each other and the relationships of people with their place. In order to facilitate relationships, critical placemaking stresses the importance of creating a dialogue wherein groups of people can affirm, interrogate, and construct the knowledge they need to make and maintain their own places.

Methods

By redefining the goal of building evaluation as placemaking, the idea of "method" is transformed to resemble more closely a way of working rather than a set of tools to be applied. We suggest that there is a set of necessary tasks to be engaged in the practice of placemaking.

The first task is to create the opportunity for dialogue about place and placemaking through the development of a relationship among the various groups within the place. This act of opening a *dialogic space* is probably the most important activity of professional placemakers and others who wish to work on the design of places, because it is within this set-aside time that the dialogue of placemaking occurs and decisions are made.

The second task involves the interplay of confirmation and interrogation that occurs in the act of dialogue. *Confirmation* is the activity that looks at the context of work with an appreciative attitude in order to understand what is and what has been taking place. It focuses on the concrete experience of place as it has been made and experienced over time by the various inhabitants. Equally important is the *interrogation* of that context by asking questions about the work in a disciplined and critical manner. The work of interrogation does not suggest "criticism" in the sense of denigration and finding fault. Rather, it seeks the gaps, disruptions, and incongruities that characterize both the material world and the worldviews of participants and brings them into the dialogue.

The third task of the professional placemaker is to facilitate the *framing of action*. The ongoing and iterative acts of confirmation and interrogation reveal the opportunities and constraints for action. These processes direct attention selectively to some aspects of the work that emerge as critical, including decisions about what and who to include in or exclude from the placemaking project.

Knowledges

People living in places know many things about their places, although this knowledge is often unstructured, informal, and hesitant. It is not the kind of knowledge normally given voice in professional arenas and could therefore be called a form of *subjugated* knowledge. A critical practice of placemaking attempts to give legitimacy to subjugated voices and to all forms of knowledge. As such, it does not favor any single interpretation or professional perspective over the dynamics of the whole place. The professional has much to contribute to this dialogue but is only one of many voices.

Conclusion

The confluence of different motivations, methods, and conceptions of what constitutes legitimate knowledge establishes a rich basis for thinking of building evaluation as placemaking. The tensions inherent in such a mix are always present in place and in people-in-places. In a democratic context, these tensions always have to be negotiated as part of any environmental intervention, including evaluation. The process of negotiation can be fundamentally emancipatory by building relationships among the people of a place and between the people and the place or it can be totalitarian and oppressive. Our conception of placemaking and its attendant tasks offers a way of thinking about our relationship to the world as part of an ongoing conversation about ourselves and our places. A dialogic space or time creates an opening for the negotiations about what we want to be and how we want our places to support us.

Place, placemaking, and dialogic space are central to designing, making, and maintaining the world. In activities such as evaluation, knowledge is constructed through dialogue, and if knowledges are brought in from the outside, they must be translated and situated within the context of the place in question. Any form of knowledge, including professional knowledge and knowledge acquired through scientific inquiry, must be made available and accessible to the dialogic space as part of the process of framing action on place. Without this opportunity for dialogue, control and responsibility for place are vested elsewhere. People surrender control over the material circumstances of their lives, and a form of tyranny

results. By contrast, building evaluation as placemaking can become part of a larger project of emancipation, empowering people to understand and control the forces that most affect their everyday lives. This process of situating knowledge through social negotiation can create places that are beloved, transcending either simply functional notions of place or more elitist conceptions of place as art. The beloved place, in turn, becomes functional and artful as it is made and remade through continuing evaluation activity.

Notes

1. See Kernohan et al. (1992) for text that strongly advocates for the users or occupants in building evaluation programs.
2. See Friedmann et al. (1978) as an example of what Campbell and Stanley (1963) describe as more experimental and quasi-experimental designs for building evaluation.
3. For a general discussion on the conflict between advocacy and the detachment of functionality, see Albrecht and Lim (1986). To see an application of the two modes applied in both practice and academic settings, see Shibley (1990) and Schneekloth and Keable (1991).
4. The postmodern concept we are referring to addresses postmodernity as a way of thinking about place and circumstance. As such, it is not specifically engaged with other aspects of the postmodern such as stylistic mandates or historic eras. To us, the postmodern movement has been fundamentally about the uncertainty of meaning in any communication regardless of its origins in science or other forms of knowing. As a way of thinking, it requires us to always be translating, situating, and constructing knowledge in place.
5. Burt, Hill, Kosar and Rittlemann Associates/Min Kantrowitz Associates, 1987.
6. *Ibid.,* p. 57.
7. See Steele (1973) for an extended discussion on the nature of environmental competence as a goal in organizational development.
8. See Gold (1973).
9. See Argyris and Schon (1974) for a more in-

depth description of the process of recording the "espoused theory" of an organizational unit or individual and contrasting it with their "theory in use." In general, the approach is to seek clarity on the way a person or group wishes to behave and then to explore with them what behaviors are actually occurring. Such an analysis often results in reconceptualizing both the espoused theories and the ongoing behaviors.

10. See Shibley (1974, 1985) and Brauer (1985) for more in-depth descriptions of the Corps of Engineers' program.

11. *Critical* here refers to the form of critical investigation discussed at length by Jurgen Habermas (1984) as the exercise of critical theory.

12. See Schneekloth and Shibley (1995) for a discussion of the intentions and tasks of placemaking and for a critique of the theory of knowledge related to the disciplines/professions of architecture and design.

evaluation practices

CHAPTER 3

Planning for Adaptability

The three contributions in this chapter describe techniques that respond to user needs, changing organizational requirements, and the continuing demand for higher productivity—particularly as they relate to the office workplace. Each of the authors stresses the importance and benefit of supplying and adapting buildings to respond to changing demands.

In Sec. 3.1, Frank Duffy suggests that organizations of the future will look for offices that add value to organizational performance and minimize occupancy costs, doing both in a way that is environmentally sustainable. Duffy discusses his firm's commitment to building appraisal, to user research into office design, and to measuring the capacity of office buildings to accommodate change. He makes reference to the ORBIT multiclient studies with which a number of our contributors have been involved. The ORBIT studies investigated the impact of information technology on office design in the United Kingdom and North America. Duffy proposes that the problem for architects and for others involved with building design and management is to plan effectively for now and for the future in an environment of rapid organizational change, influenced significantly by accelerating advances in information technology and telecommunications. Duffy suggests that we must view building appraisal as a dynamic activity requiring "relative—and changing—judgment."

Bill Sims, Frank Becker, and Kristen Quinn provide a North American perspective in their explorations of alternative ways of structuring organizations and workplaces in Sec. 3.2. They identify the benefits of a range of workplace strategies. These benefits include significant cost savings, increased adaptability, more intensive use of resources, an enhanced quality of work life, and comparable or enhanced productivity. They also make reference to the powerful effect of information technology on the nature and use of the workplace. They canvass a number of "alternative workplace strategies" offered by advances in information technology. Their approach to organizational workplace analysis introduces a number of building evaluation techniques or data-collection tools. Sims, Becker, and Quinn's case study provides a useful overview of an exploratory method that elicits specific quantitative and qualitative information. Importantly, it identifies a role and methodology for the expert evaluator or facilitator while stressing that building users must be involved in the evaluation activity if management wants them to take "ownership" of initiatives affecting their workplace.

Section 3.3, by Adrian Leaman, completes this group of contributions about the office workplace. Leaman summarizes the work of the U.K.-based firm Building Use Studies on the Office Environment Survey—the first large-sample investigation of building-related health problems in British office buildings. He describes the content and use of a standard question set that has been used without change in the study of 80 office buildings. The results provide evidence of the symbiotic relationship between human and management systems and physical and technical systems in buildings. Further, the results indicate that responsiveness to user needs and user involvement in decision making often offset shortcomings in the actual provision or controllability of the environment. Interestingly, Leaman concludes that the perception "comfort" is conditioned by the speed with which buildings can be made to respond to perceived discomfort.

3.1 Building Appraisal: Measuring the Capacity of Office Buildings to Accommodate Change

Francis Duffy
DEGW International, Ltd., London

This section is about office buildings and their use. One purpose is to give a public account of work carried out by one particular architectural practice on measuring the capacity of office buildings to accommodate change. An additional, and perhaps more important, intention is to place this specific, highly operational, pragmatic, practical set of experiences into a more theoretical framework that may help throw some light on the ongoing and ever-changing relation of buildings to users, clients, and society.

DEGW's research tradition

To understand the limitations as well as the potential for development of what is recounted here, it is necessary to give a brief account of the context in which the work was done. The work that is described has all been carried out by the consultancy arm of the Europe-wide architectural practice DEGW. This practice is unusual in three respects:

- It has specialized in the design and programming of only one building type—the office—and thus has been able to build up a considerable body of knowledge about office work and office buildings.
- It has sustained a tradition of user research into office design.
- It has always considered that it is a matter of professional responsibility for a research-based architectural practice to publish its research findings for the benefit of other architects, office clients, and office users.

Such publications include a large body of architectural criticism, designers' handbooks such as *Planning Office Space* (Duffy et al., 1976), and more formal accounts of the findings of such multiclient studies as ORBIT-1 (Duffy and Chandler, 1984) and ORBIT-2 (Becker et al., 1985), which describe investigations into the impact of information technology (IT) on office design in the United Kingdom and North America, respectively.[1] A more recent study, *The Responsible Workplace* (Duffy et al., 1993), describes trends in organizational priorities and how office interiors and office buildings are likely to have to change to accommodate such trends.

A crucial aspect of the practice's collective thinking about architectural research is the conviction that architectural knowledge, strictly speaking, cannot exist independently from the realm of practice. Architectural knowledge is defined by DEGW as those matters which comprehend the concerns of both the design of buildings and the use of buildings. Such knowledge can be distinguished from other more easily and neatly codified bodies of knowledge in more conventionally academic disciplines, in that architectural knowledge is extremely wide in scope, inherently interdisciplinary, essentially systemic, and thus, by definition, open-ended and, above all, value-laden. This is so because both architects and architectural knowledge are always and inevitably concerned with what ought to be as much as with what is.[2]

I readily acknowledge the vital importance of universities and research institutes in building up a body of architectural knowledge though research. However, it is the rich deposits of user data to which all architectural practices have such ready access and, more important, the acute pressure to resolve urgent user issues through design that make practice the better place from which to conduct much architectural research. It is in the context of active architectural practice that feedback—and what Tom Markus (BPRU, 1972) so acutely called "feed forward"—really matters.

The time-based nature of office design

Nowhere in the field of architecture is the need for feedback and "feed forward" on design and user matters currently more clear than in office design. After decades of relative stability in office architecture and interior design, during which stereotypical office solutions became accepted practically everywhere by clients as well as by architects, sudden and spectacular change in the use and design of office space is now becoming the norm. The great solvent of the old office conventions is universally distributed information technology. Familiar stereotypes of office building plan form and specification, as well as of interior layout and office furniture, are being challenged by the new ways of working made possible by IT (Duffy and Tanis, 1993).

One most important consequence of this general trend for change is the increased importance of time in office design (Brand, 1994). Users are increasingly concerned with time in their organizations and are becoming more and more inventive in the way they program the use of time in carrying out office tasks. Architects similarly, in response to accelerating client expectations of change, are becoming more concerned about the duration of the problem-solving capacity of each component, exterior and interior, of office buildings.

Such a time-based vision of office design reinforces an alternative paradigm for office design that has been evident since the early seventies (Duffy et al., 1976; Duffy, 1992) but has now a new significance for clients. This alternative paradigm is that the real design problem for architects involved in office design is not simply to design unique 50-year-life buildings or single, 7-year, one-off interiors but to design the best way to use a changing stock of space to meet changing organizational needs over time. This paradigm not only overrides many of the goals and products of conventional architectural and design services but also places a much greater emphasis on the predictive and organizational skills necessary for architects to design for time in a truly practical, effective, and measurable way.

The eighties office boom in London

The extent and rapidity of change in office design are well exemplified by what happened to the City of London in the eighties. The great model of the City

of London that was the centerpiece of the 1993 Architecture Foundation exhibit, City Changes, was color coded to show that about one-third of the entire stock of space within the "square mile" that is the City of London had been rebuilt or substantially refurbished during the eighties and very early nineties. Much of this enormous program of rebuilding was the result of the deregulation in the early eighties of London's financial services industry, which, in turn, was the consequence of the globalization of financial services, stimulated and indeed made possible by the growing communicative power of information technology. The results of the first stages of computerizing the financial services industry affected the shape of the city, rewriting, as it were, its traditional geography. Information technology also, at the micro level of individual buildings, radically changed their specification—to accommodate vast amounts of cabling and to deal environmentally with problems of local cooling caused by unpredictably mobile concentrations of heat-producing electronic equipment (Duffy and Henney, 1989). Millions of square feet of new office buildings were constructed to the new specifications, and millions of square feet of existing buildings were, in effect, rebuilt over a very short period of time to accommodate these changes.

Such were the origins and the consequences of the great City of London office boom. As we will argue later, the city changes seen in the City of London are only the forerunner of much greater and more widespread changes in the design of all office buildings in all cities.

The intellectual origins of building appraisal

It was in this exciting context that DEGW's work on measurement of the performance of office buildings, now know as *building appraisal,* was first developed and applied. The essential idea of building appraisal was conceived during the preparation of the U.K. ORBIT Study in 1982–1983. ORBIT was designed to explore the impact of information technology on office design. To quantify and compare the capacity of office buildings of different configurations and servicing designs, a simple system was devised for measuring the ease of installing and maintaining the networks of interconnected devices that the ORBIT Study had highlighted as characteristic of the new technology (Duffy and Chandler, 1984).

In 1985, the second ORBIT study was carried out in North America with Gerald Davis of Harbinger and Frank Becker and Bill Sims of Cornell University. The contribution made to building appraisal by ORBIT-2 was immense. Perhaps the most important idea was the realization that unlike what had been tacitly assumed in ORBIT-1, there were characteristic differences between various typical kinds of organizations in terms, first, of the rate with which information technology was being introduced and, second, in the priorities that were being given to a whole range of organizational factors connected with the dissemination of IT. In practical terms, these lessons had a most important consequence: Never again could it be assumed that there was such a thing as a single formula for the perfect post–information technology office building. Overprovision of IT handling capacity could be just as much an error—through waste of scarce resources—as underprovision. Since all organizations could be relied on to set—and to change—their priorities, building appraisal inherently must be a matter of relative—and changing—judgment (Becker et al., 1985).

Both ORBIT-1 and ORBIT-2 emphasized the distinction between the direct effects of IT on building design—e.g., whatever had to be done physically to accommodate cables or to disperse heat—and the indirect effects—e.g., the changes that information technology would induce in organizational structure and values. The latter were predicted to be far more important ultimately than the former.

Developing user profiles for new office developments

Many of the ideas and techniques from ORBIT-1 and ORBIT-2 were put into effect quickly from 1985 onward through DEGW's part in the rebuilding of the City of London—necessarily in a rather simpler way than had been anticipated, given the speed of events. Through the agency of developers Stuart Lipton and Godfrey Bradman, DEGW was involved in the programming first of 1 Finsbury Avenue, then decisively in the huge Broadgate development, and subsequently in other important city projects (DEGW, 1986). Simultaneous input of a similar sort was given to Lipton's business park project, Stockley Park, near Heathrow.

What building appraisal meant for DEGW in the city and at Stockley Park was the opportunity to carry out on a large scale, between 1985 and 1989, a series of investigations into the building and interior design priorities of important space users in a number of the most important sectors of the office economy. These studies resulted in user profiles that quantified the preferences of each sector in such terms as the depth of space most suitable to accommodate their activities, level of environmental servicing required, and the proportion of space for cellular offices and for specialized support spaces such as dealing and computer rooms. User profiles for seven sectors of city users were identified based on extensive focus group studies carried out on a comparative basis—e.g., the space needs and preferences of the British clearing banks, of the foreign banks, of the insurance industry, as well as of two professions, accountancy and the City solicitors. Each of these sectors differed in their requirements and priorities for office space and thus in their user profiles. Not all office buildings suit all organizations equally well (Duffy, 1989).

It was DEGW's task to identify these user profiles, to establish how consistent they were and what exactly they meant for the design specification of each building on the huge Broadgate site, to convey these preferences to the two design teams (SOM and Arup Associates) working on Broadgate in its various phases, and to demonstrate through test layouts to potential tenants from all seven sectors how they could fit into the emerging building designs.

Building appraisal, developed and applied in a spirit of optimism on the most prestigious office development in London, had an important impact on the design, lettability, and success of Broadgate. Not surprisingly, given the depth of the user research and the clarity and power of the user profiles, building appraisal has influenced many subsequent office projects in London. Perhaps more significantly, building appraisal has now achieved a quasi-legal significance, since the technique has been used and tested in several arbitrations concerned with establishing the financial value of a number of office building projects. The use value of office buildings has been made measurable, comparable, and accessible in a systematic way.

The consequences for office design of accelerating organizational change

Building appraisal, based on systematically studied user profiles, is a practical and powerful technique for improving office design performance. Essentially, building appraisal helps users because it brings them closer to designers through the consumerist process of quantifying and demystifying the choice between options. Cumulatively, however, building appraisal has even greater significance for architects because it makes possible the collection of large amounts of consistent and longitudinal data about building capacity and about changing profiles of user requirements, sector by sector, building type by building type. Just as information technology generates and accelerates change in user requirements, so IT itself, with its enormous capacity for handling data, is making possible the management of change by allowing the relationship between supply and demand in the field of office design to be studied and matched more thoroughly than ever before.

Earlier it was suggested that the scale of change experienced in the offices of the City of London in the eighties was only the precursor of even more significant changes that are likely in office design over the next decade. The potential to design the use of *time* as well as *space* is the new factor. It has become crucial for architects to accept the new paradigm that office design is less about getting individual buildings "right on the night" than about taking responsibility for fitting a changing stock of space to changing organizations over long periods of time. Through manipulating time as freely as architects manipulate space, organizations in the new era of universally available information technology will be able to increase the productivity of building use. The simplistic and outmoded conventions of the Taylorist office—which have assumed for so long that office work can only be accomplished by each individual

being glued to each office desk, within the unchanging rule of the 5-day week and the 8-hour working day—will be broken. Office organizations, already free to intensify space use, have not been slow to exploit this new dimension of freedom (Tetlow, 1994).

The value of research to architecture is threefold. First, the accumulation of accessible data increases the probability that well-trained architects will find precedents to test and inform their designs; second, measures of the performance of buildings through time enormously enhance the ability of architects to communicate the value of design to their clients; and third and most important, research—of the kind that is described above—allows theoretically minded architects to escape stereotypical solutions by giving them the power to predict the changing relation of user priorities and design resources.

Notes

1. ORBIT=ORganizations, Buildings, Information Technology
2. Duffy, inaugural address at the Royal Institute of British Architects, London, July 1993.

3.2 Organizational Workplace Analysis for Selecting and Designing Alternative Workplace Strategies
William Sims, Franklin Becker,
and Kristen Quinn
International Workplace Studies Program,
Cornell University

The office workplace is going through a period of dramatic change. New office forms such as non-territorial offices, satellite offices, telecommuting, and what has come to be called the "virtual office" are being used by increasing numbers of organizations in their quest to improve effectiveness and reduce costs. These changes are brought on by a number of forces and will have equally significant effects on the demand for office space, the quality of work life for employees, and organizational competitiveness. First is the powerful effect of information technology that initially put great stress on existing office buildings and brought about a need for buildings with better heating, ventilation, and air conditioning (HVAC), electrical and cabling capacity, lighting, and ergonomic furniture. But more recently, information technology in the form of fax machines, e-mail, voice mail, videoconferencing, low cost personal and portable computers, printers, modems, and cellular phones has made it possible to work remotely from the central office and, more important, to substantially improve the performance and quality of employees' work lives.

Global competition has forced organizations to reduce costs and improve the quality of products and services. This has been done by reducing staff sizes (e.g., doing the same work with fewer people) and reducing other costs—particularly by accommodation, the second largest cost of doing business for most organizations (after personnel costs). Also critical is the need to improve flexibility to deal with variations in staff size and to be able to respond quickly to changes in products and services. Environmental protection has emerged as a force affecting the way people work. Governmental regulations and incentive programs aimed at reducing air pollution, traffic congestion, and energy usage through programs aimed at reducing commuting by automobile in large metropolitan areas such as southern California and Washington, D.C., have encouraged new office forms such as telecommuting from home and working in satellite offices located near employees' homes (discussed more fully below). This trend is made possible by the new technologies described earlier, which make remote work both feasible and desirable. Similarly, the focus on improving the quality of family life also has encouraged a variety of flexible work responses, again chiefly telecommuting and satellite offices.

These new workplace strategies are affecting the demand for office space. The chief effect is that companies are reducing the number of office employees and simultaneously reducing the amount of space assigned to remaining employees. Also changing is the type and distribution of workspaces (e.g., fewer individual offices/workstations, more meeting rooms and project team rooms, and a wider variety of workstations). The ratio of investment between space

and information technology is changing too. Similarly, patterns such as the telework center will affect the location and size of office facilities, with the demand shifting to smaller facilities dispersed around the metropolitan area, mainly in suburbia.

What are alternative workplace strategies?

Alternative workplace strategies are new ways of working within organizations that combine a system of loosely coupled settings connected by the physical movement of people and the electronic movement of information. Some alternative workplace strategies include the following:

- *Nonterritorial offices.* Offices in which employees do not have permanently assigned desks, workstations, or offices. Employees use space and/or technology as needed on a first-come, first-served basis to accomplish specific tasks. In some settings, employees reserve a particular type of technology or workspace prior to arrival. There are various forms of non-territorial offices described in the Glossary at the end of this section.
- *Telework centers.* Sometimes referred to as *satellite offices,* telework centers provide small, fully equipped work environments in locations convenient to employee homes or client locations. These centers may be used on a scheduled or a drop-in basis, saving time, energy, and resources normally necessary for commuting to a traditional central office.
- *Home-based telecommuting.* Employees work at home for a period of the work week, utilizing technology as necessary to communicate with other members of the employer organization.
- *Collaborative team environments.* These are areas specifically designed to stimulate communication, interaction, and a sense of cohesiveness within a project team. Unlike a conference room, project rooms are dedicated to the project team for the period of the project. Although specific quiet work areas may be designated, usually team members are not assigned individual offices.
- *Other non-traditional work settings.* This is any setting in which employees are able to work productively (often through use of technology) and maintain ongoing communication with others. Examples

include client offices, airport flight clubs, specially equipped vans or cars, and hotel rooms.

Benefits of an integrated workplace strategy

The workplace strategies that have been described offer different mixes of advantages and disadvantages. They work differently for different types of jobs, organizations, managers, and employees. They work best together in a planned, integrated strategy. For example, combining a non-territorial central office with home-based telecommuting or satellite offices can both improve the performance and quality of life for employees and also substantially reduce cost. To make it work requires an integrated approach to providing the right physical settings and furniture to support the tasks being carried out, the right mix of technology and linked communication systems, and a commitment to training both managers and employees in management and work practices appropriate for work in remote and non-territorial settings.

The major benefits of a well-planned alternative workplace strategy include

- Significant, direct, and continuing cost savings.
- More intensive use of available resources such as space and equipment.
- The opportunity to use some of the savings to provide better tools such as portable computers and car phones and settings such as project rooms that increase employees' productivity and satisfaction.
- A quality and quantity of work that is about the same or better than that experienced with personally assigned workstations or offices.
- Greater potential for teamwork and group cohesion and a greater sense of vitality from the increased density of use.
- Increased flexibility to handle fluctuations in staff size without the need to add or eliminate workstations or to reconfigure the existing office.
- An enhanced quality of work life for employees with reduced commuting stress, more personal and family time, and more time for participation in community life.
- Ability to attract and retain a quality and diverse workforce. Employees are able to deal with personal and family demands.

- The potential for enhanced public image as an innovative company.

Alternative workplace strategies require changes in work patterns and management practices and the commitment to work out inevitable problems. The end result is not only cost savings on accommodation but a better way of working for employees and a more effective and flexible organization.

Selecting and designing an integrated strategy

How does an organization go about the process of deciding if alternative workplace strategies are appropriate? Because choice of one strategy affects the other (e.g., telecommuting further reduces the already low occupancy level of the typical central office), it becomes equally critical to ask how the organization can devise an integrated strategy that combines an appropriate mix of the individual strategies. It is also crucial that decisions about the physical workplace be integrated with those dealing with technology, management and work practices, training, and corporate culture. The International Workplace Studies Program at Cornell has developed an approach to this problem that we have termed *organizational workplace analysis*.

Organizational workplace analysis

The purpose of workplace analysis is to formulate strategies that enable an organization to improve competitiveness and enhance the quality of its employees' work lives. Information is collected and analyzed on

- The environmental context in which the firm operates.
- The firm's business, including its organizational culture, values, philosophy, mission, and specific processes or activities used to carry out that business.
- The kinds of organizational challenges, both internal and external, that the firm is facing and how it is (or is planning on) responding to these challenges.
- The ways decisions are made, including the roles different people play in the process and the basis on which decisions are made.

- The way in which performance is recognized and rewarded, including incentive systems.
- The kinds of information different people need to access and where, when, and how they access that information.
- The kinds of people employees need to access and where, when, and how they access those people.
- The pattern in space and time in which different activities occur, including how predictable these patterns are, the "time chunks" needed for different activities, and the human, technologic, and printed resources required for these activities.
- Significant variations in the time/space/activity patterns, seasonally, weekly, daily.
- The potential seen by respondents for changing any aspect of how, where, or when they do their work and the benefits and costs they associate with these potential changes.
- The real estate situation of the firm—the portfolio of property owned and leased and the occupancy, market, cost and terms of leases, as well as the "serviceability" of the building stock available to use (Becker et al., 1984, also Davis et al., 1993).
- The information technology infrastructure of the firm—availability of computers, printers, modems, faxes, e-mail, voice mail, teleconferencing, local area networks (LANs) and wide area networks (WANs), software, and access to databases.

Methodologic approach.   Various methods are used to collect the relevant information. The intent is to build a picture of the work the group does; how, where, and when they get it done; and the facility and information technology context within which it occurs. This picture is then used to work with users in selecting and designing an integrated set of strategies that will fit the particular needs of that organization and set of employees. It also ensures that they are committed to making it work and know how to use it effectively.

Data-collection tools. The data-collection tools (Becker and Quinn, 1994) include

- *Focused interviews* with senior management, key administrative people, and representatives of different job functions and levels. The purpose is to

understand values, philosophy, organizational challenges, etc.
- *Occupancy survey* to understand how much time staff spend in the office.
- *Demographic data* on employees and clients from archival data sources.
- *Focus groups* to obtain responses to organization and work pattern descriptions and then to proposed changes in work patterns.
- *Information technology and physical setting inventories* to document what actually exists and in what numbers.
- *A walkthrough,* essentially a tour of the office to observe what technology is available, the space and design of the office, and how it is being used. In the process of touring the office, users are also asked questions about the kind of work process they are engaged in, the information and other resources they are accessing (or need to) and what it looks like physically, why things are the way they are, and what might happen if some of the things changed.

Data-collection and analysis procedures. The first step in the data-collection process is to establish initial contact with senior management/administrative people to explain the purposes and outcomes of the project. From this contact, it will then be possible to set up individual interviews with key senior people (e.g., managing partner, chief operations officer, human resources director, MIS director) to get a sense of organizational values, culture, challenges, performance assessment/incentives, systems in place, etc. and why these things are as they are.

The intent is to identify key categories of staff and their work patterns and to select for analysis those groups which exist in some number and are fairly typical of a job function in that industry (e.g., staff-level accountants). Within these categories, two to five members of the staff are interviewed in order to identify the significant variations in the nature of the work pattern. Summaries of these individual focused interviews are then fed back to the individuals to check for accuracy and completeness. These summaries may be reviewed by a focus group of random users of similar job types/functions.

Either simultaneously or following these interviews, a walkthrough should be made to get a "gut" feeling for how the place operates and to ask questions about what you see (and do not see) happening. Ideally, at least 1 to 2 days should be spent in informal observation of the setting. After the individual interviews have been conducted and the data translated to usable information, the results of the interviews should be presented in focus groups. Also, preliminary workplace strategies should be presented within these focus groups to get a sense of what employees feel will work and what will not work (and why). The next step is to make a presentation to those key decision makers who have been involved in the process throughout with the final recommendations and suggestions for implementation.

Much of the data are descriptive. Quantitative information is most likely to come in the form of the occupancy and archival data, especially regarding employee and client demographics. Depending on the information available, the nature of work processes and work location also can be qualitative (i.e., electronic diaries that give the time, location, and nature of employees' work in the past).

Workplace strategy selection and design. Once current work patterns are understood, the team develops draft recommendations for an alternative officing strategy. This includes the implications of the strategies for physical settings and design, information technology, and management policies and practices (from values and philosophy to incentive systems and performance assessment). These draft recommendations are presented to several focus groups (representing management and staff from all the organization's business areas) for their response: What aspects of the strategy work or do not work, and why? Focus group discussions add to the team's understanding of the organization and its work processes and help generate ideas for different patterns.

Process is as important as product

The lessons learned from our research (Becker et al., 1991) also indicate that the process by which alternative workplace strategies are planned and carried out is at least as important as the end product in determining their success or failure. The leadership and the decision to proceed must come from senior management; they must be committed to making it work. Often the decision rests simply on a desire to reduce occupancy costs or space by 30 or 50 percent. Second, management also must be committed to simultaneously improving the quality of work life for employees and helping them work more effectively. In other words, the change does not just involve taking away employees' assigned offices and squeezing costs down.

Employees should take part in working out what the new workplace will be like and how to implement it. Our evidence also suggests that it is critical that employees be involved in planning the strategies to ensure that they are provided with the technology and other tools and resources necessary to enable them to be more effective. This is critical to ensure their "buy-in" and "ownership" of the new workplace. Commitment, excitement, and pride are important aspects of innovative workplaces and are present in the successful cases we studied. The advantages of these innovative practices seem certain to make them attractive to more and more organizations. To achieve these advantages, it is critical that organizations view these practices as part of a planned, integrated effort to reduce costs and to improve employee performance.

This integrated effort involves decisions about the work settings, the right technology, management practices, and training for employees in new work practices. If done right, these new workplace strategies offer great promise for companies to use their real estate resource more efficiently and improve the quality of worklife for employees—a real "win-win" situation.

Acknowledgments

Current sponsors of Cornell University's International Workplace Studies Program (IWSP) include Aetna Life and Casualty, Anderson Consulting, Chubu Electric Co, Du Pont, The Dutch Federal Building Agency, Ernst and Young, Eastman Kodak, General Electric, Herman Miller, IBM, Kokuyo, NYNEX, Osaka Gas, Project Office Furniture, Samas Group, Shimizu Institute of Technology, Silicon Graphics, Sprint, Steelcase, and Xerox.

Glossary

Non-territorial office   First used by MIT researcher Thomas Allen, this term refers to any space allocation program that does not assign desks or workstations to specific individuals. Originally applied in a team office context in which offices were replaced with a variety of activity zones available for any team member to use.

Free address   This term was first used by the Japanese to describe a space allocation program in which each individual does not have a personally assigned desk. IBM uses the term more specifically to define an area within a building without assigned desks that can be used by anyone in the company, not just people from a particular group or department. Reservations are not made in advance.

Group address   IBM uses this term to refer to an area within a building without assigned desks intended for use by employees within a particular group or department.

JIT (just in time)   Andersen Consulting in San Francisco uses this term to describe its program of not assigning offices to specific individuals on a permanent basis. Offices may be assigned on a temporary basis, ranging from half a day to several days, through a reservation system.

Hoteling   Ernst and Young in Chicago coined this term to describe its program of not assigning offices to individuals on a permanent basis. Offices are assigned using an automated hotel reservation system. This system also enables charges for space to be allocated based on use to projects.

Shared assigned   The Cornell University IWSP coined this term to describe a space allocation program where two or more employees are assigned to use the same desk but at different times.

Hot desking   This term originated in the Navy to describe bunks used by several sailors on different watches (the bunk being warm from the previous occupant). This is a slightly pejorative term for some forms of unassigned office use.

Desk sharing   This term refers generically to the situation in which the same desk, office, or workstation is used by different employees over the course of a day or week.

Red carpet   Hewlett-Packard coined this term to describe its program of not assigning workstations to employees. The intent was to create a positive image of the practice as opposed to *hot desking*.

Drop-in   This term is used by a variety of firms to describe unassigned offices that are used for a short period of time (e.g., a few hours) by employees who have not made a reservation for a workspace. Often these may be employees from a different site who "drop in" for a short period and need a place to work.

Virtual office   A generic term used to describe the idea of the workplace as wherever and whenever you are working, i.e., the workplace disassociated from a specific place and time.

3.3 User Satisfaction

Adrian Leaman
Building Use Studies, Ltd., London

Survey data

Since 1985, when Building Use Studies, Ltd., started work on the Office Environment Survey, the first large-sample investigation of building-related ill-health problems in British office buildings (Hedge

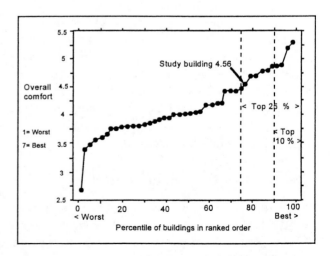

Figure 3.1 Percentile plot of overall comfort showing study building's position in the top 25 percent of all buildings (including both naturally ventilated and air conditioned) in the BUS database.

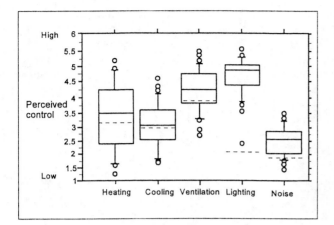

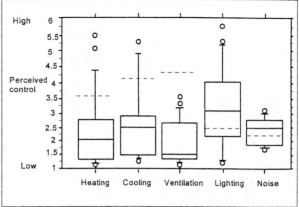

Figure 3.2 Box and whisker plots of perceived control over heating, cooling, ventilation, lighting and noise for all naturally ventilated buildings in the BUS database compared with the study (mixed-mode) building (dashed line). The bar in the box is the all-sample BUS database median (e.g., 3.5 for heating). The box shows 25 percent either way from the median, which is the solid line inside the box. The whiskers extend to values which are 1.5 times the spread from the median to the corresponding edge of the box. The circles give "outliers" which are observations that lie outside these boundaries.

The study building performs about the same as most naturally ventilated buildings for perceived control over heating and cooling, rather less well on ventilation, but not badly, but much worse on perceived control over lighting and noise.

All sample means NV n=32
Naturally ventilated buildings   Study building

	Mean	Median			Mean
Heating	3.68	3.82	Heating		3.15
Cooling	3.27	3.22	Cooling		3.01
Ventilation	4.27	4.36	Ventilation		3.67
Lighting	4.79	4.93	Lighting		2.09
Noise	2.65	2.67			

Figure 3.3 Box and whisker plots of perceived control over heating, cooling, ventilation, lighting and noise for all air-conditioned buildings in the BUS database compared with the study (mixed-mode) building (dashed line). The bar in the box is the all-sample BUS database median (e.g., 3.5 for heating). The box shows 25 percent either way from the median, which is the solid line inside the box. The whiskers extend to values which are 1.5 times the spread from the median to the corresponding edge of the box. The circles give "outliers" which are observations which lie outside these boundaries.

The study building performs much better than most air-conditioned buildings for perceived control over heating, cooling, and ventilation (the variables which in our estimation most affect work productivity), but worse on lighting (the easiest to change for the better) and noise.

All sample means AC n=20
Air conditioned buildings   Study building

	Mean	Median			Mean
Heating	2.29	2.03	Heating		3.15
Cooling	2.53	2.51	Cooling		3.01
Ventilation	1.90	1.53	Ventilation		3.67
Lighting	3.42	3.57	Lighting		2.09
Noise	2.42	2.59			

and Wilson, 1987), the company has carried out a further 80 investigations involving 7500 respondents. Each of these is a building study in its own right, carried out for purposes ranging from diagnostic investigations of humidity problems, through space planning exercises, to postoccupancy evaluation studies. Although the focus of a building study changes from one investigation to the next, Building Use Studies (BUS) has used a standard question set that does not alter from study to study. In this way, BUS has been able to build up a database that allows comparisons to be made among building types, sectors, and occupant groups.

Standard questions fall into eight groups: *environmental comfort* (36 questions), *health symptoms* (10), *satisfaction with amenities* (5 to 15), *time spent in building* (1), *time spent at task* (1), *productivity* (1 to 3), *perceived control* (5), and *background data* (3 to 10). Extra questions are added in individual studies at the clients' request. Sometimes a client will ask for question sets

	1994 survey Per cent of staff with symptoms	1991 survey Per cent of staff with symptoms	Average number of days with symptom 1994	Observation	Rank in 1994 survey 1= lowest	Rank in 1991 survey 1= lowest
Skin irritation or rash	5	6	4.35	No change	1	1
Flu-like	7	6	2.14	No change	2	2
Runny nose	13	14	3.14	No change	3	3
Dry eyes	28	15	3.68	Big deterioration	10	4
Itching eyes	16	17	2.78	No change	5	5
Dry skin	15	17	4.35	No change	4	6
Blocked nose	27	18	3.20	Worse since 1991	9	7
Dry throat	19	22	3.33	Slightly better	7	8
Headache	17	34	1.84	Much better since 1991	6	9
Lethargy	20	38	3.05	Much better since 1991	8	10
			For those reporting the symptom in 1994, this column is the average days they suffered from it.			

Figure 3.4 Building-related health symptoms.

to be removed because they consider the data too sensitive. The productivity question suffers most in this respect (BUS has productivity data on about one-third of the buildings), followed by the health questions (one-quarter). Recently, the standard question set has been applied successfully in school buildings.[1]

Thus BUS has partially overcome one of the problems that bedevil building research: sample sizes that are not large enough. The approach, however, introduces another problem: The sampling design cannot be controlled effectively, since BUS usually has to accept buildings that are offered to them rather than randomly select their own.

I think therefore that there could be a difficulty because of self-selection: Better-managed organizations will put up with the disruption caused by occu-

	Actual		Theoretical
1.Lighting	40	Per cent satisfied with 1 factor	80
2. Noise	14	Per cent satisfied with 2 factors	64
3. Winter air quality	9	Per cent satisfied with 3 factors	51
4. Summer air quality	7	Per cent satisfied with 4 factors	41
5. Winter temperature	5	Per cent satisfied with 5 factors	33
6. Summer temperature	3	Per cent satisfied with 6 factors	26

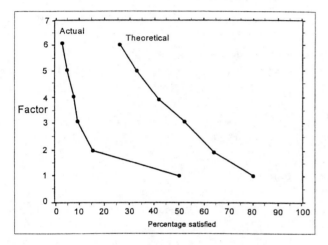

Figure 3.5 Percentages of occupants satisfied in the study building compared with a theoretical distribution based on 80 percent satisfied.

pant surveys, whereas less capable organizations will not. Not surprisingly, organizations that can make available resources for the survey also tend to have "better" management and "better" buildings. A possible consequence of this is that the conclusions about the qualities of buildings may be on the optimistic side.

Figures 3.1 to 3.5 are examples taken from our building studies. In Fig. 3.1, the score of the study building (4.56 on the overall comfort scale) is compared with other buildings in the data set, showing that the study building falls in the top quartile. The study building is compared from the perspective of occupants' perceptions of environmental control with scores for naturally ventilated buildings (Fig. 3.2) and air-conditioned buildings (Fig. 3.3). Perceptions of good control are often associated with better comfort and satisfaction. Here, the study

building has a mixed-mode ventilation system (with a combination of openable windows and partial air conditioning). For the control variable, it performs as well as other naturally ventilated buildings, except for lighting and noise, where it is worse than the norm.

Comparisons of symptom counts for the study building for 1991 and 1994 are described in Fig. 3.4. The study building has always been relatively healthy, with average person symptom index scores below 2 in both years, but the pattern of symptoms changes appreciably. In 1994, the problem was perceived as dry eyes, probably caused by excessive dust in the air-handling system or winter air-change rates set too high. Patterns of satisfaction in the study building are shown in Fig. 3.5. The chart gives the percentage of occupants satisfied with one factor, then two, and so on down to six. Only 3 percent of occupants were satisfied across all six factors, which shows the futility of trying to please everyone, and this in a relatively good building!

User satisfaction and responsiveness

A general picture of user satisfaction in U.K. offices is given in Fig. 3.6. Variables shown are overall satisfaction with lighting (LtOver), overall comfort (ComfOver), overall satisfaction with noise (NseOver), summertime temperature and air quality (TSOver and AirSOver), and wintertime temperature and air quality (TWOver and AirWOver). Variables are arranged on the diagram from most sat-

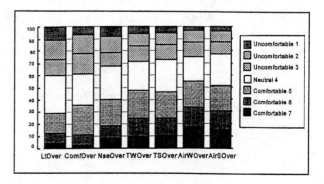

Figure 3.6 User satisfaction in UK offices
80 buildings, 7,500 respondents (UK1991–1994) 7-point satisfaction scale for seven study variables. See text for explanation.

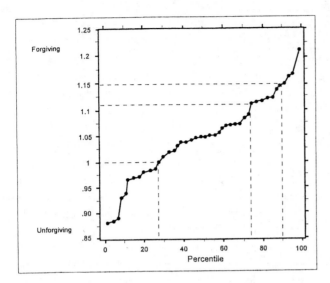

Figure 3.7 How much staff forgive the shortcomings of their office building. Forgiveness is calculated by dividing the summary variable (Overall satisfaction with temperature and air quality for both summer and winter, noise and lighting). When Overall comfort is greater than the six-variable mean, a forgiveness score of more than 1 results. The higher the score, the more forgiving staff are of the conditions. Data for 80 buildings in UK.

isfied (or comfortable) on the left to least satisfied on the right. For example, 28 percent were dissatisfied with lighting, rising to 59 percent if neutrals also are included. Over 70 percent were dissatisfied with air quality in both winter and summer, again if neutrals are included. Note how occupants tend to "forgive" some of the shortcomings of the buildings, i.e., they report satisfaction with overall comfort higher than individual variable scores, except for lighting.

Figure 3.7 shows "forgiveness" in more detail. Buildings to the top right of the diagram, those with the most forgiving occupants, also have the best developed and most responsive management systems and are also the most energy efficient. In these buildings, occupant comfort, health, productivity, management quality, and energy efficiency are linked together in a virtuous cluster, with each factor helping to reinforce the good qualities of the other.

BUS research shows that the more a building's total system (human and management systems operating in conjunction with physical and technical systems) supports occupants' needs, the more people

will tolerate whatever deficiencies are present. In the better-managed and better-designed buildings there are fewer deficiencies, and these are often tolerated by the occupants because of their perception of responsiveness in the overall system.

Responsiveness is very important. The faster buildings respond to requests from the occupants for changes to existing settings or defaults, the better they are from the point of view of occupants' comfort and satisfaction. Responsiveness operates at several levels (Leaman, 1993):

• For *individual occupants,* the way the building copes with personal discomfort is of prime concern. If environmental controls, such as blinds and light switches, are accessible, easy to understand, and provide a clearly perceived change for the better when individuals operate them, then individuals will be much more tolerant *even if the control systems are not fully effective.* This is why naturally ventilated buildings are often preferred to air-conditioned buildings, because they can potentially give instantaneous responses through openable windows or ventilators, for instance, even though the environmental conditions they create may not necessarily be "better" (Bordass et al., 1994).

• For *workgroups,* the ability to reconfigure work settings and furniture quickly is important, often because individuals within the group usually cannot agree among themselves about optimal arrangements. For example, the sun tracking around a building may create a serious glare problem in late afternoon in the summer, thereby making a particular VDU unusable for a couple of hours. Management may decide that it is not worth adding window blinds, so the occupant may respond by trying to change the orientation of the desk. If this can be achieved quickly, and *without unduly affecting colleagues in the immediate vicinity,* there will be no lasting problem. But if others' preferred locations are also affected or if the desk or VDU is fixed, there will be an enduring difficulty.

• For *departments,* the ability to reconfigure furniture quickly to accommodate changing staff numbers, without interfering with the proper operation of building services, is an important attribute of a successful building. In too many instances, management's attempts to increase densities in open-plan offices lead to desk layouts conflicting with perimeter servicing systems, thereby reducing their operational effectiveness. This will then have a cascading effect on responsiveness for workgroups and individuals, reducing their satisfaction, comfort, and productivity. The hierarchical nature of constraints at one level adversely affecting levels beneath is characteristic of buildings that underperform (Leaman and Borden, 1993).

Occupants are less concerned about the source of responsiveness than about whether or not it is present in the total building system. For example, the most comfortable building from the BUS database is a city-center, air-conditioned building with no remarkable design features other than its consistent use of robust, standard equipment. This building is rated as extremely comfortable by the occupants and is also very energy efficient—as efficient, in fact, as a naturally ventilated building. What makes the building exceptional? One major factor is that the responsiveness of the facility managers to occupants' complaints compensates for the intrinsic lack of user controllability of the services systems. If people complain, the facilities team reacts remarkably quickly (less than 1 minute is common), and even if the problem cannot be corrected, occupants appreciate the effort. Another factor was the involvement of the tenants in the brief for the fit-up, which gave them the opportunity to "own" some of the operational procedures and tailor them to their own requirements.

Design for manageability

Complexity. Rapid response is often defeated by buildings that are too complex. Complexity comes in two forms:

1. Too many functions fighting each other for inadequately finite resources
2. User uncertainty about how a system will perform over time

Conflicting functions and user uncertainty combine to make most buildings perform much less well than intended by their designers. They also reduce response times.

To bring complexity within manageable bounds, it is important to

1. Know the levels of management resources that will be available over the life of a building.
2. Define the major areas of likely functional conflicts and manage or design out these conflicts. Note that if functional conflicts cannot be managed out because of low levels of management resources (see point 1), the inefficiencies resulting from these conflicts will persist throughout the life of the building.
3. Make systems clear in their operation and responses.

Many modern buildings require more management resources over their life than their designers imagine, often because functional failures cause them to operate less smoothly than people expected. Many clients ask for "seamless" or well-integrated environments, but these often can create functional conflicts that are hard or impossible to predict at the design stage and difficult to resolve without extra human resources (e.g., security in airports). Many systems do not respond clearly or unambiguously with understandable feedbacks and diagnostics, so users are often confused or bemused (signage systems or temperature-control systems are examples). This makes them uncertain about what to do next, frustrated or exasperated with their experience, and less likely to use the facility in the future.

Comfort. The key to making people comfortable is to provide ways for them to alleviate discomfort at the moment it is perceived to occur. People need "control strategies" (Bordass and Leaman, 1993) to help them overcome discomfort wherever they are, even if it is simply the option to move somewhere else! This approach is different from the fruitless task of trying to design an automatically controlled indoor environment in which everyone is comfortable all the time. In many modern buildings, controls such as light switches or temperature controls are removed and automated, but automatic systems often do not work properly or do not respond quickly enough to make people satisfied. These systems need to be compensated for by any or all of the following:

1. Manual control or overrides of automatic systems
2. Extremely rapid complaint monitoring and response procedures
3. Clear feedback to users on the status of equipment and changes brought about by switching interventions

Opening windows, for example, are extremely popular with users because they do all three of these. Note that these options are not appropriate in all situations.

In general, the more occupants perceive that they are in control, the better. Perception of control is improved further by whether or not people sit next to a window. For example, in a study of 2379 office users, BUS found that people sitting next to windows had significantly higher perceptions of control over heating, cooling, ventilation, lighting, and noise than those without window seats. The average responses on a seven-point satisfaction scale (1=no control; 7=full control) were heating, 3.55 with window versus 2.47 without window; cooling, 3.16 versus 2.43; ventilation, 4.09 versus 3.05; lighting, 4.65 versus 3.73; noise, 2.54 versus 2.17 (all significant at $p=0.001$). The implication is that if comfort is at issue, then the more people are close to windows or have some form of outside awareness, the better. As a result of these and similar findings, office designers in the United Kingdom are resorting to shallow-plan, naturally ventilated or mixed-mode buildings in preference to deeper-plan forms and all air-conditioned environments (Leaman, 1991–1993).

Integration. Buildings are complex systems that have two types of concurrent systems:

1. A "space/performance" system, based on physical and spatial characteristics
2. A "time/performance" system, based predominantly on management and user criteria

In many non-domestic buildings, space/performance has been conceived almost independently of time/performance. The design and construction professions "supply" buildings which, it often seems from this perspective, are occupied extremely wastefully—spaces are left empty for long periods of time, and many buildings have their energy systems running very inefficiently. The criteria for assessment are usually based on relationships between spatial characteristics and the building's performance as a physical or economic system (temperature, energy, first cost, etc.). These performance measures often can be nearly independent of actual occupancy and use, especially when assessments use design criteria only and not actual performance in use.

Users and managers, though, have a markedly different perception, usually based on time criteria (bottlenecks in elevators, time taken to reach the toilets, time spent moving between departments, time spent to move the furniture, time spent waiting for log-in on the computer system, time in check-in queue, and so on). From the user's or manager's viewpoint, this time/performance system is perceived to be inefficient, usually from the perspective of time spent unnecessarily waiting or "stored" in the system. Users react strongly to time-dependent failures but pay little attention to space-dependent failures unless they are persistently affected by them.

It is obvious that integration of space/performance and time/performance systems is desirable, but this rarely happens. This is so because buildings, at briefing, design, and construction stages, are almost invariably dominated by the designer's space/performance criteria (looks, cost, buildability, function, thermal performance, structure, design parameters) and not users' and managers' time/performance criteria (response times, time spent in system, travel times, throughput, bottlenecks, etc.).

In the near future, the best buildings (and locations) will be those which can optimize on *both* time/performance criteria and space/performance criteria. Time will be perceived as an even more valuable resource than space, and it will be factored into schemes as a hidden cost or an opportunity cost (Whitelegg, 1993). Buildings that fail responsiveness tests on their control systems or cannot be switched from one use to another very rapidly or cannot accommodate rapidly changing furniture layouts or cost management time because they are too complicated to run will become increasingly obsolete.

In brief conclusion, the best buildings

1. Respond rapidly to triggers of change at all user levels (individual, group, visitor, department, etc.).

2. Are managed and operated beneath the complexity thresholds that hinder rapid response.

3. Are comfortable for the occupants most of the time but respond rapidly when they become uncomfortable.

4. Always integrate the physical and managerial environments at all production stages (briefing, design, commissioning, and use).

Buildings that have all these characteristics will almost certainly be more energy efficient and have more productive and comfortable occupants. They run "demand side" not "supply side" and offer radical benefits for the future.

Note

1. More details of these questionnaires are available on request from Building Use Studies, Ltd., from which licenses may be obtained.

CHAPTER 4

Matching Demand and Supply

An important challenge, identified by Duffy in Sec. 3.1, is for building designers and managers to achieve a long-term match of people, organizations, and the buildings they use in an environment of accelerating change. In this chapter, our contributors describe methods that explicitly explore occupant requirements (demand) as well as the capabilities of buildings to meet those requirements (supply). The methods described (physical building audits, functional suitability analysis, Building Quality Assessment (BQA), Serviceability Tools and Methods (STM), and the Real Estate Norm (REN)) provide systematic means of measuring the quality of facilities relative to the parameters of demand and objectively rating their quality with reference to defined priorities. The value of the knowledge gained for strategic decision making is demonstrated in each instance.

In his description of physical building audit procedures (Sec. 4.1), Don Sinclair outlines a two-stage method for assessing the condition of the building fabric, with implications for decision making in the management of building maintenance programs. The audit is carried out as a team "expert walkthrough" using a standardized checklist of building elements to determine the physical condition of a building.

The functional suitability assessment method described by Nigel Isaacs and Iain Hair (Sec. 4.2.) carried out for hospitals in Scotland also addresses the physical condition of buildings but is ultimately concerned with the level of care provided by the health facility. The method therefore places emphasis on the suitability of buildings for their current use and their potential for conversion to other uses.

There are similarities between the methods described in the next three contributions, each of which addresses methods for rating the usefulness of buildings for different purposes. They are essentially expert-based methods for eliciting user needs and requirements against which the performance of buildings may be measured. In Sec. 4.3, Harry Bruhns and Nigel Isaacs describe the codifying of building user–expressed preferences into a standard form suitable for use by trained assessors. The Building Quality Assessment (BQA) method is based on a scoring system and a weighted checklist of over 130 measurable factors about a building's performance.

Gerald Davis and Françoise Szigeti's serviceability tools and methods (STM) (Sec. 4.4) are directed toward making workplaces more useful, productive, and cost-effective. STM is similar to BQA in the way both employ sets of descriptors for different levels of performance, covering many features of a building. However, the BQA performance concept differs from the serviceability concept in STM in that the former focuses on investor concerns, while the latter addresses occupant concerns. The STM approach uses two scales, one for setting functional requirements (demand) and the other for rating buildings (supply).

Like STM, the Real Estate Norm (REN) (Sec. 4.5) uses a graphic profile to express the results of a comparison between the quality of existing facilities and the requirements of specific user groups. With comprehensive coverage of the qualities of both location and building in a highly accessible handbook format, the REN can be used by experts and non-experts alike.

BQA, STM, and the REN all provide systematic and rigorous means of evaluating the performance of buildings against the criteria of demand, each addressing the same issue in a different way. The direction of approach, focus, and applicability of each method are assessed in the comparative case study that concludes this chapter.

4.1 Physical Building Audit Procedures and Maintenance Management

Don Sinclair

Sinclair and Naito Architects, Ltd., Edmonton, Canada

A *physical building audit,* otherwise known as a *facility condition survey* or a *building condition report,* is the systematic gathering of information and subsequent reporting on the physical condition of a building. The extent of each audit and the form of reporting are defined by a contract with a building audit specialist.

Scope of the audit

If the purpose of the audit is to provide information required to manage the building as an asset, a large organization with many buildings or an owner of one or several buildings has essentially the same need—a condition report on only those items which are below acceptable standards. What is *acceptable* must be determined by each owner in advance of the audit.

Because the audit is an exploration of the unknown, it is best approached in stages. The basic stages are information gathering and reporting.

Information gathering

During this preliminary/initial stage, the audit specialist should

• Determine the purpose and scope of the audit.
• Review existing documentation.

• Walk through the building.
• Briefly interview the facility manager.
• Assume the role of "team leader," and select team members appropriate to the audit (usually mechanical and electrical technologists, occasionally structural). Ensure that existing documents are reviewed by team members.
• Prepare time and cost estimates for the basic stages of the audit, and receive approval from the building owner.
• Arrange for knowledgeable building staff to provide on-site guidance.

The on-site information gathering takes the form of an "expert walkthrough," with the team equipped with a screwdriver for opening access panels, a stepladder, and a good flashlight. The team records visible defects observed or defects indicated by the staff guide. *Visible* includes above-ceiling spaces, duct shafts, and crawl spaces. If team members take numerous photographs, note taking is reduced, and there is no need for a return visit to acquire more information. Selected photographs can illustrate the report.

Reporting

Organizations with many buildings usually have a computerized database with basic statistical information. If they wish to add physical condition data, the following features should be included:

• A standardized checklist of building elements, numbered so they can be identified.
• The rating of each element (e.g., 1=urgent to 9=excellent). The rating is a key for searching for maintenance information (e.g., all roofs in the inventory rated 3 and lower may form the basis of a roof upgrading program, or all elements in one building rated 3 and lower may be identified for a proposed upgrading of that building).
• An alternative to rating, FI=further investigation (e.g., to find the reason for a water-stained ceiling).
• A date beside the rating of each element, updated with each change in status, to create a "perpetual inventory" containing only current information.

An owner with only one or a few buildings does not need a database and requires simply an informal report of the results of the audit in jargon-free language so that it can be understood by everyone from maintenance worker to top management.

Further stages

The building owner must decide how to use the information reported and may then extend the audit team services to include any or all of these further stages:

- Resolve items marked "FI".
- Prepare budget costs for correction of deficiencies.
- Assign priorities to proposed corrections to create a multiyear maintenance plan.
- Discuss "value for money":
  - Will any corrections reduce operating costs?
  - Will the life of the building be extended?
  - Is disposal an alternative to the cost of renovation?
- Upgrade building documents to reflect the many unrecorded changes to partitions and building systems.

Recording building code infractions in the database may be within the scope of the basic audit. If the infractions are numerous due to changes over time or due to old buildings not designed to any code, a complete code study may be added to the tasks of the audit team.

Caution

Performing audits for maintenance information at the level discussed above can be acceptable if all involved have a clear understanding of the purpose and reliability of the audit report. The risk is that the results may be picked up and misused by people who may not be aware of the scope and limitations of the audit.

Owners seeking audits for another purpose, whether a purchase or a sale, may involve other parties, and there may be greater reliance placed on the report by those other parties who have had no direct involvement with the audit. The owner also may select the audit specialist on the basis of low bid price rather than qualifications. These and other conditions may be sufficient warning signals to the audit specialist that the report must contain limitations and disclaimers. The specialist may prefer to decline the work.

Case study: A physical condition audit of a general-purpose government office building

Building history. The subject of this physical condition audit is a building that forms part of a group of government office buildings. The building was erected 1961 in a crash program to accommodate a newly purchased mainframe computer. A three-story building, begun in 1945, also formed one wing of the 1961 building, connected at the third, fourth, and fifth levels. The building obstructs the view from the river valley of the main legislature building.

The 1961 building had problems of planning, construction, and life safety due to the lack of standards at the time and the haste with which it was designed and built. The 1945 wing was built to a lower standard of construction, which has been revealed over time. This composite building was discussed in planning reports in 1986, one option being to demolish the 1945 wing and another to demolish the whole complex. The result of the report was to place the future of the building in doubt, so maintenance budgets were reduced to emergency repairs. Eight years later, in 1993, with no decision on the future of the building, a physical building audit was conducted.

The audit. The government had an established database for the management of its properties. In 1985 it created a database for the physical condition and code conformity of its buildings based on existing checklists (NRC, 1967; Brass and Jaeggin, 1967) comprising hand-written reports, so the information was static and soon obsolete. A computerized reporting system was added to the existing main database. Each physical element reported had a quality rating (1 to 9) and a date for each entry. Building code conformity was compared with code requirements.

An experienced audit team, familiar with the database system, was selected. The team leader had knowledge of the building from involvement with interior renovation projects. The scope of this audit was to record physical defects and building code infractions. Functional problems observed could be noted for further investigation by others.

Information gathered. Defects reported in the audit were in several general categories, for example:

1. *Life safety issues in the original building design*
   - Emergency exit routes were insufficiently protected from smoke and fire. Smoke could freely migrate up five levels of the open main stairway.
   - High-risk mechanical and service rooms opened directly into exit routes without fire-protected doors.
2. *Life safety issues from changes to the building over time*
   - Smoke separation barriers and fire walls, above ceilings, were penetrated during changes to electrical wiring and mechanical piping. Access holes, crudely made, were not patched, providing uncontrolled pathways for smoke and fire. The above-ceiling space ventilation return air plenum added to this risk.
   - Insufficient emergency exit signs visible.
   - Insufficient fire alarm bells audible to occupants.
3. *Inappropriate building materials*
   - Insulation of exterior walls above the ceiling was sprayed-on asbestos, without protective cover, in a space that was the ventilation return air plenum.
   - The ceiling was a suspended metal grid with lay-in acoustical panels. The grid was not the normal interlocking type. If a number of panels were removed for maintenance, the grid could spread, causing recessed lighting fixtures to crash to the floor.
4. *Inappropriate construction of exterior building envelope*
   - Exterior walls of the 1945 wing were clay tile walls stuccoed outside and plastered inside; no insulation was provided and no air/vapor barrier. Resulting moisture movements from inside and outside had peeled paint off inside walls and caused rotting of wood window frames.
   - Flat roofs with insufficient drains caused water ponds on half the roof.
5. *Mechanical systems*
   - Lack of maintenance allowed air filters to be bypassed, causing heating coils to be plugged with dirt.
   - Due to partition changes over time, heating control thermostats were not located in the spaces they were supposed to control.
6. *Electrical systems*
   - Lighting levels were found to be excessive by current standards.
   - Obsolete fluorescent fixtures were not energy efficient.

In addition to the physical condition and life safety deficiencies recorded, concerns were noted about the underutilization of tenant space. Where staff number were reduced, they spread out rather than relinquished space. Trade shops were fully equipped but no longer in use. The main computer room was half vacant.

After the audit information was entered in the database, selected photographs and floor plans showing changes were submitted to complete the first stage of the audit. The audit team was then asked to prepare cost estimates for repair/upgrading, with priorities, to create a multiyear budget proposal.

Cost estimates. Because of original design deficiencies, many changes over time, and many years of minimal maintenance, there was no simple way to determine the proper cost for upgrading or setting priorities. To place the cost in context, the government had first to determine how long it expected to retain the building in service. Previous reports that had suggested demolition were no longer politically acceptable. The best answer available was "Nobody knows."

To help find an answer to how many years of remaining service would be appropriate, the audit team agreed to provide alternatives, with costs related to varying lengths of life expectancy. The alternatives presented were

- $200,000 to stabilize the building for 3 to 5 years to allow time for planning a major upgrading or abandonment.
- $8 million for a major upgrading of the interior of the 1961 building (mothballing or demolishing the 1945 wing) for a further life expectancy of 10 to 15 years.
- $13 million for a complete modernization of the

whole facility for a further life expectancy of 20+ years.

To prepare cost estimates for the $200,000 minor upgrading, the building had to be revisited to examine another level of detail. Examples are

- The audit reported that there were holes in smoke and fire barriers above ceilings. The detailed report listed locations and costs of sealing 333 holes.
- The audit reported that doors were required to be fire rated that did not have automatic door closers. The detailed report gave locations and costs for installing 68 closers.

The minor upgrading report was easily understood and could be given priorities to create a 2-year budget plan with life safety concerns the first priority.

Further questions. The longer-range alternatives raised further questions. The $13 million modernization solution would be close to the cost of a new building, but the resulting building would still have poor siting and a narrow floor plate unsuitable for open-area planning. What would be the justification for such a project?

The $8 million dollar interior upgrading appeared to offer the reasonable benefit of an additional 10 to 15 years extended life expectancy. However, many questions about the building were not answered by this solution; for instance:

- It may be possible to upgrade for $8 million, but is it desirable? Compared with what? If $8 million plus 10 years of operating costs were available, what facility could be leased for that sum in the commercial market?
- Considering the long-range plans for the site of the government complex, is it desirable to prolong the life of a second-class building that blocks the view of the main legislature building?
- With a general trend toward downsizing of government, reduction of staff, and the decreasing importance of mainframe computers, is there any future for this building?

The initial audit gave factual information about physical condition and code conformance. Additional reports provided costs and priorities for various options related to varying life expectancies.

The government was given further questions about the long-range future of the building to investigate. This concluded the work of the consultant team on the project.

In undertaking this assignment, there was a clear understanding that the reports from the consultant team did not offer decisions for the government to follow. Like the outcomes of many building evaluation activities, they offered information to assist the government in making its own decisions.

4.2 Functional Suitability Assessment

Nigel Isaacs
VUW Centre for Building Performance Research, New Zealand
Iain Hair
Lanarkshire Health Board, Scotland

Once a hospital building has been created, its ability to meet the changing needs of either the population it serves or medical science often goes unquestioned. For example, a Victorian-era mental asylum would originally have served young patients to whom a three-story building was not a problem. Today, the majority of patients are likely to be elderly, and since they are unable to reach the second and third stories by stair, most of the building must remain empty. On paper, the hospital appears underused, but in reality it may be utilized to its functional limit.

It is self-evident that a health service should have buildings suitable for the activities to be carried out within them. The buildings should provide a physical, spatial, and visual environment in which health care can be provided effectively and in which patients, staff, and visitors can be comfortable and safe.

In the 1960s, a period of high government investment in Scottish health buildings, the trend was to replace old hospitals and create new facilities to support the post–World War II population growth. This led to a focus on new-build strategic planning, with less emphasis on maximizing the use of the existing estate. By the early 1980s, the focus of the health sector was still on the creation of new hospitals. This led to poor investment decisions being made in relation to the existing estate, since a systematic framework and criteria for the analysis of the efficiency of the estate were lacking.

Estate management strategy

In 1983, an enquiry into underused and surplus property in the National Health Service detailed this situation and revealed how little information was available on which to base investment decisions (Davies, 1983). The recognition that the starting point of effective management of the estate was up-to-date data about the present state of buildings, equipment, and systems led to the development of the following seven-stage ESTATECODE process (Advisory Group on Estate Management, 1989).

Stage 1: Provision of an estate database

Stage 2: Performance analysis

Stage 3: Rationalization of the estate

Stage 4: Evaluation of alternative strategies for the estate

Stage 5: Preparation of an estate investment program

Stage 6: Preparation of an estate control plan

Stage 7: Estate operational plan

The process begins with the recording of information on properties (land, buildings, etc.) under the control of the health authority. Stage 2 of ESTATE-CODE involves the inspection of facilities and the evaluation of their performance in use. This "performance" is divided into five aspects weighted with respect to their importance to the ongoing operation of the building:

- *Functional suitability* is concerned with the suitability of the buildings for their current use and potential for conversion to other uses (59 percent of the total weight).
- *Space utilization* is concerned with the amount of the available space in use (31 percent).
- *Physical condition* is the repair and maintenance of the building fabric (24 percent).
- *Safety and statutory* deals with the extent to which the facility meets the requirements for a workplace and a hospital (10 percent).

- *Energy performance* considers the operational aspects of the facility's energy use (4 percent).

Except for functional suitability, these aspects have in common the availability of well-established measurement and evaluation techniques.

The Lanarkshire Health Board, with 267 hectares of estate, was the first health board in Scotland to undertake this process for functional suitability (Hair et al., 1990).

Functional suitability

The appraisal of functional suitability was concerned with the extent to which buildings, their systems, and their services supported effective health care and provided a suitable environment. Suitability for use can be measured in a variety of ways. The use of published guidance, e.g., Hospital Planning Notes by the Scottish Home and Health Department (1977), provides clear and explicit performance criteria against which the suitability of the buildings can be appraised. For any particular function, from a general medical ward to a hospital kitchen, regularly updated requirements are defined in published guidance, legislation, and recommended standards.

Rankings

In a hospital, there are too many different functional requirements and different facilities to permit a precise scoring regime to be developed for each facility. ESTATECODE instead defines a broad five-step ranking scale for scoring:

A: High degree of satisfaction

B: Acceptable/reasonable; no major change necessary

C: Below an acceptable standard

D: Unacceptable in its present condition

X: Total rebuild required

An A ranking is given to a facility that meets the present functional requirements for a facility of that type. The A score is applicable to recent purpose-built accommodation.

A B ranking is defined as requiring "no capital expenditure to improve the building." This is interpreted as requiring the facility to have good functional relationships and range of facilities when compared with current planning note standards. For example, a modern inpatient ward requires adequate numbers of toilets, six-bed rooms, and single rooms. If it lacks en suite toilet facilities for each room, as required under the present planning notes, it would be likely to be graded B. For existing facilities, the goal was to improve the functional suitability to meet a B ranking.

The ranking distinction between C and D is of minor practical concern for the functional suitability assessment but of importance to strategic planning. In both cases, the urgency to improve the situation needed to be determined. The difference is that ranking C required expenditure of under 50 percent of replacement cost in order to reach a B ranking, while for ranking D the expenditure would be over 50 percent of replacement. The functional suitability assessment team could not be expected to undertake detailed costing of the required improvements.

The X ranking could be applied on cost grounds, but it is more likely that other constraints would necessitate this ranking. For example, if space was not available immediately adjacent to accommodate missing facilities, then no amount of expenditure could raise the ranking to a B.

Assessment program

Although the assessment program was centrally managed, each assessment involved both central and local participants. A project coordinator, with the full authority of the central director of planning and estates, managed the assessment process. The central team, consisting of the project coordinator, the area maintenance manager, medical and nursing advisory staff, and an administrative assistant, established the overall strategy for the assessment program and undertook regular reviews of the results. This team provided a basis for consistency, reviewed and upgraded the methodology, and reviewed progress against plans.

For each site, a local team was comprised of central team members and medical and/or nursing advisory staff with works personnel from the hospital.

Prior to the assessment visit, each site was contacted by the project coordinator to explain the purpose of the functional suitability assessment and to obtain preliminary information.

Once on site, the project coordinator briefly outlined the objectives and timetable for the assessment and sought the availability of key data.

Ranking procedure

First, a site assessment was made to determine the suitability of the facility in meeting the requirements of its specialist service area. There were four key issues to be considered:

1. Location with respect to centers of population, transport, amenities, and other health services
2. Site characteristics and access
3. Balance of provision of facilities for the site
4. Relationships of departments on the site

Although specific requirements were established for each functional unit, a set of general issues was developed for assessing whole buildings and the individual departments or functional units:

1. *Space relationships*—critical dimensions of spaces, e.g., space around beds, walking distances, patient observation, access from beds to bathroom.
2. *Services*—suitable for function, e.g., ratio of beds to toilets, baths, storage space, etc.
3. *Amenities*—privacy of patients, staff working conditions, favorable public impression, patient facilties, e.g., day room area.
4. *Location*—with respect to other related departments and external features, e.g., entrances, loading bays, proximity to x-ray facilities if required.
5. *Environmental conditions*—heating, lighting, ventilation, noise, windows.
6. *Overall effectiveness*—overall balance as assessed based on recorded details and the local team overview.

A list of hospital departments cross-referenced to appropriate published guidance was prepared. Advice from medical and nursing specialists was obtained to establish a minimum number of proformas.

Each proforma dealt with one functional unit and provided in one page a simple checklist of the functional requirements, a tick box for the ranking (A–D,X), and space for comments. The proforma was self-documenting, recording the date of the assessment, the survey team, the site, the department, etc. Upon completion of the functional unit, the results were reviewed by the survey team and an overall ranking allocated. In general, this overall ranking was the unanimous decision of the survey team.

Although the proformas were designed to permit the ultimate development of a detailed database, it was the overall ranking that was immediately recorded, and the forms became available for review of specific information and decisions.

It was originally intended that each functional unit be subject to a comprehensive walkthrough inspection. In practice, it was found that since the buildings on a particular site tended to be of similar age and design, inspection of representative units provided adequate information about their functional suitability. After assessing a number of facilities, it was possible to develop a number of "key indicators" to further reduce inspection time, with the knowledge of the local team participants providing necessary additional information.

Strategic planning

As a result of the functional suitability survey of all sites, the Lanarkshire Health Board was able to establish objectively that a number of its hospitals were functionally unsuitable for the client groups they served. The results of the survey were correlated with other information obtained about compliance with safety statutory standards, energy efficiency, and physical condition. Each of these areas was costed and rated in a similar manner to functional suitability (i.e., A to D). With comprehensive, consistent, and objective information now available for each site, decisions could now be made on the most appropriate action to be taken on the form of estate investment, taking account of the board's strategic health care objectives.

Thus, instead of continuing to maintain old buildings at high cost, for example, decisions to close and demolish could be justified. In some cases, an investment and rationalization strategy could be prepared

for the site, and the freed surplus land could be sold. Other wards on the same site or on a nearby site that were more capable of functional upgrading could then be brought up to an acceptable standard using the available money. For example, on one site the rationalization program resulted in the release of 10 hectares of land for housing and office development, the upgrading of office accommodation using underutilized buildings, and plans to replace inpatient accommodation following the transfer of outpatient facilities to a new acute hospital being built nearby.

Conclusion

Functional suitability is ultimately concerned with the evaluation of whether the health facility is capable of providing the highest possible quality of care. Such an assessment must be based on the "standards" of the time when the assessment is undertaken. The use of published formal guidance is successful where such guidance is up-to-date and available. For example, the Nightingale-style ward (large ward with beds around the outside, each with close access to natural ventilation and lighting) met the requirements of the time it was designed, but modern social expectations for greater patient privacy and facilities have led toward comprising one-, four-, and six-bed rooms with attached en suite facilities.

It is important to recognize that the functional suitability of the buildings alone does not adequately measure the environment necessary for the wellbeing of staff and patients; that environment comprises a mixture of social, physical, and managerial issues.

Functional suitability assessment provides key information to evaluate optimal use of the existing estate, model the impact of possible alternative uses, and investigate the need for new buildings. Since the information is collected through a consistent, coherent method, evaluation can be applied across the whole estate for the development of strategic plans. The information can be used to evaluate how the introduction of new technology (e.g., day surgery) can be accommodated in the estate, the rationalization of facilities on a site, or the rationalization of the overall estate.

4.3 Building Quality Assessment

Harry Bruhns
Design Discipline, Open University, United Kingdom
Nigel Isaacs
VUW Centre for Building Performance Research, New Zealand

Building Quality Assessment (BQA) is a tool for scoring the performance of a building relating actual performance to requirements for user groups in that type of building. In practice, the BQA tool is used by trained assessors as part of a comprehensive system for assessing quality on a comparative basis, scoring performance, and reporting the findings.

The quality of a building rests in the degree to which it fulfills the requirements for that type of building. In BQA, *quality* is a relative rather than an absolute concept. The difference can be illustrated by thinking of a Rolls Royce car being used to shift loads of timber on a building site; the Rolls Royce is widely regarded as (absolutely) "the best," but on a building site a utility vehicle is (relatively) better suited to the requirements of that situation. Before building quality can be assessed, the requirements of the group or groups using the building must first be identified.

But whose requirements should be considered when assessing a building? Users of buildings are in two main groups: the *providers* of buildings, including the owner and/or investor, and the *occupants* of buildings, including tenants, visitors, and other people (with a legitimate reason for being in the building from time to time) such as maintenance and cleaning personnel (Kernohan et al., 1992). These building users have different requirements, some of which may conflict. Because a building has to satisfy different user requirements simultaneously, when designing a method for measuring building quality, a fundamental decision is necessary at the outset: whether to assess against all identified requirements (including those which conflict) or against selected requirements, such as those of the owner, investor, or tenant.

In developing BQA, the approach taken was to identify requirements that are common to most or all users of a building type *and* those of specific groups.

It is assumed that the wise investor or owner will seek to provide a building that meets the needs of existing or future occupants while also satisfying the investment requirements. Thus, although BQA is designed to be of greatest use to owners, investors, and facilities managers, it pays close attention to occupant requirements.

A particular benefit of BQA is that it provides a common basis for measurement by different people in different places at any time. This means that it is possible, with the BQA tool, to compare and score the quality of buildings of the same type, reliably and consistently.

Development of BQA

CBPR research has identified and organized common user requirements of buildings into a number of groups. These groups reflect how users perceive their requirements, based on what a building actually *does*. That is, a building

- Provides places for people to do things, e.g., enjoy public spaces, meet with other people.
- Provides places for support facilities that people use for these activities, e.g., pantry or kitchen.
- Provides access points to other resources required for the activities, e.g., telecommunication cables.
- Creates images and value-related responses in people's minds, e.g., external presentation.
- Acts as a barrier to various physical and social behaviors, e.g., provides a secure place to be at night.
- Defines status, e.g., right of entry.
- Allows for change as people and equipment come and go and move around the building, e.g., shift offices.
- Continues to meet these requirements for a considerable period of time (usually some tens of years), e.g., through the provision of building maintenance facilities.

The use of building evaluation for briefing purposes led to the development of a checklist structure with six major attribute headings: corporate, site, construction, space, internal environment, and building services (Baird et al., 1989; see also Chap. 8). The BQA research suggested further subdivision. The intention was to provide a base description of building quality on a single page, with sufficient detail for most people and further backup details when required.

BQA categories

BQA is based on nine categories that link the physical functions of buildings and the concepts used to describe them. These categories reflect what people ask for in an office building and provide a useful framework for providers and users to evaluate buildings.

The following list briefly describes the information about the building incorporated into each category:

1. *Presentation*. The building makes a statement to the world about its owners and occupants and provides for its occupants an aesthetic environment.
2. *Space*. The building provides spaces for its occupants and the activities they carry out in the building.
3. *Access and circulation*. The building also must allow and aid (and, where necessary, inhibit) the entry and exit of people and the various goods and tools they use to, from, and among those spaces.
4. *Business services*. The building also should provide various services (e.g., electricity, telecommunications) to aid the work functions of its occupants.
5. *Personnel amenities*. The occupants will require some amenities, e.g., washbasins and toilets at the very least and possibly showers, gymnasiums, and other recreational features.
6. *Working environment*. Since the function of an office is to provide suitable space for the work of people, it is necessary that the building provide a suitable environment (temperature, light, sound, etc.).
7. *Health and safety*. The building should avoid putting occupants, visitors, and passers-by at risk.

Categories 1 to 7 are concerned with what the building does for its users, i.e., the service it provides. Categories 8 and 9 are concerned with retaining that level of service.

8. *Structural considerations*. The building is robust for both the day-to-day activities carried out in it

(e.g., lack of floor bounce) and long-term viability (e.g., that it will survive a reasonable storm or earthquake).

9. *Manageability*. Buildings need cleaning, maintenance, and the provision of various services to retain a given level of service within categories 1 to 7 above.

BQA structure

Figure 4.1 illustrates the development of BQA for a particular building type. The nine *categories* establish a broad classification of user requirements. These are divided into *sections* that represent the effects of the building that a user will be aware of—what the user feels, sees, hears, etc. The overall structure of BQA aims for a homogeneity of issues at and within the section levels.

Each section comprises a number of measurable *factors* for use in the assessment process. The user may not be concerned with or even wish to understand individual factors. For example, a typical building user does not know all the technical issues that contribute to air quality, but he or she does know that he or she wants a well-ventilated building. At the factor level, a range of issues can be explored as to how the building provides acceptable air quality, while the results are reported in summary at the section level.

Plateaus provide a scoring scale for measuring each factor ranging from 10 down to 0. The plateaus

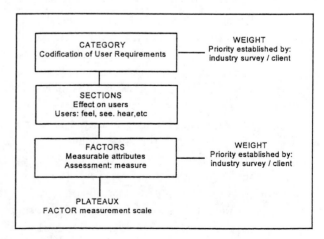

Figure 4.1 Steps in the development of a BQA module.

cover the range of practice for each factor (considered as if in isolation), with the highest score set at the level of best current practice. In addition to the numerical score, the assessor provides a written commentary on issues affecting each factor.

Neither the categories nor the factors are all of equal importance. Are the number of toilets as important as the floor-to-ceiling height? Each factor requires a priority to establish it within a clear framework. The BQA encapsulates these priorities by a system of weighting. In order to permit the BQA to be used for a standardized comparisons between buildings, it was decided to use weightings based on a user opinion survey. It was recognized that no two users will have exactly the same requirements, and it was decided also to incorporate the ability for any BQA user to assign his or her own (possibly unique) weighting to both factors and categories.

Factor scoring plateaus

Scoring plateaus have been prepared based on a review of current industry practice. For example, the factor that examines the provision of emergency power supply or standby electrical generation facilities for an office building has the following scoring plateaus:

SCORE	DESCRIPTION
10	100 percent standby generator—automatic cut-in: minimum lapse period; supports all building and occupant operations; maintenance record available.
8	50 percent standby generator—automatic cut-in: minimum lapse period; supports all essential building operations as well as some nonessential operations; provision and space to upgrade to 100 percent.
6	Standby generator—automatic cut-in: lifts and emergency operations only.
4	Standby generator—manual start: lifts and emergency operations only.
2	Standby generator—manual start: emergency operations only.
0	No standby generator.

Thus a building with a standby generator that automatically starts operating in case of power failure but is only supporting lifts and emergency operations would score 6. This factor does not deal with the provision of emergency lighting, which is considered elsewhere.

Where there are no predetermined plateaus, a scale is used ranging from 10 (excellent—exceptional or rare quality, top international class) to 6 (good—typically acceptable quality for this building type) to 0 (none—feature is not implemented or hopelessly so).

A *null* score may be used where a feature does not exist in a particular building; e.g., if it is a single-story building, then no stairs are required and hence that factor cannot be scored.

Factor scores also may be *split,* where different parts of the building have features at different plateaus. For example, if the entrances of a building differ in their presentation, the factor dealing with entrance presentation can be split, with a different score allocated to each entrance, with the proportions based on the relative importance of each.

Calculation of BQA scores

The overall BQA is a weighted combination of the category and factor scores. As discussed, each individual factor is scored from 0 to 10. The factor score is then multiplied by a factor weight (from 0 to 100), and the weighted factor scores are then summed for each category and normalized by the sum of the weights for that category. The category score (out of 10) is multiplied by the category weight and summed across the nine categories to give the overall BQA.

Figure 4.2 provides a sample of Category 3 scores for a central city office building. Factor scores are given in cross-hatched bars, and refer to the top scale. The factor scales are combined for the section score (given in capital letters) based on the section weight (given in parentheses). The section score is given in solid bars and refers to the lower scale.

Applications

BQA may be used to evaluate buildings on a common basis while retaining the ability to differentiate

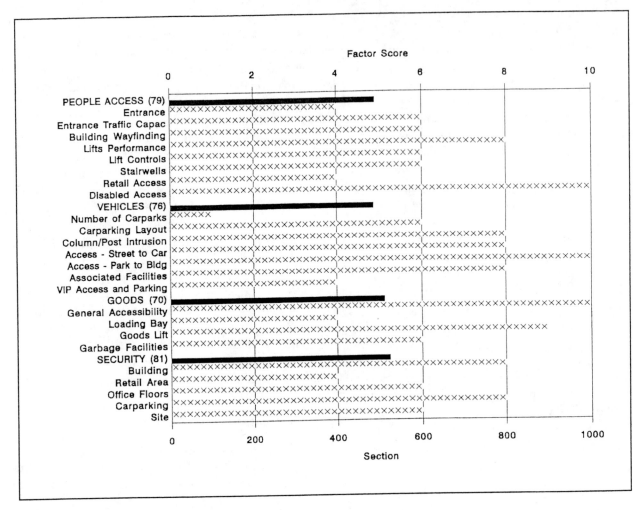

Figure 4.2 Example of Category 3 scores

according to the requirements of a particular organization. This is achieved by the provision of graded levels of information. Comparison of category scores permits the identification of general areas of particular concern, which can then be traced through the sections and then to specific factors.

For example, the owners of a large vacant 1970s central city office building were competing in a market with considerable vacant office space. BQA was one of the tools used to evaluate opportunities for improving the attractiveness of the building. The BQA analysis revealed that the building scored significantly less than market-leading buildings in Category 6, Working Environment. This covered

aspects of acoustic conditions, lighting, thermal environment, temperature, humidity ventilation, and air quality. The refurbishment design concentrated on improving these elements. With this work completed, a reevaluation of the plans gave a 39 percent improvement in this category. The final upgrade specification met the owners' investment criteria. The energy efficiency work led to a national award, and the building is now rented.

BQA also can be used to compare competing buildings. A large financial organization found itself with two head offices in the same city as a result of a merger. Both buildings provided apparently suitable facilities, but objective information was required to

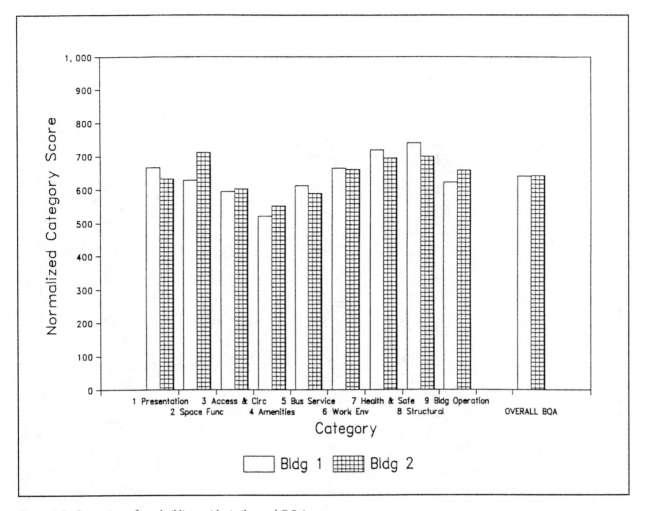

Figure 4.3 Comparison of two buildings with similar total BQA.

support the retention of only one building. BQAs were carried out on both buildings, and the assessments were then used to identify the benefits and drawbacks of each building.

Figure 4.3 compares BQA category scores for the two buildings. The overall BQA scores are very close (646 and 650), but there is considerable difference in the scores for each category. The use of a profile comparison is not uncommon, but the advantage BQA offers is that it is also possible to progress through two further levels of information.

In this example, both buildings have very similar Category 3, Access and Circulation, scores. Figure 4.4 provides information on the section scores, where it

can be seen that building 1 has better *people access* than building 2, while building 2 has better *security* than building 1. Further information is available from examination of the individual factors. The result was that one building was selected to be retained.

Obviously, to make full use of BQA, an organization must be in a position to make major decisions about the physical attributes of the buildings it uses or to relocate to more suitable buildings. Assuming the organization is in a position to make such decisions, procedures based on comprehensive and enumerated frameworks provide additional assistance to strategic planning. In particular, they provide the

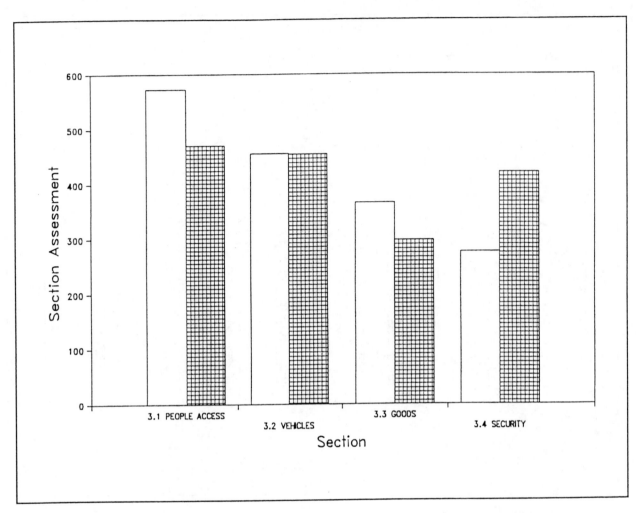

Figure 4.4 Category 3 by section for two buildings.

various groups within the organization with a common language for dealing with its buildings and a framework for the storage of management information. The comprehensive nature of the BQA ensures that aspects of present or future interest can be investigated and recorded in a consistent, coherent structure.

Acknowledgments

BQA was developed for Quality Assessment International, Ltd., a company owned by Rider Hunt, Ltd. It is now distributed in Australia, New Zealand, the United Kingdom, and the United States.

4.4 Serviceability Tools and Methods[1] (STM): Matching Occupant Requirements and Facilities

Gerald Davis and Françoise Szigeti
International Centre for Facilities, Ottawa, Canada

Buildings are among the largest, most complex, and long-lasting "products" that we humans create. Their purpose is to provide shelter for human activities; therefore, they are responding to what is, after food, one of the primary human needs.

In many developed countries, the building industry is one of the biggest in terms of output and employment (e.g., the construction industry alone accounts for 10 percent of the gross domestic product of the European Union and EFTA countries combined and for one in eight jobs in the EU). Yet it is a fragmented industry, with a poor institutional memory, little research about the building product as a whole, and almost no feedback loop.

"Customers" for these "products," unless they are on the staff of large organizations, are at a disadvantage. They probably make a buy decision or sign a lease for this product only a few times in their life and have no *Consumers Report* to guide them. More often, as occupants, visitors, and other users or stakeholders, they have little or no say in why or how facilities are built, renovated, selected, or evaluated.

Over the years, many project-specific building programs have been written, often "reinventing the wheel" and treating each project as a unique, one-off event. Buildings have been evaluated, but there has been no consistent format or link between the programs and the evaluations.

For building evaluations to be meaningful and effective, they ought to relate directly to a comprehensive description of what the "customers" and other stakeholders need in a format and language that can easily be understood by nontechnical people. One of the major goals in developing the *Serviceability Tools and Methods* (STM) approach was to create such a comprehensive framework and a process for involving all stakeholders, where possible.

After outlining key points about STM and responses to the questions most often posed to us, we will illustrate how STM is used in practice based on an example from The Netherlands.

What is serviceability?

Serviceability is the capability of a building to perform as required. A serviceable workplace is capable of meeting occupant needs, now and in the future.

What is STM?

The serviceability tools and methods (STM) approach to programming and building assessment was designed to bridge between facility programs written in user

language on the one side and outline specifications and evaluations written in performance language on the other. For organizations with many facilities that house similar types of functions, STM captures a systematic and consistent record of the institutional memory, speeds up the functional programming process, and provides comprehensive ratings in a short time without being simplistic. STM is a set of macro, broad-brush tools appropriate for strategic overall decision making. STM includes tools to deal both with *demand* (occupant requirements) and *supply* (serviceability of buildings). It is therefore far more than the building evaluation technique that it includes.

At the heart of STM is a pair of matched multiple-choice questionnaires. One is a set of scales for setting functional requirements (demand) using nontechnical words. The other is a set of scales for rating the serviceability of buildings and building-related facilities (supply) using technical and performance terms to describe indicators of capability for combinations of building features. These scales cover over 100 topics of serviceability (see Fig. 4.9) and assess more than 340 building features. Each set of scales can be used separately and independently of the other. Each can be used to add understanding and information about the other. STM is an open, standardized approach that can be adapted easily to reflect the particular needs of a specific organization.

STM includes several kinds of tools, along with procedures, documents, and computer templates for using them. These are descriptive text profiles, functional requirements, bar-chart profiles, quantity spreadsheet profiles, a building loss features rating table, a footprint and layout guide, and building serviceability bar-chart profiles.

Three generic versions of the functionality profiles have been developed up to now. These versions set out the levels of serviceability typically needed in North America for office workplaces for basic general office functions, offices with much public contact, and workplaces requiring basic functionality with enhanced protection for sensitive information or for valuable papers such as checks. Others are being developed.

On the demand side, the STM requirement tools were developed intentionally as a comprehensive set of questions that can be used separately by occupant groups to define the main components of a "basic functional program or brief." This can be done with as much or as little participation from the occupants and other stakeholders as is appropriate in each situation. We recommend using a participatory, sociotechnical approach, as described in the STM manuals and American Society for Testing and Materials (ASTM) standard practice.[2]

On the supply side, serviceability ratings provide an overview of the capabilities of facilities and buildings. Serviceability ratings often will point to the need for further investigations when deficiencies are uncovered. The STM ratings complement but do not replace other building evaluation techniques such as building condition reports, in-depth technical evaluations, walkthrough/touring POEs, special audits for specific issues, occupant satisfaction studies at move-in or during occupancy and other "expert" investigations. STM does not itself prescribe solutions. Serviceability ratings do assess the performance of building features as noted during a building tour without requiring that the rater use specialized equipment.[3]

Although STM can be used simply to rate the serviceability of buildings, it is much more powerful because it focuses primarily on defining the needs and expectations of the "customers" and provides direct links between occupant requirements (demand) and specific combinations of building features (supply).

Individuals without a lot of technical knowledge and skills can apply the STM tools effectively after 1 week of training. STM requires no technical knowledge from the occupants, users, and other stakeholders participating in the process other than the knowledge of who they represent, of what they do and need now, and of the range of changes they expect in the future. For the process to be most effective, however, it is useful to add an "informed" facilitator to the team when defining user requirements.

When can STM be used and for what purposes?

The STM method is a versatile set of tools that can be used in many different ways to help plan, cost, design, procure, use, maintain, operate, and manage facilities. STM can be of use to select properties to rent or buy, prepare an asset management plan, investigate occupant complaints, manage a portfolio of properties, review architectural designs and rehabilitation proposals, or plan new construction projects. The STM kit of processes and tools provides a "road map" to

- Describe the occupant group or organization, its mission, structure, staff, workflow, etc.
- State the functional requirements, current and future, and produce a "requirement profile."
- Estimate "effective" floor area requirements of the group or groups to be housed.
- Rate the capabilities of buildings and facilities and produce a "facility serviceability profile."
- Assess building and space planning loss features in existing buildings or proposed designs.
- Match "demand" and "supply" and highlight the shortfalls as well as the surpluses.
- Find "best fit" for a specific occupant group within a given financial envelope.

What are the benefits of using STM?

- It is a quick, low-cost way to compare what is required to what exists, is proposed, or is delivered.
- It is normally used in a participatory manner or as part of sociotechnical planning.
- It is a tested and proven communication tool between facilities management groups and their "customers."
- It is a way to inform the occupants, to build trust, and to include them on the team.
- It can easily be used with all stakeholders and provides a common ground for discussion.
- When used in difficult situations, the consistent result has been increased occupant/user satisfaction.

How was STM developed, and what is its current status?

STM was developed as a management aid for Public Works Canada (now PWGSC), building on the multisponsor project ORBIT-2[4] and on many years of practice in functional programming and evaluation. It was approved as a component of government policy by the federal government of Canada in late 1993.

How long does the STM process take for one project at one site?

To define the requirements of one occupant group for generic office functions can take from 2 to 5 days, based on the existing scales. To rate one facility can take 1 to 3 days, including preparation of reports.

Does the involvement of "customers" and other stakeholders increase project cost?

Not in our experience. On the contrary, it is an effective way to avoid specifying facilities with higher levels of requirements than occupants or the market actually requires. Building design professionals may know what constitutes a "good" building, but occupants and property managers know what requirement levels they need to do their work or operate a building. Allocation of funds can therefore be adjusted more appropriately.

How is STM calibrated?

The scales use a 9 to 1 gradation, 9 representing more and 1 representing less, rather than good to bad. For example, a building might provide more or less security, be more or less easily identified by the public, or be more or less flexible and able to cope with churn and change. Level 5 of the rating scales is calibrated to reflect the level of functionality and normal construction of what, in a town of 50,000 people, the North American Building Owners and Managers Association (BOMA) defines as a class B building. Level 5 of the requirement scales would be satisfied by the performance of the building features described in level 5 of the rating scales.

Why is STM expressed as a profile of performance topics and not a "bottom line" score?

A serviceability profile is far more informative than a single score and far less misleading. A profile can be

scanned quickly and permits "management by exception." Buildings and facilities are not necessarily better or worse, although they may have different levels of quality and capability. An existing building or facility can be quite appropriate for one occupant group and unsuitable for another. Tradeoffs will be made, depending on the functional needs of an occupant group and its location requirements, the rent, fit-up, and cost-to-cure of selected facilities on offer, and the financial envelope for the project. Adding the numbers for all the topics together would not be meaningful and would lump together many more fruits than just apples and oranges.

Why is it so important to consider building features in combination rather than separately?

More than one building feature normally contributes to the capability of a facility to respond to any one stated requirement. A building is more than the sum of its parts. Until now, however, building elements and systems have been tested and assessed separately from each other. Yet, for example, the performance of the lighting system will depend, in part, on the color of the paint and the light absorbency of the carpet. For STM, the wording and sequence of requirements, and corresponding combinations of building features, were derived from the years of experience of the International Centre for Facilities (ICF) team and ICF senior advisors, reviews by PWGSC and ASTM, and several years of pilot testing with real occupant groups, in real buildings, and on real projects. The resulting scales are what have worked best so far in practice. As with any standard documents, the scales are likely to be edited and added to over the next 5 years to incorporate the lessons from further experience in use.

Can the Building Loss Features (BLF) of buildings and designs be estimated?

STM specifically addresses this question. It is common knowledge that the "usable area" as defined in ANSI/BOMA Z65.1 still contains some space that an occupant group cannot use. It may be space used by columns and convectors or space that cannot be used effectively for space planning purposes because of building features such as space required for internal circulation and access to fire exits or conflicts between different building grids, etc. In our experience, the cumulative impact of these building loss features can range from a low 2 percent to a high 32 percent of the "usable area." Using the STM Table A.7.A in scale A.7.3, "Influence of Building Loss Features on Space Needs," one of the Canadian provincial government agencies rated the complete inventory of its owned properties and now uses this table to review all new architectural and fit-out designs.

Can STM be used for quality assurance and accountability in design?

Yes, STM provides a key element for accountability in design. The starting point for quality assurance programs is the ability to determine and define customers' needs, expectations, and the product requirements and to document them in a systematic and orderly manner as part of a quality management system. The goal is to ensure the satisfaction of "the customer." A quality management system should include the means to monitor the compliance of all production phases and be able to verify that the final product meets the *stated and implied* needs of the customer. Quality is recognized as the "totality of features and characteristics of a product or service that bear on its ability to satisfy stated and implied needs" (ISO 9004-2, 1991, p. 312). STM provides a means to determine customer needs and expectations in a systematic and orderly manner and to translate them into an outline specification in performance language.

Is STM applicable outside North America?

Yes indeed, as illustrated below.

Assignment.[5] During the spring of 1994, the International Centre for Facilities was invited by the Dutch government (Rijksgebouwendienst, RGD) to demonstrate STM at one building in Gouda, The Netherlands. At the same time, RGD invited

demonstrations of the Real Estate Norm (REN) and of the Building Quality Assessment (BQA). The illustrations of STM are based on the actual findings for that demonstration.

Site. The demonstration site was a district office of the Dutch Income Taxation Department (Belastingdienst). The ICF team included three senior programmers. The data gathering, report writing and presentation for both the requirement and rating processes were spread over a 2-week period. The building had been built for this specific occupant group and had been occupied for about 2 years. Therefore, this demonstration was considered as a form of post-occupancy evaluation. Because of the context for the demonstration, the process for defining the occupant requirements was not used in full. Only a few staff and managers of the occupant group participated in the interviews and in setting the requirements with the scales.

Findings. The building rated very well overall compared with the occupant requirements. It compared even more favorably against North American generic requirements for "basic general" office space, which are much less demanding than the requirements of this occupant group. In particular, the capability of the building for easy, effective facility management, operations, and maintenance rated much higher than would be typical for a comparable building in North America.

The building failed significantly to meet the occupants' requirements on only two topics: A.11.6, Identity Outside Building, and B.2.7, Energy Consumption. With respect to Energy Consumption, the building was far below average for North America and for The Netherlands, but it fell short of the occupants' requirement to be a national leader in reduced energy use. With respect to Identity Outside Building to the general public, the design team had not responded to a requirement that the occupants considered to be exceptionally important. The building blended with the surrounding buildings to such an extent that the RGD staff person taking the ICF team to the site had passed right by it and circled for 15 minutes before finding the building. It was clear during the presentation at the end of the demonstration that this topic had been a source of complaint on the part of the occupant group but had been ignored by the architect and by the project staff of the central facilities group. Once pointed out, this shortcoming could be remedied easily at relatively low cost.

Response to the STM Process and Report

- *Enthusiastic response from occupant group.* The staff and managers from Belastingdienst involved in the project were enthusiastic about the STM process, scales, and results. The demonstration showed that STM is the only system that addresses the occupant requirements from the point of view of both occupants and the organization, that makes an explicit direct link between the requirements of the occupants and the serviceability of the facility and which therefore shows how the facility meets the stated requirements. The contents of the findings, report, and presentation were perceived as straightforward by RGD staff.
- *Development for the future.* Experience has show that there is a demand for further development of STM. Issues under consideration include a module to deal explicitly with assessing location from a real estate point of view, improving the ease of use, and improving the documentation style.

The STM approach proved resilient, and the demonstration was successful despite cultural and regulatory differences between The Netherlands and North America. For extended use in Europe, minor adjustments would need to be made to some of the scales to take into account the impact of local regulations and building practice, such as maximum distance from windows and natural light, position and use of the radiators under openable windows, etc. A new scale will be needed to deal with the provision of facility management services by outside organizations. Overall, probably 10 percent of the scales would require adjustments or additions.

Can STM be used for benchmarking and worldwide standardization?

As illustrated, STM provides a sound basis for benchmarking worldwide. The generic profiles have been calibrated and tested both in North America and in Europe. Most scales work well in all jurisdictions, although a few will need some adjustments to make them applicable worldwide in developed and industrialized countries. The STM scales were purposefully designed to be generic, regardless of local code or regulation. They are not intended to be used for code compliance or regulatory purposes, although noncompliance, where evident, is flagged for further investigation.

Throughout its development, STM has been reviewed and pilot tested within the government of Canada. Requirements profiles and facility serviceability profiles can be benchmarked and compared against the generic profiles that have been established and tested over 2 years during the development of the STM package. STM also has been reviewed widely as part of the normal ASTM standardization process. The STM rating process has been an ASTM standard practice since 1987. It has now been revised to incorporate recent experience and to simplify the process. The current STM scales and processes became ASTM standard documents in 1995.

The following figures illustrate, for topic A.11.6, Identity Outside Building, how the scales are used and how the results are presented. (The first three are excerpts from the actual workbooks and data for the demonstration at the Belastingdienst district office, Gouda, The Netherlands.)

To give the reader an overview of the comprehensiveness of STM, the complete listing of topics currently covered in the STM scales is included (Fig. 4.5).

Notes

1. STM was developed by a team from the International Centre for Facilities (ICF) led by Gerald Davis and including Lynn Y. Blair, John Gray, Cynthia Manuel, Donald Sinclair, Françoise Szigeti, Carroll Thatcher, Guy Thatcher, and several other senior advisors. Public Works Canada provided major funding for this work. That support is herewith gratefully acknowledged.
2. For further information about the STM manuals and ASTM standard documents related to STM, contact the authors at the International Centre for Facilities.

3. The rating process includes an analysis of plans and other documentation. Refer to STM manuals and ASTM practice.
4. The ORBIT-2 (ORganizations, Buildings, Information Technology) project was led by G. Davis, F. D. Duffy, F. D. Becker, and W. Sims.
5. We express our thanks to the management and staff of Rijksgebouwendienst and Belastingdienst for their support and cooperation during this demonstration and for allowing ICF to use the findings from this project in publications and presentations.

Serviceability Aspect A.11: Image to Public and Occupants

Scale A.11.6. Identity outside building

■ 9 Operations require maximum "exposure" to the public. The address, building and signage must be very easy for pedestrians or motorists to find and recognize, even for those unfamiliar with the locality.

□ 8 . . . .

□ 7 Operations require above average "exposure" to the public. The address, building and signage must be easy to find and recognize, even for those not very familiar with the locality.

□ 6 . . . .

□ 5 Operations require average "exposure" to the public. The address, building and signage must be easy to find and recognize, for those familiar with the locality.

□ 4 . . . .

□ 3 Operations do not require much "exposure" to the public. Most visitors are "regulars". Corporate image is not a high priority.

□ 2 . . . .

□ 1 Operations require that the office is obscure to the public, e.g. for security reasons.

■ Exceptionally important. □ Important. □ Minor importance.	
■ Mandatory minimum level (threshold) = __7__	□ NA or NR

Notes: *Space for handwritten notes.*

"Nearly always need to be in a very visible location where the public can easily find us."

"We can't make it nicer for you, but we can make it easier."

Policy is to be helpful and honest with our clients.

— 105 —

Figure 4.5 The level of the organization's functional requirements, the minimum threshold level, and the relative importance of that topic.

Serviceability Aspect A.11: Image to Public and Occupants

Scale A.11.6. Identity outside building

9 ☐ O IDENTITY OF BUILDING: The building is a well known landmark. The building and entrance are clearly visible and recognizable.

O CORPORATE IDENTITY AND SIGNAGE: The organization's identity is clearly recognizable, and readily visible from all directions. Direction signs are placed at main nearby transit stops.

O QUALITY OF EXTERNAL SIGNS: The building has special custom signage, e.g. stand-alone elements, special lighting, and full information. All signs are in as-new condition.

8 ☐ ....

7 ☐ O IDENTITY OF BUILDING: The building and building entry are clearly visible to passing motorists and pedestrians, and recognizable.

O CORPORATE IDENTITY AND SIGNAGE: The organization is well identified from all directions. Signage is adequate, and clearly visible on every approach to passing motorists and pedestrians.

O QUALITY OF EXTERNAL SIGNS: Building signage is appropriate and typical, e.g. street address, building name, principal occupant group(s). Signs have no visible deterioration.

6 ☐ ....

5 ☐ O IDENTITY OF BUILDING: The building and building entry are visible to passing motorists. The building is identifiable, and not easily confused with its neighbours.

O CORPORATE IDENTITY AND SIGNAGE: The organization is identified to a minimum level. Signage is generally visible to passing motorists and pedestrians.

④ O QUALITY OF EXTERNAL SIGNS: Building signage is appropriate and typical, e.g. street address, building name and, if appropriate, principal occupant group(s). Signs have no damage or major deterioration.

4 ☐ ....

3 ■ ● IDENTITY OF BUILDING: The building is obscured by other buildings from some directions, and from people approaching along the street from one direction. The building is very similar and hardly distinguishable from adjacent buildings.

● CORPORATE IDENTITY AND SIGNAGE: The organization is not clearly identified. Signs are obscured from some directions or are in poor light.

O QUALITY OF EXTERNAL SIGNS: Signage is minimal or impaired, e.g. minimal information, weathered surfaces, partly damaged.

— 162 —

Serviceability Aspect A.11: Image to Public and Occupants

Scale A.11.6. Identity outside building

2 ☐ ....

1 ☐ O IDENTITY OF BUILDING: The building is obscured by other buildings until viewed from directly in front, or, the building is not distinguishable from adjacent buildings, e.g. facades are almost the same.

O CORPORATE IDENTITY AND SIGNAGE: There is no evidence of the organization's identity on the exterior of the building. Signs are obscured, e.g. by vehicles or other buildings. Signs are very poorly located or hard to read, e.g. signs are too high on the building, too small, the lettering is too small or low in contrast, or signs are in shadow.

O QUALITY OF EXTERNAL SIGNS: Signage is minimal or badly damaged, with incomplete information, e.g. no street number or building name.

Notes: *Space for handwritten notes.*

— 163 —

Figure 4.6 The level of serviceability of the building it occupies.

SAMPLES: 1. Required Levels of Functionality.
2. Serviceability Rating of a Building.
3. Comparison of the Facility Rating to the Required Functionality

Requirem't Threshold Rating *Importance*

Part of A.11 IMAGE TO PUBLIC AND OCCUPANTS

				Item	1 2 3 4 5 6 7 8 9
5	3		2	*Exterior appearance A.11.1*	
5	5		5	Public lobby of building A.11.2	
4	5		5	Appearance and spaciousness of office spaces A.11.4	
9	7		8	Identity outside building A.11.6	

Part of B.2. MANAGEABILITY

7	7		8	Reliability of external supply B.2.1	
7	5		5	Ease of operation B.2.3	
6			2	*Ease of maintenance B.2.4*	
9	9		8	Energy consumption B.2.7	

1. Part of required levels of functionality, and minimum threshold levels.

Part of A.11 IMAGE TO PUBLIC AND OCCUPANTS

		1 2 3 4 5 6 7 8 9
5	Exterior appearance A.11.1	
6	Public lobby of building A.11.2	
6	Appearance and spaciousness of office spaces A.11.4	
3	Identity outside building A.11.6	

Part of B.2. MANAGEABILITY

7	Reliability of external supply B.2.1	
NA	Ease of operation B.2.3	
6	Ease of maintenance B.2.4	
6	Energy consumption B.2.7	

2. Part of a serviceability rating of a facility.

Part of A.11 IMAGE TO PUBLIC AND OCCUPANTS

					1 2 3 4 5 6 7 8 9
5	3	5	2	*Exterior appearance A.11.1*	
5	5	6	5	Public lobby of building A.11.2	
6	5	6	5	Appearance and spaciousness of office spaces A.11.4	
9	7	3	8	Identity outside building A.11.6	

Part of B.2. MANAGEABILITY

7	7	7	8	Reliability of external supply B.2.1	
7	5	NA	5	Ease of operation B.2.3	
6		6	2	*Ease of maintenance B.2.4*	
9	8	6	8	Energy consumption B.2.7	

3. Comparing the facility rating to the required functionality.

Legend for the columns above:
Extremely important Important *Minor importance*

Legend for the bar charts:
Requirement = striped. Threshold = black Rating = white

d:\act\STM\barchart\UOFV-BAR.XLS p=1994-12-05 17:46

© 1994 International Centre for Facilities

Figure 4.7 A sample of three barchart profiles to illustrate how functional requirement levels, serviceability rating levels, and their match, are graphed.

Chapter 8. Introducing the Serviceability Scales

Figure 8-A. Example of a pair of Serviceability Scales

This is the name of aspect A.11.

There are seven topics in aspect A.11. This is the sixth.

The occupants use this left-hand column as though it were a multiple choice question, to set their required level of serviceability on this topic. They decide which of these statements comes closest to describing their requirement.

This is the name of a feature. The number of features in a topic will vary from one topic to another. Most typical are three to five.

A.11 Image to Public and Occupants

Scale A.11.6. Identity outside building

Occupant Requirement Scale	Facility Rating Scale

This is a requirement statement at level 9.

9. Operations require maximum "exposure" to the public. The address, building and signage must be very easy for pedestrians or motorists to find and recognize, even for those unfamiliar with the locality.

7. Operations require above average "exposure" to the public. The address, building and signage must be easy to find and recognize, even for those not very familiar with the locality.

If the actual requirement is between level 5 and 7, then the required level would be 6.

5. Operations require average "exposure" to the public. The address, building and signage must be easy to find and recognize, for those familiar with the locality.

3. Operations do not require much "exposure" to the public. Most visitors are "regulars". Corporate image is not a high priority.

1. Operations require that the office is obscure to the public, e.g. for security reasons.

9. ○Identity of Building The building is a well known landmark. The building and entrance are clearly visible and recognizable.
○Corporate identity and signage The organization's identity is clearly recognizable, and readily visible from all directions. Direction signs are placed at main nearby transit stops.
○Quality of external signs The building has special custom signage, e.g. stand-alone elements, special lighting, and full information. All signs are in as-new condition.

7. ○Identity of Building The building and building entry are clearly visible to passing motorists and pedestrians, and recognizable.
○Corporate identity and signage The organization is well identified from all directions. Signage is adequate, and clearly visible on every approach to passing motorists, and pedestrians.
○ Quality of external signs Building signage is appropriate and typical, e.g. street address, building name, principal occupant group(s). Signs have no visible deterioration.

5. ○ Identity of Building The building and building entry are clearly visible to passing motorists. The building is identifiable, and not easily confused with its neighbours.
○ Corporate identity and signage The organization is identified to a minimum level. Signage is generally visible to passing motorists and pedestrians.
○ Quality of external signs Building signage is appropriate and typical, e.g. street address, building name and, if appropriate, principal occupant group(s). Signs have no damage or major deterioration.

3. ○Identity of Building. The building is obscured from other buildings from some directions, and from people approaching along the street from one direction. The building is very similar and hardly distinguishable from adjacent buildings.
○ Corporate identity and signage The organization is not clearly identified. Signs are obscured from some directions or are in poor light.
○Quality of external signs Signage is minimal or impaired, e.g. minimal information, weathered surfaces, partly damaged.

1. ○ Identity of Building The building is obscured by other buildings until viewed from directly in front, or, the building is not distinguishable from adjacent buildings, e.g. facades are almost the same.
○ Corporate identity and signage There is no evidence of the organization's identity on the exterior of the building. Signs are obscured, e.g. by vehicles or other buildings. Signs are very poorly located or hard to read, e.g. signs are too high on the building, too small, the lettering is too small or low in contrast, or signs are in shadow.
○Quality of external signs Signage is minimal or badly damaged, with incomplete information, e.g. no street number or building name.

These three features, taken together (in combination) meet the required level of the serviceability specified in the left column.

To rate the serviceability of a building, see which combination of features in the right-hand box best describes what is physically present in the building.

☐ Exceptionally Important. ☐ Important. ☐ Minor importance.

☐ Mandatory minimum level (threshold)=   ☐ NA or NR

NOTES Space for handwritten notes on Requirements or Ratings

Relative importance of the requirement.

For some topics there is a minimum level below which serviceability may not fall. This threshold level may be the same as or different from the required level, depending on other options and possible tradeoffs.

Figure 4.8 A page from the manual, showing how the two scales, requirement and rating, are matched. The different parts of the scales are annotated.

Topics of the Serviceability Scales

Each serviceability scale is a multiple-choice questionnaire. There are more than 100 scales, in three groups. Scales in Group A, which cover the primary concerns of occupants and users, focus on requirements for group and individual effectiveness. Scales in Group B are about the property and its management. Group C scales are being developed, and will provide a scan for issues involving laws, codes and regulations. The titles of the scales are listed below.

A.1 Support for Office Work
A.1.1 Photocopying
A.1.2 Training rooms, general
A.1.3 Training rooms for computer skills
A.1.4 Interview rooms
A.1.5 Storage and floor loading
A.1.6 Shipping and receiving

A.2 Meetings and Group Effectiveness
A.2.1 Meeting and conference rooms
A.2.2 Informal meetings and interaction
A.2.3 Group layout and territory
A.2.4 Group workrooms

A.3 Sound and Visual Environment
A.3.1 Privacy and speech intelligibility
A.3.2 Distraction and disturbance
A.3.3 Vibration
A.3.4 Lighting and glare
A.3.5 Adjustment of lighting by occupants
A.3.6 Distant and outside views

A.4 Thermal Environment and Indoor Air
A.4.1 Temperature and humidity
A.4.2 Indoor air quality
A.4.3 Ventilation air (supply)
A.4.4 Local adjustment by occupants
A.4.5 System capability and controls

A.5 Typical Office Information Technology
A.5.1 Office computers and related equipment
A.5.2 Power at workplace
A.5.3 Building power
A.5.4 Data and telephone systems
A.5.5 Cable plant
A.5.6 Cooling

A.6 Change and Churn by Occupants
A.6.1 Disruption due to physical change
A.6.2 Illumination, HVAC and sprinklers
A.6.3 Minor changes to layout
A.6.4 Partition wall relocations
A.6.5 Lead time for facilities group

A.7 Layout and Building Features
A.7.1 Influence of HVAC on layout
A.7.2 Influence of sound and visual features on layout
A.7.3 Influence of building loss features on space needs

A.8 Protection of Occupant Assets
A.8.1 Control of access from building public zone to occupant reception zone
A.8.2 Interior zones of security
A.8.3 Vaults (secure rooms)
A.8.4 Security of cleaning service systems
A.8.5 Security of maintenance service systems
A.8.6 Security of renovations outside active hours
A.8.7 Systems for secure garbage
A.8.8 Security of key and card control systems

A.9 Facility Protection
A.9.1 Protection around building
A.9.2 Protection from unauthorized access to site and parking
A.9.3 Protective surveillance of site
A.9.4 Perimeter of building
A.9.5 Public zone of building
A.9.6 Facility protection services

A.10 Work Outside Normal Hours or Conditions
A.10.1 Operation outside normal hours
A.10.2 Support after-hours
A.10.3 Temporary loss of external services
A.10.4 Continuity of work (during breakdowns)

A.11 Image to Public and Occupants
A.11.1 Exterior appearance
A.11.2 Public lobby of building
A.11.3 Public spaces within building
A.11.4 Appearance and spaciousness of office spaces
A.11.5 Finishes and materials in office spaces
A.11.6 Identity outside building
A.11.7 Neighbourhood and site
A.11.8 Historic significance

A.12 Amenities to Attract and Retain Staff
A.12.1 Food
A.12.2 Shops
A.12.3 Day care
A.12.4 Exercise room
A.12.5 Bicycle racks for staff
A.12.6 Seating away from work areas

A.13 Special Facilities and Technologies
A.13.1 Group or shared conference centre
A.13.2 Video teleconference facilities
A.13.3 Simultaneous translation
A.13.4 Satellite and microwave links
A.13.5 Mainframe computer centre
A.13.6 Telecommunications centre

A.14 Location, Access and Wayfinding
A.14.1 Public transportation (urban sites)
A.14.2 Staff visits to other offices
A.14.3 Vehicular entry and parking
A.14.4 Wayfinding to building and lobby
A.14.5 Capacity of internal movement systems
A.14.6 Public circulation and wayfinding in building

B.1 Structure, Envelope and Grounds
B.1.1 Typical office floors
B.1.2 External walls and projections
B.1.3 External windows and doors
B.1.4 Roof
B.1.5 Basement
B.1.6 Grounds

B.2 Manageability
B.2.1 Reliability of external supply
B.2.2 Anticipated remaining service life
B.2.3 Ease of operation
B.2.4 Ease of maintenance
B.2.5 Ease of cleaning
B.2.6 Janitors' facilities
B.2.7 Energy consumption
B.2.8 Energy management and controls

B.3 Management of Operations and Maintenance
B.3.1 Strategy and program for operations and maintenance
B.3.2 Competences of in-house staff
B.3.3 Occupant satisfaction
B.3.4 Information on unit costs and consumption

B.4 Cleanliness
B.4.1 Exterior and public areas
B.4.2 Office areas (interior)
B.4.3 Toilets and washrooms
B.4.4 Special cleaning
B.4.5 Waste disposal for building

C.1 Fire and Life Safety
C.1.1 Egress facilities, building is sprinklered
C.1.2 Egress facilities, building is not sprinklered
C.1.3 Exits, number and design
C.1.4 Fire protection, active
C.1.5 Fire protection, passive
C.1.6 Fire department support

p=94-12-05 18:42   r:\act\wrtg-p\uofvtopi.doc

Figure 4.9 Topics of the serviceability scales.

4.5 The Real Estate Norm (REN)

Hans de Jonge
Delft University of Technology, The Netherlands
John Gray
VUW Centre for Building Performance Research,
New Zealand

The *Real Estate Norm* (REN) is a method for evaluating office locations and office buildings.[1] REN was initiated in Holland in the early 1990s by the international real estate advisors DTZ Zadelhoff and Jones Lang Wootton and the project management firm of Starke Diekstra. These firms saw a growing demand for a tool that would enable the objective comparison of office facilities. They felt that a clear and unambiguous method for rating the quality of offices would improve mutual understanding between the users and providers of office real estate. Communication between professionals and the users of office space is increasingly difficult, since each group speaks a different language. From the outset, the initiators of REN saw it as a user-oriented standard to bridge communication gaps occurring in practice. For example, one use of REN is to enable user groups to decide the quality of accommodation they need and then to communicate those requirements to professional providers of offices.

The initiators of REN introduced it to the Dutch market in November 1991. They subsequently invited some 50 companies and institutions to participate in workshops to test, review, and refine the method. Edition 2 of REN was published in November 1992 by the Real Estate Norm Netherlands Foundation, which had been established to manage its further research and development.

This section has two parts. First, we describe the REN structure and application, and second, we outline the results of a study that compared REN with two other methods for measuring the quality of office facilities. These other methods are *Serviceability Tools and Methods* (STM), developed in Canada by the International Centre for Facilities, and *Building Quality Assessment* (BQA), developed in New Zealand by the Centre for Building Performance Research and quantity surveyors Rider Hunt. Both are described earlier in this chapter.

The structure of REN

Office facilities have to serve certain basic organizational and individual requirements, including comfort and well-being, security, and functionality. However, although words such as *comfort* occur in everyday discussions about office accommodation, many such commonly used terms are unreliable as a basis of measurement. To be reliable, a classification system for assessing office quality must use terms that are unambiguous and understood by everybody with an interest in using the tool. In practice, this means that most things included in the classification have to be observable physical features.

REN's primary structure: Two main headings and five subheadings. From the user's point of view, two fundamental considerations in assessing or selecting office accommodations are quality of location and quality of building. In the REN system, the primary categories are *location* and *building*. Location is further divided into the *site* itself, and the *surroundings* to the site; building is further divided into *general features* of the building, the *working area* of the office, and the building's *facilities* (Fig. 4.10).

Cost is another major consideration in decisions about office accommodations. The REN Foundation has plans to research the relationship of quality to life-cycle costs, but at this time, cost is not part of the REN system. This is so because the cost of a thing is not necessarily a measure of its suitability; even as an indicator of quality, cost is not always a reliable measure of what users require. It is true that

Heading	Subheading
LOCATION	Surroundings
....	Site
BUILDING	General
....	Working Area
....	Facilities

Figure 4.10 The primary structure of REN.

rental cost (when accepted by a tenant) is a measure of the market value of a particular building in its particular location. The problem is that rental cost does not reveal the various qualities that make one facility suitable for a particular user group and another facility unsuitable.

Aspects and features of office quality. The five sub-headings in the REN structure are subdivided into aspects. Most aspects are further subdivided into more detailed and specific features that affect quality. Aspects and features are the levels at which the qualities of the site and building are measured. For example, *flexibility* is one of seven aspects listed under the main category of *building,* subheading *general.* Flexibility is subdivided into 11 features, each of which is scored in the assessment process. Taken together, these 11 features make up the observable qualities of an office building that describe its flexibility of use.

In the REN structure there are 135 aspects and features to be considered in assessing an office. Figure 4.11 shows part of the REN classification under the main heading of building.

Measuring quality with REN. Users of REN score each aspect and feature on a scale of 1 to 5. Each point on the scale is a *level*. Level 5 is usually a more demanding or "higher" level of performance than level 4, but it is not necessarily the case that the performance at a higher level is *better* than one at a lower level. A more appropriate way to see the levels in REN is that they represent *different kinds of performance* for the particular aspect being rated. What is "good" or "bad" performance depends on the particular requirements and wishes of a user group.

The authors of REN have prepared a booklet containing a specification or description for each level of each aspect. This booklet is designed to be understood and used by experts and nonexperts alike and in this way contributes to improving communication between users and professional providers of offices. Technical language is kept to a minimum so that an assessment can be carried out reliably by any person with a good general knowledge of buildings. However, for some aspects, such as acoustic performance, an assessor may need to draw on expert opinion. Typically, entries in the booklet comprise diagrams or photographs that provide visual clues to the performance features at the different levels. Figure 4.12 shows a sample two-page spread from the REN booklet.

The booklet serves two purposes—one is to assess an existing facility, and the other is to help in establishing the requirements of a specific user group. These have been called the "supply" and "demand" sides of the real estate business. REN provides a tool for checking the degree of match between demand (what the user requires) and supply (what the facility provides) in a particular situation.

The REN booklet does not specify different degrees of importance for the aspects. This is so because the importance of the different aspects depends on the requirements of each organization making use of the REN method. Figure 4.13 shows a sample of one way to record and present the results of a REN assessment. It also illustrates how the relative importance or "weighting" of each item can be included in an assessment. The structure of aspects and features is listed on the left side of the format. On the right of the format there are columns for displaying

- The relative importance of each aspect for a specific user group.
- The performance levels required (on the "demand" side).
- The scores for the performance of a specific facility (on the "supply" side).
- The variance between "demand" and "supply" side scores for each aspect.

Some typical uses for REN

The REN method gives a systematic and reliable foundation of information for many aspects of the real estate business. Some common uses are

- *Defining users' requirements.* An organization can define its requirements for quality of accommodation as a program or brief for supply-side professionals.

- *Accommodation check.* A user group's requirements can be compared periodically with the performance

BUILDING

1	General	1	flexibility	1	vertical zone layout				
				2	horizontal	1	structural		
						2	construction		
						3	demountability		
						4	installations		
				3	access to building				
				4	main structure				
				5	load(s)				
				6	design module subdivision				
				7	self-contained unit				
				8	access of daylight into the building				
		2	main entrance	1	recognition				
				2	ease of operation				
				3	draft prevention				
				4	access for the disabled				
				5	spaciousness				
				6	visitor reception				
				7	reception facilities				
		3	transport	1	people	1	route from parking area		
						2	sense of direction in the building		
						3	lifts		
						4	main staircase	1	capacity
								2	walking comfort
						5	secondary (emergency) stairs	1	access
								2	walking comfort
						6	excess front space compared with area required near lifts		
						7	walking distance		
				2	goods	1	access		
						2	access to building		
						3	vertical movement		
		4	communication	1	company sign attached to or on the building				
				2	multi media facilities	1	central network room for telephone and PCs		
						2	clear height in the central network room		
						3	permitted floor load in the central network room		
						4	communication distribution facilities		
						5	flexibility	1	main structure
								2	moveability
								3	connection point density
						6	network cabling		
						7	utilisation of the cabling		
		5	maintenance	1	cleaning	1	premises/site		
						2	facade / elevation		
						3	inside the building		
						4	separation of waste products		
						5	waste removal		
		6	energy management	1	thermal insulation				
				2	alternative energy sources				
		7	security	1	access	1	parking		
						2	buildings		
				2	burglary prevention				
				3	fire				
				4	potential problems	1	lightning		
						2	vandalism		

Figure 4.11 Portion of the REN structure for measuring office quality: aspects and features under the main heading of "Building."

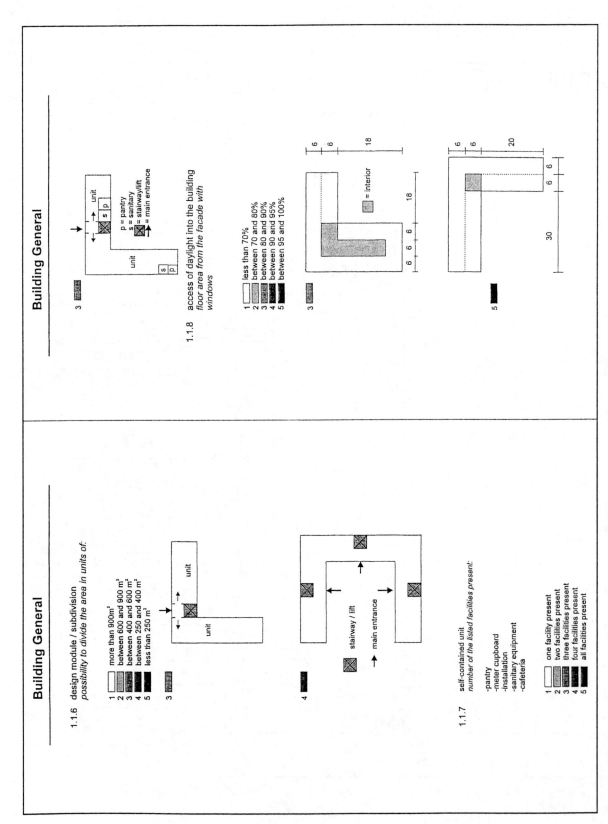

Figure 4.12 Sample pages from the REN booklet, illustrating how each aspect is measured at five levels of performance.

LOCATION

					importance	demand	supply	match -4	-3	-2	-1	0	+1	+2	+3	+4
1 surroundings	1 representativeness	1 urban classification			B	5	5					5				
		2 town planning			B	4	4					4				
		3 image			B	3	4					3	4			
		4 landscaping			C	1	1					1				
	2 accessibility	1 car	1 proximity to highway		A	4	5					4	5			
			2 traffic flow		B	5	3			3		5				
		2 public transport	1 proximity to railway		A	5	5					5				
			2 type of railway station		A	2	4					2		4		
			3 proximity to fast tram		A	4	5					4	5			
			4 proximity to a bus stop		A	5	5					5				
			5 bus routes		B	5	5					5				
		3 air transport			C	1	1					1				
	3 service amenities	1 shops for daily needs			C	1	1					1				
		2 restaurants			C	1	1					1				
		3 hotels			C	1	2					1	2			
		4 banks			C	1	5					1				5
		5 post office			C	1	1					1				
		6 relaxing or recreational facilities during lunchtime, parks, sports, libraries			B	3	1			1		3				
	4 public safety	1 social climate			A	5	5					5				
	5 potential personnel	1 educational level				n.a	n.a					–				
	6 available housing	1 housing facilities				n.a	n.a					–				
2 site	1 visual aspects	1 prominence to passers-by			A	3	5					3		5		
		2 obstruction to view	1 view		A	5	5					5				
			2 frontage		B	3	5					3		5		
	2 accessibility of the site entrance from the main road				B	3	5					3		5		
	3 parking	1 public parking			B	3	5					3		5		
		2 on site parking	1 type		A	2	3					2	3			
			2 capacity		B	3	4					3	4			
			3 dedicated spaces		A	5	5					5				
			4 size	1 width	C	3	3					3				
				2 length	C	3	3					3				
			5 manoeuvering space		C	3	3					3				
			6 use of on site parking space		B	3	5					3		5		
			7 prevention of unauthorised parking		A	5	5					5				
			8 moped and bicycle storage		A	4	5					4	5			
	4 site characteristics	1 potential for extending premises on site			A	2	1				1	2				
		2 landscaping			C	3	1			1		3				
	5 security	1 public accessibilty			B	1	5					1				5
	6 levels				A	5	3			5		5				
	7 soil pollution				A	5	5					5				

Figure 4.13 Sample pages from the REN assessment, showing how performance and weighting may be displayed.

of their existing premises to check how well the present accommodation meets their requirements and identify significant concerns.

- *Accommodation search.* A user group's requirements can be compared more easily and reliably with assessments of optional premises to select the most suitable accommodation at the best price.
- *Investment portfolio analysis.* Demand profiles for typical client (user) groups can be compared with quality profiles of buildings in a portfolio, providing information for better portfolio management.
- *Negotiation.* Variance between demand and supply standards can be made explicit and can provide an agreed foundation for negotiating rents and other aspects of tenancy agreements.
- *Communication aid.* A common language can provide the basis for better understanding between supply professionals and users.

A comparison of three assessment methods

In 1994, the Dutch government (Rijksgebouwendienst RGD) invited demonstrations of the REN, BQA, and STM quality assessment methods. The agency's objective was to gain an independent picture of the capabilities of each method and, more specifically, to assess their potential for use in the Dutch market. This subsection reports on the method of inquiry and the main lessons and conclusions to be drawn from the study.

The method of comparison. The Rijksgebouwendienst set out to compare each method in relation to three topics:

- *Customer orientation.* Questions included: What market or range of interest groups is served? How accessible and user-friendly are the processes of assessment and the forms of presentation? How applicable or adaptable is the method for international use?
- *Scope and content.* Questions included: How comprehensive is the content? What are the main uses of each method, e.g., supply and demand profiling, matching requirements to optional buildings, or choosing between buildings?

- *Method of measurement.* Questions included: How valid and reliable is the system of measurement (including degree of objectivity, empirical accuracy, feasibility)? What checks are there, if any, on the effects of combinations of building features (as distinct from measuring one thing at a time)? How are scores aggregated, and to what extent? How are specific or special needs of a specific user group given due weight in the assessment of a facility?

The agency approached the study from theoretical and practical directions. The theoretical side of the study comprised an analysis of the three methods, assessing their relative strengths and weaknesses in relation to the research questions posed by the agency.

The practical side of the study consisted of independent assessments of the same building with each of the three methods. An occupied office building in Gouda, Holland, was selected to be the subject of the comparative assessment. It has a net usable area of 4500 m^2 and houses 280 staff working for one government department. The agency invited three organizations, each with intimate knowledge and practical experience of one of the three methods, to demonstrate their use in practice. The organizations were the REN Foundation, Holland (managers of REN), the International Centre for Facilities, Canada (authors of STM), and DEGW London Limited with Bernard Williams Associates (European licensees of BQA). Each assessor group was asked to independently assess the building and, if possible with the method, prepare a user demand profile.

Findings. From the agency's analysis of the results of the study, we have compiled the following list of findings to illustrate the differences among the three methods.

Customer orientation

- The aims and audiences differ. STM and REN are designed for communication between users and providers. Both methods are oriented to the users, mainly to enable them to select an office facility that matches their requirements for quality; BQA is designed as a tool for building providers and owners, mainly to provide comparative information to assist in portfolio decisions.

- Different levels of expertise are needed. REN and STM are designed to be operated, if necessary, entirely by nonexperts. The STM manual recommends that a "knowledgeable person" should be available to an assessment team, but otherwise the process can be carried out reliably by people with an average knowledge of buildings. The BQA method is only operated by experts trained in the method and licensed to conduct BQAs.

Scope and content

- The basic questions differ. REN and BQA are based on the question, "What does the building offer, and how well does it perform at the present time?" STM focuses on the question, "What is the capability of the building to provide for the needs of different users, now and in the future?"
- Differences in scope reflect the different uses for which each method in designed. Each enables the assessment of building performance, but in addition, STM provides a method for establishing requirements and the means for comparing demand and supply profiles.
- There are differences of emphasis. For example, STM places emphasis on the quality of workplaces, space, and facilities for occupants based on the operational requirements of occupants. Both REN and BQA reflect the professional provider view of what occupants need, focused on the "hardware" aspects of a building.
- Cost information is excluded from all methods. None of the methods (to date) relate differences in the qualities of accommodation with differences in capital or operating costs.

Method of measurement

- The precision of measurement differs. REN is especially suitable for a "rough selection" and is intended as a tool for "scanning" a building to build a picture of its main qualities. Both BQA and STM are more precise in measurement terms than REN, adopting descriptors for the various levels of perfor-

mance that are much more detailed than is to be found in REN.

- BQA and REN focus on the physical attributes and performance of parts of the building, taking one feature at a time. STM measures combinations of features because the interaction between attributes and parts of a building may produce a result that is different from the sum of the parts.
- There are different approaches to the aggregation of scores. Each method provides scores for many aspects (in each method there are well over 100 aspects to measure), but they differ in the ways scores are aggregated and the manner of presenting the results of an assessment. BQA aggregates the scores for various aspects into nine "category" scores and then sums these to give a single score for the building. For example, the case study building scored 624 from a possible score of 1000). STM and REN both deliberately avoid the single score approach, relying instead on presenting a graphic "profile" of the various qualities of the building. This is somewhat like a personality profile. For example, a typical STM serviceability profile comprises 14 bars on a chart, the length of each bar representing the score for each aspect of the building.

Conclusion

The target audiences, the aims, and the applications of the three methods are different. REN is especially suitable for a rough selection in the process of finding accommodations and for broad-brush monitoring of existing premises. The method is easy to use and comprehensible for nonexperts and best serves the needs of building users. BQA is best suited to the needs of investors and owners or their professional advisers. It provides precise (numerical) scores of the building attributes most likely to affect market value, allowing simple comparison of buildings. STM deals explicitly with the different needs of occupants and owners or managers but is biased toward occupant needs. It provides separate but related tools for establishing user requirements and rating the serviceability of buildings.

Both STM and BQA are more detailed and comprehensive than REN, and probably more reliable, but they are also more complex to use. For example, nonexperts can assess a building successfully using STM, but first they should undertake a short training program to learn the process. BQA assessments are only undertaken by experts licensed to operate the method.

Despite the differences among the three methods, they have much in common. For example, in the comparative study referred to earlier, all three methods required 2 days to assess the building and report the findings. More fundamentally, all three methods use systematic and rigorous means to measure the performance of office buildings. But the most significant agreement is that REN, STM, and BQA all address the question of office *quality*. In sharing this mission, these assessment methods give new heart to a real estate industry seemingly obsessed with quantity and cost at the expense of quality and value.

Note

1. In addition to a REN for offices (1992) there is also a REN for industrial buildings. A REN for shopping centres is expected to be ready in 1996.

CHAPTER 5

User Participation

Many evaluation techniques enable a systematic check of the fit between people and their facility and can be used to inform decisions on change and development in a cost-effective manner. A range of these techniques is presented in this chapter. They advocate various levels of user participation that extend from predesign to post-occupancy evaluation and throughout the lifetime of a building.

The generic participatory evaluation method developed by Kernohan et al. (1992) has many applications, two of which are cited here. The work of Kantrowitz and Preiser is geared to post-occupancy evaluation activity, while Sanoff's approach involves users in clarifying their objectives and focuses on demand leading supply in design. Not only does user participation bring designers and users closer, it enhances the participants' sense of ownership of the resulting change to the built environment.

In Sec. 5.1, David Kernohan and John Gray describe a generic participatory evaluation process that enables representatives of building providers and users to determine action about the physical and social issues in the building. Essentially, the generic process is a robust and flexible tool that sets up dialogue between people with different interests in a building and enables decision making about the building to be enacted in an open and collaborative manner.

In Sec. 5.2, Duncan Joiner discusses how the same generic participatory evaluation method can be used specifically for post-occupancy evaluations. Drawing on a New Zealand case study, he advocates the use of such an evaluation method as "an instrument of accountability for design quality in architecture" and also suggests that the outcomes of evaluation activity should allow the creation of knowledge databases that can be useful for design and other decision-making activity.

In Sec. 5.3, Min Kantrowitz and Jay Farbstein describe the results of a 10-year research program for post office buildings in the United States. They explain how post-occupancy evaluation has become a central part of the corporate culture of the U.S. Postal Service Facilities Department and how important decision makers within the organization have developed an "evaluative attitude" to new facility design concepts. Central to the research activity has been development of a standardized building evaluation approach and publication of a *POE Guidebook* for dissemination throughout the postal service.

Wolf Preiser's approach to post-occupancy evaluation is described in Sec. 5.4. It has similarities to that of Kantrowitz and Farbstein in that it employs a mix of building evaluation techniques—in this case archival and document evaluation, a generic evaluation checklist, walkthrough evaluations, and interviews. However, Preiser's contribution also highlights a role played by many evaluation experts: training others to facilitate their own evaluations.

Finally, in Sec. 5.5, Henry Sanoff demonstrates how building evaluation techniques are used to support a participatory approach to building facility design. He describes how a range of evaluation techniques was used to promote the collaboration of students, teachers, the local community, and central authorities in the design of a new elementary school in North Carolina, which ultimately reflected strongly their views. Sanoff reflects on a post-occupancy evaluation of the school conducted 4 months after occupancy. His conclusion is applicable to the other forms of building evaluation described in this segment on user participation, namely, that "having a sense of ownership, achieved through participation, can have far-reaching positive effects."

5.1 Selecting Accommodation

David Kernohan and John Gray
VUW Centre for Building Performance Research,
New Zealand

Architects, developers, engineers, facility managers, and others who provide, manage, and operate buildings think they have the answers about what people need in buildings. The providers say, "You tell us what you think you want—we know about buildings, and we will give you what you need, trust us." Unfortunately, this is fiction. At present, however, this is about the extent to which building users are involved in decision making about their daily lives in the buildings in which they live and work.

Yet the people who really know about buildings *in use* are the people who use them—they are the experts in what buildings have to do. The trouble is that this information doesn't find its way back to the providers. The providers do have a great deal of technical knowledge that users do not have yet depend upon. But users too have a great wealth of experience and knowledge that the providers could use to do a better job. Sadly, there is little contact between users and providers, too few opportunities for user knowledge and provider knowledge to be integrated.

We believe that users and providers can and should negotiate the quality of the places they use. We have developed a generic process of participatory building evaluation as a way to bring providers and users together. For us, negotiation has two components: discussion and a means of reaching agreement that promotes action. The process we have developed is designed to be adapted to the specific needs of the

people who use it and for different situations. The process is equally useful for any type and size of facility, for design proposals in preparation, and for buildings in use. It can be applied to any built form or space that is used by or intended for people with distinctly different interests—users and providers.

The generic process

The generic process is based on the very simple idea of asking people what they know about a building. The process gives opportunities for different groups representing users and providers to focus on a building and determine action about whatever physical and social issues in the building concern them. Each group engages in a three-part process. They meet to agree on the procedure for the evaluation. They then walk through the facility, identifying and commenting on issues that are important to them. Finally, they

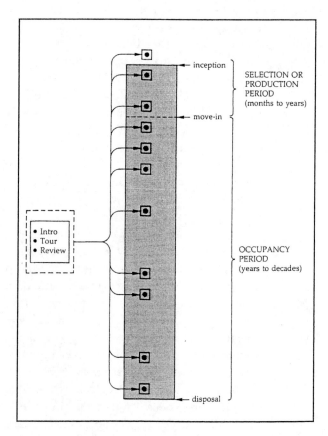

Figure 5.1 Evaluation in use. The generic evaluation process can be used at many stages in the life of a facility, for different purposes.

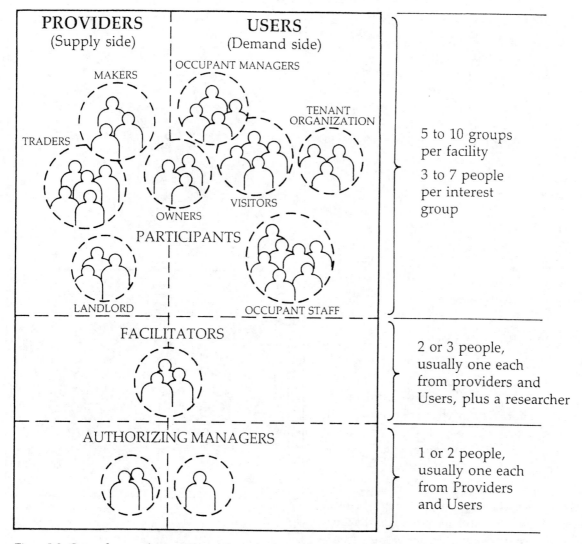

PROVIDERS
(Supply side)

USERS
(Demand side)

MAKERS

OCCUPANT MANAGERS

TENANT
ORGANIZATION

TRADERS

VISITORS

OWNERS

PARTICIPANTS

LANDLORD

OCCUPANT STAFF

FACILITATORS

AUTHORIZING MANAGERS

5 to 10 groups
per facility

3 to 7 people
per interest
group

2 or 3 people,
usually one each
from providers and
Users, plus a researcher

1 or 2 people,
usually one each
from Providers
and Users

Figure 5.2 Groups for an evaluation. The number and composition of participant groups varies with the context and purpose of the evaluation, and the size of the facility being evaluated.

meet to discuss and negotiate recommendations about those issues. We call the three parts

• Introductory meeting
• Touring interview
• Review meeting

These three events are the core of the generic process and recur at every evaluation. While the core of the process is present in each evaluation event, each evaluation itself is unique. Each has its own pattern and is designed to respond to its own purpose, objectives, and context, each of which will vary every time. The core of the process is surrounded by other events

that are directed specifically toward the different building design and management purposes. Thus we have a generic evaluation process that is used in various ways in different contexts for different purposes throughout the lifetime of a building (Fig. 5.1).

Who takes part in an evaluation?

Evaluation involves three sets of people with distinct roles. Figure 5.2 illustrates who takes part:

• *Participant groups*. These people are the building evaluators. They represent the different interests in a building, both users and providers. By interests, we mean that a group has a common concern in the building . The interests typically include those of occupants, visitors, owners, tenant organizations, makers, traders, and maintainers. Each participant group evaluates the building from their point of view as representatives of their interest.

• *Facilitators*. These people do not evaluate the building. They support and assist participants to make their evaluations. Facilitators (usually two or three) have a neutral role throughout.

• *Managers*. These people authorize the evaluation event. They are not normally involved with the on-site activities, although they may be represented in a participant group. They may initiate, approve, and authorize an evaluation and have responsibility for managing action on the outcomes.

What happens in an evaluation?

The on-site evaluation involves participant groups and facilitators in the three core events of the generic process (Fig. 5.3). The introductory meeting, touring interview, and review meeting are repeated with each different participant group. Typically, there will be anything from 5 to 10 groups with 3 to 7 participants in each.

1. *Introductory meeting*. To start an evaluation, the facilitators meet with a participant group to explain the evaluation process and procedures for the touring interview and review. Participants are encouraged to discuss their involvement with the facility and raise topics they wish to be part of the evaluation. The group then agrees on the route they will take in a tour of the building.

2. *Touring interview*. Now the participant group walks through the building with the facilitators. They visit spaces of significance to their interest and to topics raised at the introductory meeting. The touring interview is primarily a chance for the group to discuss and reflect on its views of the facility. Standard open-ended questions are used as prompts, but leading or directed questions are avoided. Topics raised by participants are noted by one of the facilitators for recall at the review meeting.

Figure 5.3 A staff group (users) engaged in an evaluation (a) Introductory meeting (b) Touring interview (c) Review meeting

3. *Review meeting*. This is where the essential negotiation event of the process takes place. Here, ways for dealing with the outcomes of the evaluation are formulated and agreed on. Topics raised from the touring interview are discussed and formed by consensus into participant group recommendations for action.

Later, all participants may be brought together at a general review meeting to develop and agree on prioritized recommendations for action.

The generic evaluation process is flexible and robust. We use it for many purposes in a variety of building design and management contexts. These purposes include

- *Fixing*. Evaluating occupied buildings for fine-tuning purposes or troubleshooting in buildings with ongoing performance problems. This also has involved the use of specialist skills for focused studies of particular issues.
- *Selecting*. Assisting the selection of accommodations from a range of existing facilities either for purchase or rental.
- *Programming*. As an aid to the briefing and design of new and refurbished facilities.
- *Developing knowledge*. As a means of gathering information to form a corporate knowledge database.

Case study: Selecting office accommodation for a major government department

A major government department asked us to help with their search for new accommodations that would bring together, under one roof, a staff of about 300 people previously housed in six different locations. The department had placed the task in the "too hard basket" for a time because (in their words) "We really didn't know how to start to look for accommodations or what our needs would be. During that time we were being approached by real estate agents and developers offering us buildings. We had no way of assessing whether these were good or bad buildings, and we really wondered how we were going to deal with this whole issue."

We began by assessing the client's needs and then formed a brief against which possible accommodations could be assessed. We discussed with management the kinds of things that produce a good fit between buildings and their occupants, including health and safety. For us, the greatest source for information about how an organization can operate in a new situation is the *people* who are affected by the change. We therefore directed our evaluation activities to obtaining accurate and comprehensive information on users' responses to their existing accommodations.

We set about obtaining information from all levels of the client organization. Our prime activity was an evaluation of the major accommodation then occupied by the department. Ten participant groups were organized to carry out the evaluation. They included groups of occupants, managers, cleaners, the designers and builders of the accommodation, the people who maintained the building, and regular visitors to the department.

The core evaluation process activities of introduction, touring interview, and review meeting were followed with each group. The recommendations negotiated at each review by each participant group were recorded and collated. They addressed the nature of future accommodations, covering not only the physical "hardware" of the accommodations and how it worked but also "software" items like building operation and management, corporate policy, and so on.

The outcomes of these activities formed an information base for the first brief, aimed at developers and agents with the intention of finding a suitable building. Topics were accordingly selected to deal specifically with building shell, structure, and services and less to do with fit-up and finishing. The brief described the ideal building from the client's perspective. It emphasized environmental quality as well as functional requirements. For instance, 9 of 10 staff members wanted to have opening windows, so that was prescribed. The brief was sent to about 40 developers and agents, and proposals were received in respect of 30 buildings. A selection was made (Fig. 5.4) from a short list using an evaluation checklist developed from the first brief.

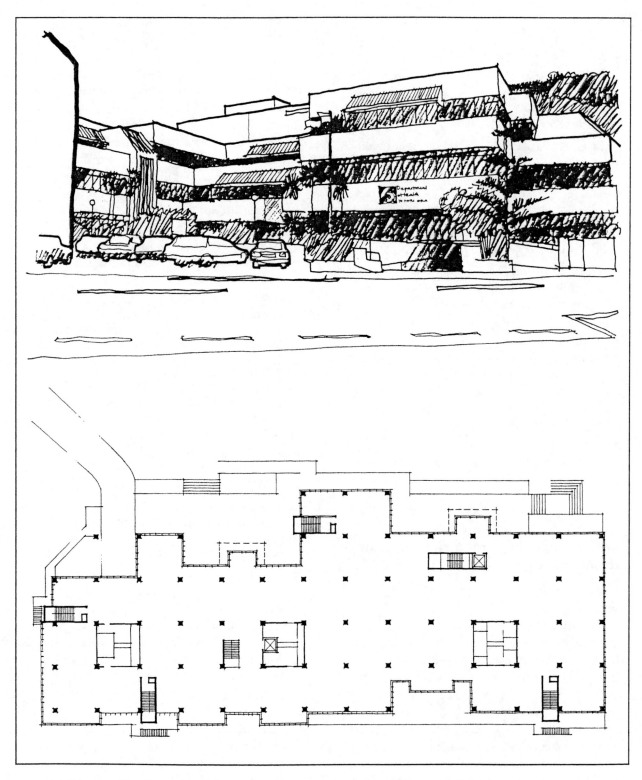

Figure 5.4 The selected building was one of four shortlisted from among 30 options. Each of the short-listed facilities was evaluated in detail against the brief.

Figure 5.5 General review meeting.

The fit-up of the building was designed by an independent architectural firm and took the form of a full internal refurbishment, which, interestingly, has since won a number of architectural awards. Seven months after occupancy, the building was evaluated for fine-tuning purposes. Again, 10 participant groups were identified to represent an interest in the building. Some had participated in the earlier evaluation of the department's old accommodations. The facilitators comprised two people from our own research team, the department's facility manager, and a union representative. Our concern was with getting the building right for its users.

The process of introduction, touring interview, and review meeting was carried out with all participant groups over 4 days. The recommendations of each participant group were recorded verbatim and were later transcribed and categorized under keyword titles by the facilitators in preparation for the general review meeting, which was held 4 weeks later. Prior to that, we met with senior management to discuss the recommendations and their attitude toward implementing them. Issues of policy, particularly with regard to space equity and workplace use, required consideration. Management was able to express its attitude toward several possible scenarios to be developed at the general review meeting.

Over 60 of the 250 staff attended the general review (Fig. 5.5), which lasted 2 hours. Ten topics were identified for discussion and were shaped by the whole group into prioritized consensus recommendations for action. The principal recommendations concerned ventilation, space equity, and workplace design. The first brief had been explicit about the standards required of the ventilation system, and the building's owners had previously accepted that the standards were not being met. Thus they were contractually obliged to achieve them. Participants at the meeting were informed about actions to date and the owner's intention to meet the department's standards.

Management acknowledged that there were anomalies apparent with space allocations for different sections of the organization. Due to uncertainties about staffing levels and the reuse of an existing office furniture system, the open-plan work areas had been designed with a limited range of layouts. This had reduced the opportunities for customized spaces for individual staff. Explanation also was given for some of the limitations of the generic workstation plans that had been caused by the building services infrastructure and the furniture system.

For many of the participants at the meeting, these circumstances had not been known. They expressed a view that if they had been told earlier they would have felt less stressed by some of the resulting inconveniences. Their mood moved from animosity toward management to a certain degree of sympathy. All agreed that unit managers should now take a proactive responsibility for discussing and negotiating individual requirements for space and equipment within overall department policy. In a sense, lines of communication were reestablished.

Other recommendations addressed issues of lighting, noise, signage, meeting rooms, slipping at entrance, coffee bar layout, and safety. Finally, a "catch-all" recommendation was made to ensure that all issues not addressed specifically at the general review would be addressed as part of normal building management activity. The meeting concluded with some "on the spot" undertakings for work to be carried out. Intentions for action in response to other recommendations also were declared, and the mechanism for keeping staff informed of progress was made clear. Senior management commented, "The whole process came at a time when we were moving to a new organizational setup. So we found it really useful to look at the way in which we worked and the way in which we wanted to work in the future. The evaluation process made that possible."

A by-product of conducting this evaluation was to find evidence of how major issues of concern to people may be overlooked if a general participatory approach is not adopted. In parallel with our participatory evaluation, we carried out a direct comparison of the building's performance against the objectives set out in the first brief. We created a checklist of over 100 required items as stated in the first brief and used this to check conformity in the occupied building. Only three failures to conform were identified. However, the impact of the items that failed, as identified in the participatory evaluations, was given

great significance and importance by the participants. A failure rate of 2 or 3 items out of a checklist of 100 seems trivial at first glance. However, if use of the checklist had been the only approach to evaluating the building, the strength of participants' concern with these issues would have been missed. Our use of the checklist demonstrated to us some of the limitations of evaluation methods that remain remote from users.

Conclusion

Our evaluation process set in train a dialogue that we have termed *social negotiation*. The evaluation process creates social situations in which people have free and equal opportunity to engage in negotiation through dialogue, and while differences are acknowledged, no one group's view is privileged. Equal credence has to be given to values, intentions, and perceptions. We have found that people develop a commitment to knowledge that emerges through dialogue.

However, in addition to dialogue, there is a need to reach agreement and promote action. Ensuring that action is taken to implement what has been negotiated is critical to the success of the intervention. We have shown that there are multiple benefits from using the generic evaluation process—physical and social, immediate and long term. Often the changes recommended are organizational, a result of at last talking about an issue and sorting it out face to face. If there is no resulting action, then the facility remains unchanged, and the purpose of the intervention remains unrealized. Once the evaluation event is over, everyone needs to know what happened—What are the outcomes, and what is to happen now? Dialogue must continue in some form. To maintain the goodwill generated, communication needs to be as much as possible face to face, through meetings and seminars.

Where issues about designing and managing building facilities are concerned, providers' interests currently dominate or are privileged over those of users. The result is facilities skewed to the providers' view of the world, a world in which users' needs are absent or at least relegated in importance. Our response has been to develop a generic evaluation process to transform this situation so that user experience, knowledge, and values gain a rightful place. Both users and providers depend on each other. However, dialogue alone will not transform anything until users and providers, in particular, acknowledge their interdependence and the need for better understanding. Participatory building evaluation based on the generic evaluation process is a means of achieving this better understanding and negotiating improved quality in the buildings we use.

5.2 POE Practice

Duncan Joiner
Duncan Joiner and Associates, New Zealand

Building evaluation as an accountability measure

The building evaluation practice described here began with the development of a method for accounting for design quality in the New Zealand government architect's office. The method used is based on the generic participatory building evaluation process described in the preceding section by Kernohan and Gray. The method was prepared initially as an instrument for property management and building design and, since the abolition of the government architect's office in 1987, has continued as a general architectural practice design and property management service offered to clients.

In the late 1970s, the New Zealand government architect's office was under political pressure to demonstrate its effectiveness in delivering an architectural service to government departments and agencies. The experience of the government architect at the time was that accountability for financial and physical performance of both architectural services and building designs was relatively easy to establish, since they can be measured using conventional accounting and engineering practices. But the government architect was unable to show that buildings delivered on time and within cost were working well for those who used and managed them (Joiner, 1983). There were no conventional practice methods to hand that could help to demonstrate how well a

building was working for those who used and managed it. There was no simple way to account for quality.

The government architect commissioned a research team from Victoria University of Wellington to help his designers develop a method of assessing the performance of government buildings in use. The development of the building evaluation method and its applications is fully described elsewhere (Kernohan et al., 1992). Advice also was taken from other experts, notably Robert Shibley, who was at that time directing a program of postoccupancy evaluation (POE) on behalf of the U.S. Army Corps of Engineers—one of the few government agencies in the world then successfully operating a POE program (Shibley, 1985). Note also was taken of studies into perceptions of design quality for public buildings, which show that designing, making, and using buildings involve processes of social negotiation and that it is through negotiation that definitions of design quality are achieved (Joiner and Ellis, 1985).

The government architect's office had working relationships with many other government departments and agencies for whom it designed buildings. A number of these became important partners and participants in the development of the building evaluation process. The development of evaluation practice was therefore itself a process of social negotiation between designers, providers, and users of buildings and reflected ideals for both building delivery and evaluation.

Requirements for accountability

As an instrument of accountability for design quality in architecture, there were a number of things the government architect expected building evaluation to address:

• It must account for physical and sociocultural phenomena simultaneously. It had to account for how well buildings accommodated the expectations of occupants and their organizational structures. Perin (1970) described how each person who uses a building has his or her own expectations associated with that building. It seems reasonable to suggest that design quality is related to the extent to which expectations are met.

- Findings must be useful for design and more than just judgments on historical events. They must be presented and referenced in ways that make them easy to use and accessible in design. There was concern that many of the results of building and behavioral research remained inaccessible to designers (Joiner et al., 1987).

- There was an intention to build a database from the accumulated findings of building evaluations that would inform the design and modification of government buildings. There was a belief that without a commitment to a database, building evaluation would not be effective (Zeisel, 1989).

- It was acknowledged that if building evaluations were going to be undertaken when necessary and to be effective as a process of negotiation, they must be structured as a process that could be arranged within an organization from the bottom up. It must be a participatory and nondirected procedure that could be initiated by anyone (Kernohan et al., 1992).

Use of the generic process in practice

As noted earlier by Kernohan and Gray, the generic participatory building evaluation process offers much more than a record of how well a building is working. Because it is set up as a process of social negotiation, it is easily integrated with other building design and management activities, and it has been used for building briefing, design development, and facilities management.

The success of the process in practice comes from its flexibility—when it is used in a noninstitutionalized way as an "approach to finding out about" rather than as a research method. The experience of many designers is that the results of conventional research instruments such as surveys, questionnaires, and interviews are of limited use (Joiner et al., 1987). This is largely because such methods separate the participants from their subject matter, and their structure predetermines the responses. The generic process has a directness and immediacy that is not available in conventional structured research methods. Findings

are presented in the form and structure in which users perceive buildings rather than being structured by the research design. Recommendations from evaluations are based on actual comments of building users.

Many users of building evaluations believe it is important to build a database and that building evaluation will be ineffective without one (Joiner and Ellis, 1989). But a database of information from building evaluations has yet to be established. This may be for organizational and resource reasons—no one building owner seems interested, and since there is no longer a government architect's office in New Zealand, there is no centralized agency that would see this as its role. Yet building evaluations continue to be commissioned in increasing numbers as a recognized part of building programming, design, and delivery.

A direct benefit of participation in an evaluation is that it enables people to understand facility decision making and to become aware of options, possibilities, and limitations in the use of their buildings. The understanding brought about by an evaluation can reduce frustrations and engender a sense of pride among staff in the facility they are operating. Staff members need to know how to make the best use of the building they work in—its benefits and shortcomings—in order to provide a good service to customers. This has been referred to as the *therapeutic* aspect of building evaluation in practice (Joiner and Ellis, 1989).

In addition, it is important to acknowledge that building evaluation is an intrinsic part of design practice. The work of Watson (1985) and others who have used the generic evaluation process in design development shows that it can provide empowerment through understanding for all who participate in building processes. The result of this can only be more satisfied people.

Case studies

Use of the generic building evaluation process for post-occupancy evaluation (POE) purposes is described in two groups of case studies. The studies were carried out for the New Zealand Department of

Justice. The first group, the Napier and Palmerston North courthouse POEs, was undertaken in 1988–1989 by direct commission. The commission for the second group, Auckland High Court, Wellington District Court, and Porirua District Courts, was let after competitive tendering for the POE work.

The five courthouse buildings were built to briefs that had been developed as part of major changes within the New Zealand justice system in the late 1970s and early 1980s. These changes included a redistribution of court facilities and shifts in the distribution of functions among high courts, district courts, and tribunals. Significant changes to children and young persons court and family court arrangements came into effect after the briefs had been written. In an overall sense, the five POEs were commissioned as part of the management of change in the court system.

Group 1: Palmerston North and Napier courthouses. In commissioning POEs of the Palmerston North and Napier courthouse buildings, the Department of Justice believed that the studies would assist them to acquire information useful for the design of future courthouses. To ensure this, the studies and the reporting methods highlighted aspects of the brief, design, construction, and building use that were worthy of being reproduced, modified, or deleted in future buildings. Modifications that could be made to improve the existing buildings also were identified in the studies.

The Department of Justice required these two POEs to meet the following objectives:

- To identify the extent to which the buildings matched the briefs.
- To find out how well the buildings satisfied the requirements of the building users.
- To recommend modifications to improve the Palmerston North and Napier courthouse buildings.
- To recommend knowledge considered likely to be helpful in the provision of future new courthouses.

To meet these objectives, the POEs consisted of two main tasks. The first comprised a short building survey and discussions with designers, court staff, and the Department of Justice executives, in which the buildings were compared with the brief documents and disparities noted. The second task was to determine how well the buildings met the expectations and requirements of the users. Representatives from up to 10 groups of users and people involved with the buildings in each case participated in this part of the post-occupancy evaluations.

In carrying out these tasks, four principal sources of information were used:

- Examination of the building briefs, job correspondence files, drawings, and associated documents and schedules.
- Static interviews with representatives of 10 interest groups associated with the buildings.
- Touring interviews with representatives of 10 interest groups associated with the buildings.
- Interest groups were invited to submit written comments about the buildings, and most did.

The interviews were not structured to seek responses to preset questions. Participants were encouraged to raise issues which they thought were important. In the touring interviews or walkthroughs, participants were invited to take the interviewers to the parts of the buildings that interested them and to demonstrate on location their points of criticism or appreciation.

Recording methods. Handwritten notes were made during all interviews and walkthroughs. Complete audiotape recordings were made of all interviews, and parts of some of the walkthroughs also were recorded on tape. All the principal spaces inside the buildings and the exterior of the buildings were photographed. Photographs also were taken during the walkthroughs to record particular details or items of concern pointed out by participants. Comments from each participant group were recorded in a report, and the requests or recommendations of all participants were summarized. These were categorized as items to be fixed immediately, items for attention in the long term, items for consideration when planning new court buildings, and items requiring further study.

Group 2: Auckland High Court, Wellington District Court, and Porirua District Court. The terms of reference for the Auckland High Court, Wellington District Court, and Porirua District Court post-occupancy evaluations were based on the tender and contract documents for those evaluations. These defined that the Department of Justice required evaluations of the buildings in terms of their operational effectiveness, and it sought to confirm which design features should be repeated or improved for future buildings serving similar functions.

The reports from these three post-occupancy evaluations focused on the following issues:

- The extent to which the buildings matched the design briefs.
- The functional effectiveness, layout, design, quality, value, user occupancy, management, operation, and maintenance of each building.
- Features for inclusion or exclusion in future developments.
- Conditions of engagement and performance of the design consultants.
- Documentation, tendering, contract award, construction, administration, and commissioning in delivery of each project.

The contract documents required the POEs to include touring interviews with people from a range of building user groups to systematically compile users' assessments of the buildings. The users' assessments were recorded under 20 headings suggested by the Department of Justice.

Evaluation structure. Participants were drawn from building users and other interested parties selected by the Department of Justice. The interested parties were invited in writing to nominate their participants. Participants were interviewed within interest groups for what was typically a 2-hour structured meeting. Each of these meetings included a walkthrough of the building during which participants' comments were noted. The comments made by each group were then confirmed at review meetings. The agenda of a typical interview included introduction, walkthrough, and review. At the end of every review session, each participant was invited to comment on the process through a questionnaire. These com-

ments were to be used to fine-tune the design of future post-occupancy evaluations of court buildings for the Department of Justice.

Reporting. There was a difference between the reports on the Palmerston North and Napier courthouses and the three later post-occupancy evaluation reports on Auckland High Court, Wellington District Court, and the Porirua District Court. In the first two, the findings were reported separately for each participant group. In the subsequent three reports, findings and recommendations were reported under 20 headings suggested by the Department of Justice. These ranged over aspects such as the design brief, building contract issues, issues of space functionality, and planning for the various parts of the courthouse. In the second group, as in the first, recommendations were classified according to urgency of action or the need for further study.

The format used for reporting the second group of three post-occupancy evaluations reflects changes and developments in the Department of Justice's expectations about post-occupancy evaluation and how they intended to use the results.

Summary. These case studies involving the generic building evaluation process as a method of post-occupancy evaluation demonstrate several important characteristics of developing POE practice:

- The growing changes in recognition of the place of POE in practice from a unique research-based activity to a service that practices could deliver. The contracts to undertake the POEs were won on a competitive basis from other tenderers.
- The acceptance of POE as a means of assisting with the provision of essential information for developing and adapting accommodations to meet changing needs in organizations.
- The evolving expectations of POE within one organization as a result of its experience with POE.
- The range and multiplicity of agendas and expectations for POE existing within an organization—officially and unofficially and within each POE event—including checking that things have been done as required, treating it as something to badger the head office with, and understanding and managing change in the justice system.

The biggest change between the first two post-occupancy evaluations and the second three is the extent to which the Department of Justice took ownership of the process. The tender documents for the second group set out a clear structure for each study and a list of headings for the reports. This suggests that the Department of Justice had become clear about why it wanted post-occupancy evaluation. The driving force was accountability in a climate of change—wanting to know how things had gone and where they should go next. The Department of Justice saw POE as the means of integrating business policy and premises policy.

5.3 POE Delivers for the Post Office

Min Kantrowitz
Min Kantrowitz and Associates, New Mexico

Jay Farbstein
Jay Farbstein and Associates, California

Background: Why the U.S. Postal Service uses building evaluation

Since 1978, the United States Postal Service (USPS) has operated as a quasi-public corporation requiring rate and administrative approval of the U.S. Congress, which mandates it to deliver mail to all addresses in the United States. The USPS is the largest nonmilitary organization in the country, with more than 750,000 employees and 35,000 facilities. Postal facilities range in size from just over 2m² to about 200,000m² and are located in all parts of the country. Most of the facilities (especially smaller ones) are leased rather than owned by the Postal Service, although many of these are built to USPS specifications. Postal facilities accommodate a diverse but specific range of functions that are housed in a somewhat repetitive set of building types. Given this recurring set of functional and technical needs and a large building stock, the USPS is an organization that could effectively leverage the results of building evaluations.

Over the past 10 years, the USPS has been investigating ways to make its operations more efficient and responsive to customers and looking at how facilities could contribute to this effort. In 1985, the Facilities Department experimented with its first

building evaluation project, a national study of the image of postal facilities. Following that, in recognition of the potential usefulness of systematic feedback information, the Facilities Department initiated a design evaluation and research program that has been changing the way facility standards and designs are developed, refined, and communicated.

The overall research program has consisted of several major components:

- Studying the image of post office buildings.
- Developing new "demonstration" design concepts for postal retail lobbies, and evaluating those lobbies, and then creating design guidelines for future retail lobbies based on the evaluation findings.
- Developing and testing a "standardized" building evaluation approach, leading to a field-tested post-occupancy evaluation (POE) guidebook to disseminate POE methods throughout the USPS.
- Testing customer and employee response to experimental approaches to post office services and design, including a variety of types of retail services and automated self-service equipment.

The approach to research over the 10-year period combines consultant teams and Postal Service personnel in a mutually supportive way. Research concepts and issues are developed collaboratively; methodologies are proposed, refined, and adopted based on intense, iterative interactions; and the data are gathered using both USPS and consultant staff. As it has developed, POE has become a central part of the corporate culture of the Facilities Department; program managers developing innovative design concepts now assume that evaluations are a normal part of the process of testing and refining new design ideas. Important decision makers within the organization have developed an "evaluative attitude" toward the development of new facility design concepts.

Case study example: A new design approach to postal retail lobbies

One area in which the evaluation system has proven particularly effective is the development of new approaches to retail operations. Similar to other major corporations, the USPS was interested in developing less labor-intensive, more cost-effective, and more consumer-oriented retail operations. The new approach incorporates a number of innovative ideas affecting design, site selection, operations, and personnel selection and training. The approach emphasizes customer choice, self-selection, and ability to perform a variety of postal retail activities without interacting directly with a postal clerk. These new types of post offices, originally called the "Store of the Future" (but now known as "Postal Retail Stores"), are similar to other retail establishments, designed primarily to sell stamps and other postal products rather than to sort, process, or distribute mail. Design innovations include

- A focus on retail image and marketing, including an attractively designed self-service retail display where a variety of prepackaged, shrink-wrapped, bar-coded stamp packets are arranged on a display wall.
- An expanded self-service area called "Quickpost" that offers a set of new self-service stamp vending machines and various devices to allow customers to weigh packages themselves and determine the appropriate postage.
- Letter and package drop boxes that are close to the front of the "store" and easily accessible to customers.
- A revised layout and supportive graphics that emphasize the quickest and most cost effective service options and which expose customers to new products and services, encouraging increased sales.

This approach is aimed at improving customer satisfaction and postal service efficiency by

- Saving customer time, since customers do not have to wait on long lines for simple transactions such as stamp purchases.
- Increasing customer choice; customers browse through a variety of stamps that are displayed in the open and make their own selections.
- Saving postal clerk time. Since stamps are prepacked and bar coded, clerks can simply scan the package electronically to determine the price rather than guiding the customer through a time-consuming selection process.
- Increasing the percentage of clerk time performing complex transactions and calculations that require

assistance from trained personnel. Overall, the aim is to lower the cost per sale by reducing clerk time.

Research

The first evaluations of retail facilities were carried out in 1986 on a set of demonstration lobbies distributed around the country. Based in part on the findings, the Postal Service developed the concept of the "Store of the Future" and built two prototypes in the Washington, D.C., area in 1988; they were evaluated shortly thereafter, and the results used immediately to develop the next generation. The time frame for this input was so short that the evaluation team presented initial finding at the architects office before the report could be prepared.

By 1993, the Postal Service was committed to "rolling out" the new concept, now called the "Postal Retail Store," and two prototypes of these facilities were evaluated, one in Kalamazoo, Michigan, and one in Washington, D.C., (the Union Station Post Office).

Union Station is a national landmark that recently received a multimillion-dollar renovation. In addition to serving as the major terminal and transfer station for regional trains and the Metro underground lines, it now houses a variety of mostly upscale retail shops and restaurants. The post office is located at the end of a busy passageway, outside the main stream of shopping traffic but near the Metro entry.

The post office displays an array of prepackaged stamp stock, provides two mail drops, a self-service scale with rate display, multicommodity and individual stamp vendors, and a parcel slide (see definition below). A retail products clerk and a full-service postal clerk staff two counter positions at the rear of the store.

Methodology

In order to measure a variety of responses and evaluate a number of issues, several information-gathering techniques were used. These included

- *Presite visit forms*. Facility managers and postal operations personnel completed detailed description forms prior to the site visits, providing construction history, building configuration, postal operations, and manager assessments of the facility.

• *User interviews.* As they exited the post office area, a random sample of users was selected for interviews. Customer interview questions focused on issues related to patterns of use, design, quality of service, and the concept of providing a post office with characteristics of a retail environment.

• *Clerk interviews.* Clerk interviews focused on how the unique operations and architectural design supported customer service and retail operations.

• *Store manager interview.* The station manager was interviewed to explore operational issues unique to the Postal Retail Store.

• *Touring interview.* A touring interview was scheduled for the first day of the site visit. The approach involved taking a slow tour through the facility with a variety of people who were or had been involved in its planning, design, operation, and maintenance. At designated places along the route, the facilitator asked the participants about the characteristics of the area, their opinions about how well it functions, its appearance, and other features.

• *Focus groups for customers and staff.* Researchers conducted two focus group sessions, one for staff and one for customers. The participants were asked questions about a variety of design issues, and their responses were recorded and videotaped (with informed consent) from behind a mirrored window.

• *Space-use observations.* From an unobtrusive vantage point, we systematically observed patterns of use at specific locations throughout the store. This was done at varying times of day (opening and closing, lunch hour, and busy after-work times).

• *Physical environment checklist.* A checklist was used to record physical characteristics of the post office, including such factors as door type and operation; types, sizes, and placement of signs; floor and wall materials; lighting; and dimensions of key fittings (such as the customer service counter).

• *Assessment of systems and details.* We examined technical issues such as construction detailing and installation; selection of materials, fixtures, and finishes; and the performance of HVAC, lighting,

security, and electrical systems. Review of the construction documents also was conducted to evaluate their overall clarity and completeness and to confirm field observations.

• *Photographic documentation.* Photographs were taken to document use patterns such as queuing, interactions, and merchandise selection as well as design features such as lighting, details, materials performance (wear and tear), and so on.

Summary of findings

In general, both the Postal Retail Store concept and its expression in Union Station were very well received. Customers and employees alike commented on the convenience, positive image, and more efficient service encouraged by this approach. Customers made many spontaneous comments about how the post office was attractive, well organized, and convenient. However, several issues were identified that need to be improved in future designs.

The store projects an up-to-date, professional image. However, while the signage mounted directly on the facade is readable from directly in front of the store, it is not very visible to the majority of users, who approach from either side.

The post office left customers with a very positive impression of fast service. Almost everyone who was interviewed responded favorably, commenting on the efficient and friendly staff who went out of their way to serve customers. Focus group participants appreciated the short waiting times, typically less than 5 minutes, and the quick, efficient service. Customers strongly supported locating Postal Retail Stores in other retail settings, such as shopping malls. People appreciated the ability to self-select stamps. A significant number commented that they made repeat visits to the store to look over the stamps and even brought friends and relatives. Many people were observed to browse through the stamp display.

During the site visit, there were difficulties caused by nonoperational machines and by operation of the policy not to sell display or single stamps (except from the machine that was out of service). Many customers wanted less postage than the clerks could sell. Some bought additional postage, some were sent to the full-service station across the street, and several left in anger.

A parcel slide (a fixture that is meant to channel circulation to the correct location for queuing) is immediately apparent to the entering customer. Contrasting floor tiles also indicate the direction for queuing. Despite these gestures, queuing was sometimes confusing to customers, who did not realize that the lines provided different services, despite a sign to that effect.

The work room is crowded and appears to have insufficient storage. There are also several operational issues at Union Station that need policy consideration. These include customer complaints about the lack of availability of single stamps, problems obtaining stamp stock in a timely manner, frequent false alarms from the electronic surveillance system, and problems getting the vending equipment fixed in a timely manner.

Recommendations

While most elements were functioning well, the following items were identified for future improvement:

- Reduce queuing problems through improved signage, allowing all counter clerks to provide all services, or customer education (so they will know which queue to select).
- Allow clerks to sell single stamps or provide reliable single stamp vending equipment.
- Improve vending machine maintenance to include coverage and quick response at all times.
- Clearly identify the range of services available (and not available) at each station that does not offer all services.
- Resolve technical problems resulting in false alarms from electronic surveillance systems.

These findings and recommendations are being incorporated into the Postal Services program of continual improvement and refinement of the Postal Retail Store. They illustrate some of the ongoing relationships between evaluation and decision making about physical and operational aspects of building programs. Using both USPS and consultant staff in the data gathering and social interactions of the program is developing a mutually supportive corporate culture characterized by an "evaluative attitude." This contributes to ownership not only of the program but also of innovations in postal retail operations.

5.4 POE Training Workshop and Prototype Testing at the Kaiser Permanente Medical Office Building in Mission Viejo, California

Wolfgang F. E. Preiser
School of Architecture and Interior Design
University of Cincinnati

Facility visit

A *facility visit,* like an indicative post-occupancy evaluation (POE) (Preiser et al., 1988), does what the name implies. It provides an indication of major successes and failures in a building's performance. This type of visit is usually carried out within a very short time span, from 2 to 3 hours to 1 or 2 days. It presumes that the evaluator/evaluation team is experienced in conducting facility visits and is familiar with the building type to be evaluated, as well as the issues that tend to be associated with it. The following is an overview of data-gathering methods that are typical of a facility visit.

Typical issues identified in facility visits. According to my experience with facility visits, the most common issues in building performance range from technical performance (e.g., poor airflow) to psychological concerns (e.g., lack of patient privacy): leakage, poor signage, lack of storage, lack of privacy, hallway blockage, poor air circulation, poor temperature control, handicapped accessibility, security problems, health and safety problems, aesthetic problems, entry door problems with wind and accumulation of dirt, inadequacy of space for equipment (e.g., copiers), maintainability of glass surfaces (e.g., skywalks or inaccessible skylights), and so on.

While this list of issues appears to identify only negative performance aspects in facilities, *positive* aspects of building performance are usually identified also. This is evidenced by the executive summary of the Kaiser Permanente Medical Office Building facility visit that I guided at the Longview/Kelso, Washington, facility (see below). It showed that *both* positive and negative performance aspects were found and prioritized by the facility visit team, which consisted of architects, planners, and facilities personnel of the Kaiser Permanente Northwest Region headquartered in Portland, Oregon. I then carried out a very similar project, which is reprinted here, for the Southern California Region headquarters of Kaiser Permanente in Pasadena, California, where a facility visit was conducted at the Mission Viejo Medical Office Building.

In the past, I found that approximately *80 percent of all important issues and information can be identified* during a 1-day or half-day visit to a facility in a very efficient and cost-effective manner.

It is useful to prepare the respondents at a health care facility for the impending facility visit by sending both the structured interview schedule and the quality profile survey to the administrator of the facility. This helps the administrator focus on the types of issues in which the facility visiting team is interested. It is helpful if a limited number of supervisory staff responds to the quality profile survey, which is returned to the facility visit team prior to the visit (see Appendix for generic interview and survey questions). Thus the team will get a good sense of where the problems and priorities lie or where the excellent features are to be found in the facility, even *before* the site visit occurs.

Archival and document evaluation. If possible, as-built drawings of the facility to be evaluated are obtained and analyzed before the visit. In addition, space utilization schedules, safety and security records, accident reports, remodeling and repair records, and any other historical/archival data that may be pertinent are obtained and analyzed. These activities do not necessarily occur on the building site.

Performance issues. A list of generic building evaluation questions (see Appendix) is submitted by the evaluators to the client organization *prior* to the site visit. It is common that the facilities manager or

committee delegated to deal with questions of space planning and building performance reply to open-ended questions concerning the performance elements. These questions deal with technical building performance as far as environmental conditions are concerned. In addition, they deal with functional appropriateness (adequacy of space and health, safety, and security issues, for example) and behavioral or psychological concerns such as the "image" of the facility. Replies to such questions represent management's knowledge not only of problems but also of successful features of a given facility.

Walkthrough evaluation. Following a discussion with management about the responses to these performance issues, a walkthrough evaluation is conducted, covering the entire facility and addressing the issues raised earlier. In addition, the evaluators use direct observation and, if warranted, still photography or video to identify and record building attributes that may deserve particular attention. Within a few hours, a walkthrough can comprehensively cover a given building.

Interviews. Individual or group interviews with selected personnel responsible for and familiar with the facility and a debriefing of the client representatives conclude the on-site visit with the client organization. Subsequently, a brief summary of indicators of successful and unsuccessful features of the evaluated facility is submitted to the client organization for final verification and review.

Outline of facility visit phases and steps

This outline of facility visit phases and steps is intended to be generic, to provide the reader with a basic understanding of each step's purpose and results. The phase and steps do not necessarily apply to all facility visits, nor are all items listed, needed, or available in every facility visit.

Phase 1: Planning the facility visit overview. There are several preliminaries to observe in initiating and organizing a facility visit prior to on-site data collection. Liaison with the client organization is a critical aspect of all visits. The client must be briefed on the nature of the visit, the types of activities involved, the resources needed, and client responsibilities in carrying out the visit. After agreement is reached on how extensive a visit will be conducted, historical and other background information that may assist in planning the evaluation is identified and obtained. Coordination with user groups within the building is begun, and potential benefits for participants are outlined.

At this point, on-line searches and reviews of the state-of-the-art literature, including preparation of an annotated bibliography, are carried out (in this case focusing on health care facilities).

Resources for conducting the evaluation are organized, and a preliminary schedule, work plan, and budget are established in which project team members' tasks and responsibilities are defined. At the same time, appropriate research methods and analytical techniques are determined, and sources for evaluation criteria are identified. The three steps included in this first phase are reconnaissance and feasibility, resource planning, and research planning.

Phase 2: Conducting the facility visit overview. The activities, resources, and results involved in conducting the facility visit are based on the planning steps and tasks developed in phase 1, the planning phase. The main objectives in conducting the facility visit are the collection and analysis of data, ensuring the quality of data collection and analysis, coordinating the many tasks involved, and continuing the liaison with the client.

Phase 3: Applying the facility visit. In this phase of the facility visit, findings are reported, conclusions drawn, recommendations made, and eventually, the resulting actions reviewed. The findings of the facility visit are organized, and an effective reporting framework is devised. Usually, recommendations imply that the results from the facility visit must be prioritized, a task requiring continued liaison with the client. Finally, actions resulting from the facility visit are reviewed to ascertain that benefits envisioned in initiating the evaluation have, in fact, been achieved.

The steps involved in this phase are reporting findings, recommending actions, and reviewing outcomes.

Synopsis of workshop

A 3-day POE training workshop was held at the Kaiser Permanente Northwestern Regional Office in Portland, Oregon. The purpose was to train Kaiser Permanente staff in facility visit and POE methodology and more important, to evaluate a prototype medical office building in Longview/Kelso, Washington, which had recently been completed and occupied. The structure of the 3-day training workshop was as follows:

Day 1: Facility visit and POE training. Approximately 20 Kaiser Permanente facilities-related staff members participated in lecture presentations on the history, evolution, and methodology of post-occupancy evaluation and facility visits in particular. The presentations included slide lectures and videotapes of previous POE case studies. At the end of day 1, three subteams were formed that would address different areas of the building to be evaluated. Base documentation on the building such as floor plans, organizational charts, mission statements, etc. were reviewed. This included questionnaire surveys that had been sent to the administrator and supervisory staff of the medical office building prior to the workshop.

Day 2: Data gathering. On this day, on-site data gathering was carried out in the medical office building. Methods included interviews with administrators and supervisory staff, as well as walk-throughs and still photography of all major building areas. Subteams covered the assigned building areas and personnel, and they gathered intermittently for review meetings and reports to the workshop coordinator. At the end of day 2, subteams were assigned summary draft reports to be presented on day 3. Photographic slides were processed overnight.

Day 3: Reporting. Subteams reviewed their findings and drafted preliminary written and verbal reports to be presented in a final wrapup session with senior management. All the recommendations in both the written and oral presentations were organized into major sections by area or department.

Furthermore, recommendations were made in three categories of issues:

Category 1: issues that could be addressed immediately.

Category 2: issues to be incorporated in future buildings.

Category 3: issues that require policy changes.

In addition, issues were grouped according to the views of staff and patients (called *members* at Kaiser Permanente). Findings of the POE training workshop are reported below in summary format.

Selected findings and results

Category 1 issues: Items that can be addressed immediately, not necessarily in order of priority

Member issues

- Install outside covered benches for members awaiting rides. Many elderly people use Dial-a-Ride and must wait for extended periods of time to be picked up. Currently, there is neither outside seating nor an inside location to sit and see vehicles as they arrive. Also, outside telephones and a clock would be helpful.
- Reorient kiosk in lobby so the building layout and directory face both entrances.
- Install diaper-changing tables in rest rooms (especially near pediatrics), and affix appropriate signage indicating location of changing tables throughout the medical office building.

Safety maintenance issues

- Install electronic safety mats for automatic exterior doors. These doors have caused multiple injuries due to children not being detected by the electronic eye and having the door swung open on them. While the installation of guard rails has helped alleviate this, mats that activate the door by stepping on them would help more.
- Provide vision panels in doors opening into heavy traffic hallways.

- Install exterior lighting on main entry sidewalk. Because the MOB is open in the evening, this is needed for member safety.

Employee issues

- Install outdoor eating area for staff.
- Remove wall between adjacent reception areas. This would allow receptionists to provide coverage for one another and reduce member confusion.
- Install half door with writing shelf in administration area. Currently, members and staff walk into the secretarial office uninvited.

Category 2 issues: Items to be incorporated in future buildings

- Avoid use of automatic swing-open exterior doors. Sliding doors are preferable to avoid injury and are not prone to staying open during windy periods. Also, vestibules would provide a waiting area to see approaching vehicles and would minimize the wind tunnel effect in the building.
- Waiting room chairs should always have arms. This helps frail people get in and out and encourages members to sit in all available seats.
- Provide covered outside waiting areas for members.
- Plan for a cot in the blood-drawing areas. Space is needed for pediatric patients and adult patients who need to lie down while blood is being drawn.
- Plan staff lounge areas in departments that are open after hours. It is not feasible or safe for staff to travel to other areas of the building.
- Provide adequate staff lockers within departments
- Always have ramped sidewalk outside acute care area for ambulance access, as well as a loading and unloading zone.
- Put vision panels on heavy traffic hallway doors.
- Replicate the open, quiet, and naturally lit area in physical therapy.
- Do not put smoked glass (only clear glass) at pharmacy in/out counter. Short members cannot be seen.

Category 3 issues: Strategic and policy issues

- Evaluate service area strategies for the number and size of MOBs. This includes what services should be available at smaller remote facilities. The addition of unplanned specialists creates a strain on both the facilities and staff.

- Evaluate if we should be designing for flexible space to accommodate inclusion of a limited specialty presence. This may include a "bullpen" for rotating physicians and slightly larger, multipurpose exam/procedure rooms.
- Complete evaluation of centralized versus decentralized reception is needed. This would include evaluating staffing impacts, member preferences, and variations on the amount of decentralization.
- Develop a system to orient staff to the intent and use of buildings. This may include final walkthroughs with architects and planners, "owner's manuals," and lists of who to call for what problems.
- Evaluate the use of additional hallway alcoves to avoid clutter. This would add square footage, and would it really be used?
- Evaluate the number and location of computer terminals.
- Evaluate the actual use of the materials management system. Space is designed for decentralized, minimum storage, yet supply levels are causing overcrowding.

Conclusions

The shortcut POE methodology outlined in this section has proven to be quite effective in troubleshooting and/or prototype testing of building designs. This success is partly due to the following conditions:

- The POE/facility walkthrough is carried out in-house, i.e., by staff members of the client organization.
- The POE results are fed directly into future medical office building designs and thus have strategic importance for the organization.
- Top-level management initiated and supported the POE. They subsequently received and helped implement the findings and recommendations.
- Information control is absolutely essential for this type of POE to be effective. Too often, negative findings lead to finger-pointing and ill feelings about those who committed mistakes. As long as information is released to the public *only after* clearance by the client organization, this problem should be resolved.
- Training of in-house staff is one of the most effective ways to promote continuous use of POE without having to resort to expensive external consultants.

Experience has shown that the approximate cost of carrying out walkthrough-type indicative POEs or facility visits is $0.50 per square foot of evaluated space. This benchmark value held true in this project also, and it shows that significant findings and recommendations can result from a rather inexpensive and expeditious POE effort.

Building profile

1. Architect: HMC Architects
2. Completion date: September 1988
3. Total gross area: 27,500 square feet
4. Construction cost: $4,165,000
5. Number of staff employed: 75
6. Number of patients seen per year: 83,000

Acknowledgments

The excellent contributions to this project by Kaiser Permanente staff (especially Mr. Axel Gumeson) at the Southern California Regional Office in Pasadena, California, are gratefully acknowledged.

Appendix: Checklist of useful documents for facility visits

Client-related information

1. Client mission statement, organizational chart, and staffing
2. Initial program from building
3. As-built floor plans (may require updating)
4. Space assignments and schedules
5. Building-related accident reports
6. Records of theft, vandalism, and security problems
7. Maintenance/repair records
8. Energy audits or review comments from heating/cooling plant manager
9. Any other feedback concerning the building that may be on record

Building type–related information

1. Identification of selected recent, similar facilities
2. Review of programs and other pertinent information on the building type being evaluated
3. Identification and assessment of state-of-the-art literature (e.g., technical manuals and design guides)

Building evaluation interview questions for health facility visits. We would like to know how well your health facility performs for all those who occupy it. Successes and failures (if any) are considered insofar as they affect occupant health, safety, efficient functioning, and psychological well-being. Your answers will help improve the design of future, similar buildings.

Below, please identify successes and failures in the building by responding to the following broad information categories and by referring to documented evidence or specific building areas wherever possible:

1. Adequacy of overall design concept
2. Adequacy of site design
3. Adequacy of health/safety provisions
4. Adequacy of security provisions
5. Attractiveness of exterior appearance
6. Attractiveness of interior appearance
7. Adequacy of activity spaces
8. Adequacy of spatial relationships
9. Adequacy of circulation area, e.g., lobby, hallways, stairs, etc.
10. Adequacy of heating/cooling and ventilation
11. Adequacy of lighting and acoustics
12. Adequacy of plumbing/electrical
13. Adequacy of surface materials, e.g., floor, walls, ceiling etc.
14. Underutilized or overcrowded spaces
15. Compliance with ADA handicapped accessibility requirements
16. Other, please specify (e.g., needed facilities currently lacking)

Facility quality profile: An occupant survey. We wish to conduct a facility visit of your building(s). The purpose of this visit is to assess how well the building(s) performs for those who occupy it in terms of health, safety, security, functionality, and psychological comfort. The benefits of a facility visit include identification of good and bad performance aspects of the building, better building utilization, and feedback on how to improve future, similar buildings or remodeling of your own building.

In the survey that follows, please respond only to those questions which are applicable to you. Indicate your answers by marking the appropriate blanks with an X.

1. In an average work week, how many hours do you spend in the following types to spaces (specify):

Space A _____

Space B _____

Space C _____

Space D _____

Space E _____

Hours	A	B	C	D	E
0–5	( )	( )	( )	( )	( )
6–10	( )	( )	( )	( )	( )
11–15	( )	( )	( )	( )	( )
16–20	( )	( )	( )	( )	( )
21–25	( )	( )	( )	( )	( )
26–30	( )	( )	( )	( )	( )
31–35	( )	( )	( )	( )	( )
35–40	( )	( )	( )	( )	( )
40+	( )	( )	( )	( )	( )

Key for the following quality ratings:

EX=excellent

G=Good

F=Fair quality

P=Poor quality

2. Please rate the overall quality of the following areas in the building:

	EX	G	F	P
a. Space category A	( )	( )	( )	( )
b. Space category B	( )	( )	( )	( )
c. Space category C	( )	( )	( )	( )
d. Space category D	( )	( )	( )	( )
e. Space category E	( )	( )	( )	( )
f. Restrooms	( )	( )	( )	( )
g. Storage	( )	( )	( )	( )
h. Elevator(s)	( )	( )	( )	( )
i. Stairs/corridors	( )	( )	( )	( )
j. Parking	( )	( )	( )	( )
k. Other, specify	( )	( )	( )	( )

3. Please rate the overall quality of space category A in terms of the following:

	EX	G	F	P
a. Adequacy of space	( )	( )	( )	( )
b. Lighting	( )	( )	( )	( )
c. Acoustics	( )	( )	( )	( )
d. Temperature	( )	( )	( )	( )
e. Odor	( )	( )	( )	( )
f. Aesthetic appeal	( )	( )	( )	( )
g. Security	( )	( )	( )	( )
h. Flexibility of use	( )	( )	( )	( )
i. Other, specify	( )	( )	( )	( )

Questions 4, 5, 6, and 7 use the same format as question 3 for space categories B, C, D, and E, respectively.

8. Please rate the *overall quality* of design in this building:

	EX	G	F	P
a. Aesthetic quality of exterior	( )	( )	( )	( )
b. Aesthetic quality of interior	( )	( )	( )	( )
c. Amount of space	( )	( )	( )	( )
d. Environmental quality (lighting, acoustics, temperature, etc.)	( )	( )	( )	( )
e. Proximity of views	( )	( )	( )	( )
f. Adaptability to changing uses	( )	( )	( )	( )
g. Security	( )	( )	( )	( )
h. ADA compliance (handicapped accessibility)	( )	( )	( )	( )
i. Maintenance	( )	( )	( )	( )
j. Relationship of spaces/layout	( )	( )	( )	( )
k. Quality of building materials				
(1) Floors	( )	( )	( )	( )
(2) Walls	( )	( )	( )	( )
(3) Ceilings	( )	( )	( )	( )
(4) Other, specify	( )	( )	( )	( )

9. Please select and rank in order of importance facilities that are needed but currently lacking in your building:

10. Please make any other suggestion you wish for physical or managerial improvements in your building:

11. Demographic Information:
   a. Your room number/building area:_____
   b. Your position: _____
   c. Your age:_____
   d. Your sex:_____
   e. Number of years with the present organization: _____

5.5 A Collaborative Process for Designing a Responsive Elementary School

Henry Sanoff
School of Design, North Carolina State University

The amount of time young people spend in school, from preschool to the twelfth grade, is so significant that it is important to recognize that much of this time is devoted to living as well as learning. Consequently, the quality of this living is an important matter (Gump, 1987). The quality of student life and the quality of education are directly affected by the quality of the school environment. School environments include not only the physical provisions but also the patterns of a school's operations. Students' perceptions of their environment, whether supportive or hostile, interesting or boring, are also integral to an understanding of the school environment.

There is a gulf between what is known to be the needs of adolescents and their experiences in schools (Lipsitz, 1977). Decisions about schooling are more often made on the basis of budgets and buses rather than on an understanding of the physical, intellectual, psychological, and social needs of adolescents. Schools that encourage the developmental needs of young people do not look the same nor do they have identical programs. Safety and academic achievement are necessary for all schools, but they are not sufficient in themselves to produce responsive schools for adolescents.

Since young people vary in physical development, intellectual capability, and interests, the need for diversity would be an important characteristic of a responsive school. In such a setting, students and teachers would be engaged in different learning activities, where a variety of teaching methods would be used. Small group work, lectures, individual projects, and experiential learning, combined with flexible scheduling, are features that would respond to the need for diversity.

Client

The school district located in the Charlotte-Mecklenburg area of North Carolina is undergoing educational reform that can have a substantial effect on the design of school buildings in the county. The results of numerous workshops and teacher in-service training programs in 1991 have created a climate conducive to team teaching in the county's elementary schools. The growing population and the inadequacy of older schools in the area have prompted the school administration to construct four new elementary schools in 1992 on four different sites. The Davidson site is the only one containing an existing school building, located in a well-organized community with an appearance commission, a historic district commission, and active citizen's groups. The school planning administration selected the firm of The Adams Group architects because of their experience producing effective results working with a variety of community groups and a previous award-winning elementary school addition. Davidson Elementary School already had a committee structure examining excellence in education and a group of teachers and parents anxious to be involved in the process of designing their new school.

Project process

The Davidson Elementary School was designed to accommodate the teachers' and parents' vision of an appropriate environment for 600 children, kindergarten through fifth grade. Community involvement was perceived to be instrumental in achieving any changes in the traditional school delivery process,

which normally bypasses the teachers' expertise and results in a building produced by a formula. To begin, an assessment process was developed that included the use of extensive interviews with teachers at each grade level, as well as the use of workshops aimed at identifying educational objectives for different grade levels and the complementary teaching methods for achieving those objectives. Integrating findings from the educational literature with the expertise of the teachers is believed to be an approach for producing school environments relevant and satisfactory for its diverse users.

As the design consultant, the process I developed began with an introductory meeting with the Davidson Elementary School principal to outline a strategy for parent, teacher, and student involvement. The first step consisted of individual interviews with each of the school's 30 teachers to review the educational specifications provided by the Division of School Planning. The specifications consist of a quantification of spaces and a listing of classroom equipment for each grade level. The obvious limitation of the "ed specs" is that they presume a set of educational objectives and a style of teaching. During the interview process, many discrepancies were found between teachers' requirements and the ed specs, such as the location of teachers' workrooms, location of the counselor's office, and general requirements for proximity between academic and administrative areas. Teachers preferred several small workrooms to be adjacent to their classroom to allow for parent tutoring and sharing ideas with other teachers rather than the required work area designated for clusters of classrooms that would be remote from the individual classrooms. The teachers also discussed teaming and the opportunity for teachers to collaborate more effectively. With respect to spatial concerns, they were fearful that the long, noisy corridors in their present school might be repeated.

The interviews were followed by a walkthrough evaluation by the teachers of the existing two-story school building. The walkthrough revealed many negative features of their building, such as noisy corridors, desks located in the corridors for tutoring purposes, and play areas separated by parking.

Objectives

- developing language fluency
- encouraging a sense of community identity
- reinforcing individual effectiveness
- developing cognitive skills
- developing motivation for learning
- encouraging self expression
- reinforcing positive self image
- developing a sense of confidence
- developing a persistence towards a goal
- developing communication skills
- developing concept formation
- channeling biological drives constructively
- encouraging resourcefulness
- developing initiative and spontaneity
- developing introspective skills
- developing social competence
- developing tolerance of differences
- developing a sense of responsibility
- learning by conditioning
- encouraging group interaction
- learning through execution
- stimulating curiosity and imagination
- developing a sense of reality
- achieving intra-sensory integration
- developing motor skills
- learning by example
- developing memory skills
- developing self actualization
- encouraging a sense of trust
- constructive use of fantasy
- developing perceptual acuity
- involving parents in the program
- developing social awareness

Methods

- competition
- parent-teacher-student collaboration
- group problem solving
- student participation
- self preservation
- field trips
- small group discussion
- voucher system
- direct experience
- role playing
- nongraded classes
- parent participation
- lecture/demonstration
- graded grouping
- remedial workshops
- self directed activities
- independent study
- student testing and evaluation
- open classroom
- programmed instruction
- individualized instruction
- paraprofessionals
- community resources
- community involvement
- peer counselling
- contract teaching
- audio visual aids

Figure 5.6 Listing of educational objectives and corresponding list of teaching methods assembled from the literature.

The combined interviews and walkthrough evaluation disclosed the features of the building that were valued, as well as giving voice to the aspirations for the new building. A parent-staff-teacher workshop followed the more individual activities that occurred on the previous days. This workshop was intended to create a dialogue between teachers about their educational objectives, the variety of teaching methods generated from those objectives, and the types of places or physical settings that would be supportive. This workshop was designed to prepare the partici- pants for the second meeting that would engage them in the site design of their new building.

Group interaction approach

Prior to planning and designing appropriate environments for adolescents, the objectives for that environment must be discussed, considered, and decided on by the teachers, administrators, and students. The relationship between the objectives, the activities students engage in, and the places that accommodate

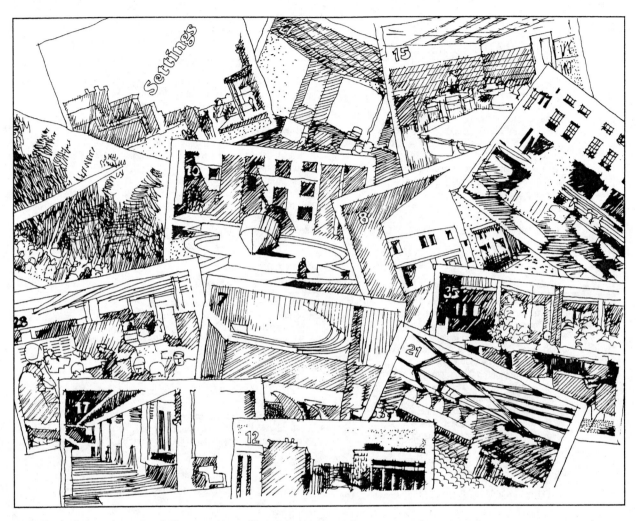

Figure 5.7 Photographs used to facilitate participant discussion on settings.

those activities is the basis for designing. The objectives that are found in the educational literature describe concepts that are paramount to the development of the young adolescent. These objectives (Dorman, 1981) include personalization of the learning environment, student control of movement, provision of adequate meeting and social gathering places, environmental flexibility to accommodate different student activities, and the ability for students to facilitate projects and studies in their areas of interest (Fig. 5.6).

While there is agreement within the education profession that these objectives may be crucial to the development of young adolescents, there is a lack of agreement about the relationship of these objectives to the places in which they ought to occur or to the variety of possible spatial arrangements. The interpretation and philosophy of an educational program have a significant impact on how the educational objectives are evidenced and realized in the learning environment. For example, "personalization of place" is an important objective because, as the educational literature points out, the young adolescent needs to have a stake in his or her environment (Sommer, 1974). An important aspect of personalized space is the presence of designated places where

FIRST GRADE CLASSROOM

1,000 square feet

OBJECTIVES:

- Develop sensory skills.
- Develop basic skills in all subject areas.
- Develop motor skills.
- Develop socialization skills.
- Develop communication skills, both verbal and written.
- Develop concepts and understanding in all areas.
- Develop sound work and study habits.
- Develop purposeful activities which will lead to greater utilization of leisure time.
- Develop self discipline.
- Develop learning opportunities to encourage maximum learning.
- Develop positive self image.

EXPERIENCES PLANNED:

- Basic instructional activities to develop fundamental skills commensurate with student needs.
- Use of manipulative aids and materials.
- Independent work for individualized instruction.
- Small group instruction for diagnostic teaching.
- Gross motor and fine motor activities.
- Utilization of audiovisual equipment.
- Arts and crafts activities.
- Use of resource personnel (parent volunteers, guest speakers, instructional aids, etc.).
- Large group instruction in specific subject areas.
- Recreation activities inside and outside, for large and small groups.
- Students will be able to utilize computers within the classroom environment.

CAPACITY:

- 25 students
- 1 teacher
- 1 assistant

TEACHING METHODS:

METHODS	TCR*	NO.	AGES
• Parent-Teacher-Student Integration	TR	4-5	6-7
• Student Participation	CD	1-6	6-7
• Group Problem Solving	C	6	6-7
• Role Playing	CD	1-3	6-7
• Individualized Instruction	TR	1-3	6-7
• Small Group Discussion	TD	3-6	6-7
• Community Involvement	C	25	6-7
• Field Trips	TD	25	6-7

* TEACHER CHILD RELATIONSHIPS:
  TD - Teacher Directed
  CD - Child Directed
  TR - Teacher as Resource
  C - Collaborative

GENERAL REQUIREMENTS:

- Ceiling height shall be minimum 10'-0".
- Walls shall be concrete masonry or gypsum board.
- Pin-up / Display space on one full wall (eg. gypsum wallboard with wall fabric covering.
- Provide windows for natural light and ventilation. Minimum sill height shall be 32" above finish floor. Windows shall have one (1) operable vent.
- Provide 1" mini-blinds for light control.
- Floors shall be carpet and vinyl composition tile.
- 12' or 16' white marker board for dustless markers.
- Tackable strip on top of marker board with map/chart holders, flag holders (2) and hooks (4).

SPECIAL REQUIREMENTS:

- Individual toilet room with outswing door.
- Countertop sink for handwashing located near the toilet.
- Equip sink with bubbler for drinking water.
- Provide wet area of vinyl composition tile for 1/4 of floor area to include floor at outside entrance, sink and toilet.

ENVIRONMENTAL VARIABLES:

THERMAL:
- Thermally treated for year round use.
- Ventilation in lavatories and storage area.
- Particular attention to external equipment noise.

VISUAL:
- Mixture of artificial and natural lighting.
- Each area should be able to be darkened for A-V use.

ACOUSTICAL:
- Provide acoustical treatment as required to isolate sounds made in these areas and/or external sounds.

STORAGE:

- 10' base cabinet with sink near toilet room. Provide plastic laminate countertop.
- Wall cabinets with adjustable shelving above.
- 26 cubby holes and space for 26 coat hangers. Space shall be 13" wide, 12" deep and 59" long.
- Provide shelving above cubby hole unit in 2 layers 12" high and 12" deep.
  Teachers coat closet 12" wide and 84" high.
- Storage cabinet 36" wide and 84" high.

Figure 5.8 Detailed first grade classroom program.

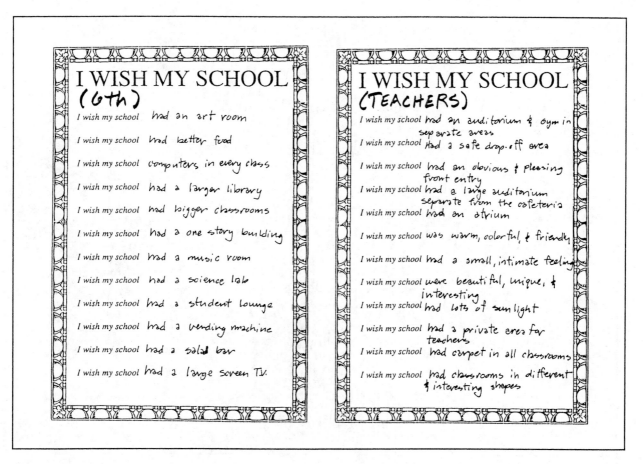

I WISH MY SCHOOL (6th)

I wish my school had an art room

I wish my school had better food

I wish my school computers in every class

I wish my school had a larger library

I wish my school had bigger classrooms

I wish my school had a one story building

I wish my school had a music room

I wish my school had a science lab

I wish my school had a student lounge

I wish my school had a vending machine

I wish my school had a salad bar

I wish my school had a large screen TV.

I WISH MY SCHOOL (TEACHERS)

I wish my school had an auditorium & gym in separate areas

I wish my school had a safe drop-off area

I wish my school had an obvious & pleasing front entry

I wish my school had a large auditorium separate from the cafeteria

I wish my school had an atrium

I wish my school was warm, colorful, & friendly

I wish my school had a small, intimate feeling

I wish my school were beautiful, unique, & interesting

I wish my school had lots of sunlight

I wish my school had a private area for teachers

I wish my school had carpet in all classrooms

I wish my school had classrooms in different & interesting shapes

Figure 5.9 Participants' wish poem.

adolescents can gather, free from danger, to engage in stimulating activities, conversation, and exploration of ideas. Such places may take the form of outdoor courtyards, outdoor tables and benches, or interior places such as student lounges or corners of a larger room.

After initial discussion of the process, the school community members were ready to consider features of the physical environment through small group discussion sessions that stressed consensus decision making. The process described as "relating objectives for learning to education" (Sanoff, 1984) allows parents and teachers to discuss, clarify their differences, and seek common understanding. The opening discussion was devoted to establishing commonly agreed-on objectives. The teachers were divided into six small groups of five according to their teaching focus. They selected objective statements from a prepared list generated from the educational literature. Participants were asked to make their decisions based on group consensus to ensure that all voices were heard in the deliberations. In addition to work groups clarifying their ideas and intentions about classroom education, there was a strong support for the school's interaction with the Davidson community. Developing a sense of community emerged as an important focus for the teachers.

The ability to link teaching methods to physical settings was a new experience for the teachers, since their teaching methods were always constrained by the existing classrooms. The use of photographs corresponding to the physical settings allowed participants to explore and discuss a wide range of traditional and nontraditional settings used to accommodate various teaching methods. Most important, the photographs describe a variety of outdoor settings suggesting the

Figure 5.10 A review of the site planning results of the six teams of teachers.

need for a more integrated indoor–outdoor environment for learning (Fig. 5.7).

This exercise was instrumental in successive interviews with groups of teachers in using the model of linking objectives to teaching methods. Teachers were able to expand the physical characteristics of the ed specs to include the objectives for each grade level, the corresponding experiences planned to achieve those objectives, and the teaching methods that might be employed. This concept allowed teachers to envision the classroom as a spatial setting that should accommodate a variety of teaching methods (Fig. 5.8).

The opportunity to use the outdoors for a variety of different activities, for small or large group activities, and for reading, art, eating, and gardening expanded the teachers' awareness of new opportunities for their new school building. This discovery found its way into the building design in the form of outdoor areas adjacent to each classroom, covered porches, and a variety of different courtyard spaces.

Children, too, were involved in offering their ideas and perceptions about the new school through their art and poetry. The school's art teacher and The Adams Group staff met with all the students in the school for 2 successive days through an art exercise where the students were asked to draw a picture of their ideal or dream school. The students made different types of drawings including floor plans, sections, and elevations. Images such as towers, clocks, and clerestory windows all appeared in the students' drawings. One of the interesting ideas that emerged from these sessions was that the media center could open to the outdoors, a feature that was included in

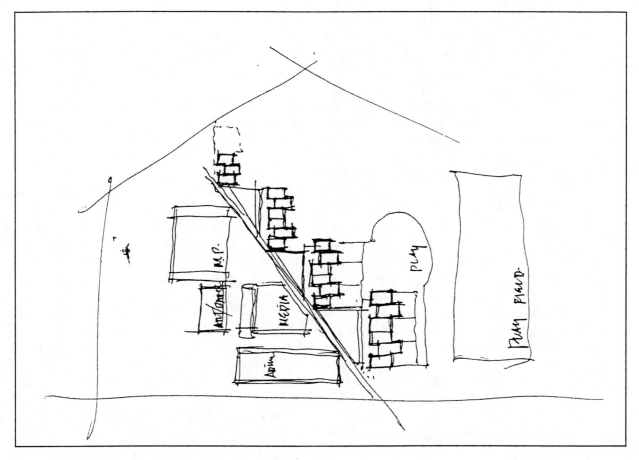

Figure 5.11 Preliminary plan sketch for the Davidson school.

the building design. The students also stressed the need for daylight in the classrooms and other areas of the building. In addition, teachers, parents, and students were asked to write a wish poem stating their desires for their new school. All participants were asked to complete the phrase, "*I wish my school...*" shown on Fig. 5.9 (Sanoff, 1984).

The results from each grade and the parents and teachers responses were summarized and presented on large sheets of newsprint paper. Many of the wishes stressed the exploration of teaching methods, including team teaching and an environment that supported innovative teaching methods. There also was interest in particular physical features, such as atria, bright colors, and extensive use of outdoor learning environments. The results of the wish poem, students' drawings, and all subsequent work were on

exhibit in the school as an ongoing record of events, as well as serving to inform those who were not participating about the events that had occurred.

The final workshop consisted of a building image study and site-planning exercise in which 35 teachers, parents, and school-planning officials worked collectively. The building-image study began with a slide show depicting 10 different school buildings, each representing different regional characteristics and design features. Each building was rated by the participants, and an overall priority list was established. The purpose of this exercise was to increase the participants' level of awareness about the possible variations in the visual character of school buildings. In effect, the exercise was intended to expand their vision of building images beyond their everyday experiences with school buildings.

The final event was the site-planning exercise, where participants were given a scaled drawing of the new site (located several blocks away from their present school) and scaled building components representing all the spaces in their school building. All building components had labels fastened to the styrofoam pieces. Each of the six groups was asked to develop a building plan located on the site, considering bus drop-off, parking, soccer field, cluster patterns of classrooms, outdoor space, and appropriate orientation and daylight. At the completion of the 2-hour exercise, representatives from each team presented their solution for discussion and debate. All the solutions were then displayed for review by the participants (Fig. 5.10).

Similarities between solutions occurred in the deliberate use of open space and courtyards and the clustering of kindergarten, first and second grade classrooms, separated from the third, fourth, and fifth grade classrooms. Team teaching appeared to guide many of these design decisions. While group members had some dissatisfaction with their solutions, they all agreed that they had a better understanding of the complexity of issues requiring simultaneous consideration. They readily admitted being more sensitive to the role of the architect and were willing to leave the resolution of problems to the architect.

The Adams Group and myself as design consultant met after the workshop to synthesize the workshop results and to arrive at several alternative concepts that would satisfy the requirements developed through the interviews and workshops (Fig. 5.11). One scheme was developed and proposed to the client group by posting large-scale drawings in key locations in the present school building and a request for teachers to write comments directly onto the drawings about positive and negative features (Fig. 5.12).

After several days of allowing the teachers to discuss the proposal and to comment, the drawings were retrieved and reviewed by the design team, only to find the comments very minor in detail. All the teachers seemed to identify elements of their design ideas in the architect's submission. At this point, and until preliminary drawings were completed, the involvement of teachers was limited to personal interviews clarifying details of classroom design.

The building design contained features that were not typical of traditional schools in the area, namely, clustered classrooms to facilitate team teaching and nongraded classes corresponding to the curriculum changes occurring within all Charlotte-Mecklenburg schools, single loaded corridors with classrooms oriented toward the south, and outdoor play areas for each classroom. This arrangement allowed each classroom to have a relatively private outdoor area (Fig. 5.13).

A plan review conducted by the North Carolina State Department of Public Instruction raised questions about these and other unusual design features, some of which might increase the operating cost of the building. The Davidson School proposal was very different from any other school plan they had reviewed. Since the original intention of this project was to create a building that satisfied the needs of the teaching staff and administration, as well as the historic concerns of the community, it was agreed to allow the community to make the final decision. A review with the teachers and principal indicated strong support for the opportunity for greater teacher collaboration. The superintendent's office, too, supported the building concept and believed it would enhance their curriculum goals. The Adams Group commented: "If the teachers and administrators had not been involved in the process, it is pretty clear that the state and county plan reviewers would have been very forceful to have the architects change the plan. It was only through the intervention of the teachers and administrators, and the arguments they made for the curriculum, that allowed the slightly higher cost for heating to be overpowered by the gains of the curriculum."

Post-occupancy evaluation

Construction was completed on the Davidson Elementary School in January 1994, at which time students and teachers took occupancy (Fig. 5.14). A post-occupancy evaluation (POE) was conducted (by Jennifer Hyder and James Rice, graduate architecture students from North Carolina State University) using a walkthrough evaluation, systematic observations of classroom and public space behavior, and a student-teacher questionnaire. The thrust of the POE was to

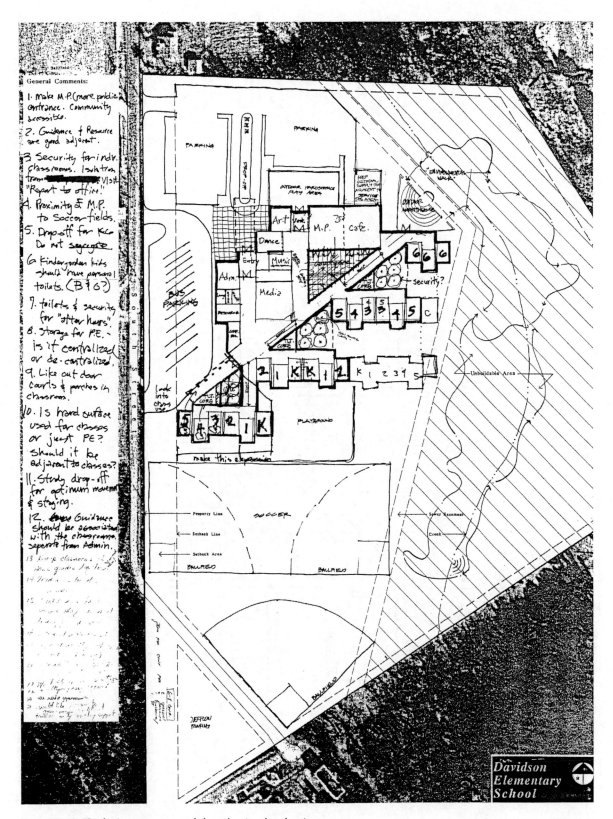

Figure 5.12 Teacher's comments recorded on the site plan drawing.

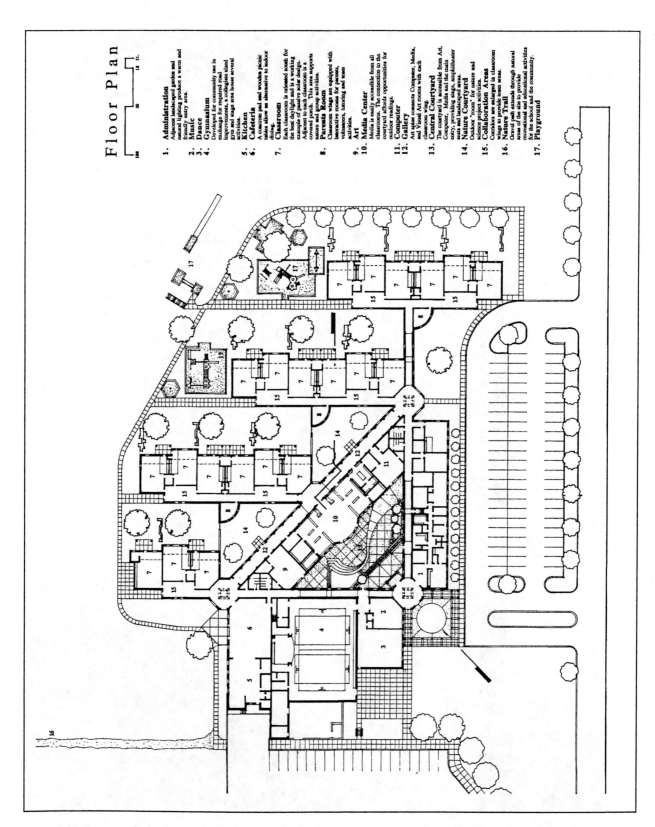

Floor Plan

1. **Administration**
   Adjacent landscaped garden and natural lighting produce a warm and friendly entry area.

2. **Music**

3. **Dance**

4. **Gymnasium**
   Developed for community use in exchange for required road improvements, a collegiate sized gym and stage area house several activities.

5. **Kitchen**

6. **Cafeteria**
   A concrete pad and wooden picnic tables allow an alternative to indoor dining.

7. **Classroom**
   Each classroom is oriented south for the best daylight and is in a working triangle of passive solar design. Adjacent to each classroom is a covered porch. This area supports nature and group activities.

8. **Parents Room**
   Classroom wings are equipped with interactive rooms for parents, volunteers, tutoring and team activities.

9. **Art**

10. **Media Center**
    Media is easily accessible from all classrooms. The connection to the courtyard affords opportunities for outdoor readings.

11. **Computer**

12. **Gallery**
    Art space connects Computer, Media, and Visual Art rooms with each classroom wing.

13. **Central Courtyard**
    The courtyard is accessible from Art, Computer, Media and the main entry, providing stage, amphitheater and landscaped areas.

14. **Nature Courtyard**
    Outdoor "room" for nature and science project activities.

15. **Collaboration Areas**
    Corridors are enlarged in classroom wings to provide team areas.

16. **Nature Trail**
    Gravel path extends through natural areas of the site to provide recreational and educational activities for the school and the community.

17. **Playground**

Figure 5.13 Private outdoor areas associated with each classroom.

Figure 5.14 The completed building.

validate initial design assumptions about student ownership in the building and its positive effects on their learning. Ownership was operationally linked to students' ability to personalize their environment. Additionally, learning through social interaction with peers and teachers was a factor that influenced the design of areas inside as well as outside the classroom.

To this end, observations were conducted of children's behavior in eight different classrooms. The results indicated that classrooms of younger children exhibited versatility in seating arrangements, well-defined activity areas within the classroom, and continuous use of the adjacent outdoor area. Classrooms of the older children were arranged in such away that the focus was on the teacher. Interestingly, all classrooms were designed to discourage rows of desks facing the teacher.

Thirty-six teachers and 60 students from the fourth and sixth grades were surveyed. Both questionnaires focused on the classroom and adjacent areas and how they contributed to the learning process. Distinctions were made between the influences of the teacher and the classroom environment. It was apparent from the results that the teachers' attitudes toward education directly influenced the ability of students to personalize their environment. In fact, while teachers generally agreed that it was important to provide a variety of work spaces within the classroom to allow for spontaneity of group activity, the students felt teachers exerted considerable control over their use of the classroom environment. Consequently, personal space was perceived by the students to be limited to their desk. Teachers, however, were enthusiastic about the way in which the classrooms were designed to facilitate group activities and with the overall design of the building. Students, too, had very favorable comments about their new environment.

Although the students and teachers had occupied this building for only 4 months prior to conducting the evaluation, it was apparent that a training program would benefit the teaching staff in allowing them to more effectively manipulate the classroom to accommodate their educational objectives.

Conclusion

The intent of this project was to narrow the gap between what we know about the education of young people through the literature and what we observe happening in everyday school environments. Observations of school buildings and classroom behavior has provided some insight into space use that often denies the existence of variations in types and styles of learning. Also, buildings produced without the involvement of those who will use the building can further exacerbate the rising alienation found in many schools. It is evident that having a sense of ownership, achieved through participation, can have far-reaching positive effects, especially in terms of confronting the viability of traditional school building standards.

Focused Evaluations

The types of evaluations described in this chapter are more specific than those presented so far. Largely quantitative in their results and conducted by experts, they focus on particular aspects of building performance rather than giving an overview. To begin, Kroner, Stark-Martin, and Willemain reinforce fur-

ther the productivity-design link in Sec. 6.1. Their West Bend Mutual office building study demonstrates that individually controlled "environmentally responsive workstations" increase worker productivity. This finding is consistent with other studies that have demonstrated a strong link between user satis-

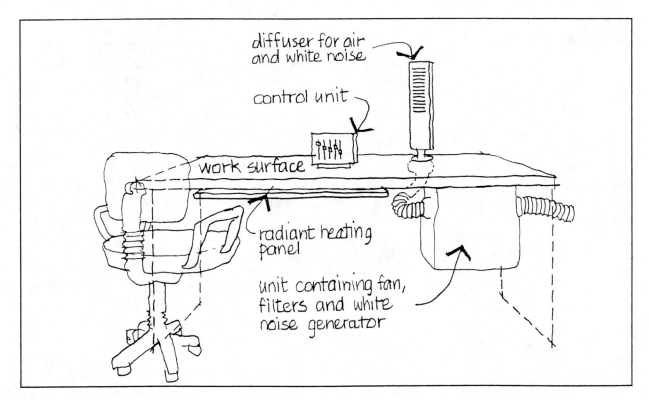

Figure 6.1 An environmentally responsive workstation that gives the occupant individual control over temperature, air supply, light, and acoustic conditions.

faction and control. Alan Hedge then describes in Sec. 6.2 a method of indoor air quality evaluation that enables cost-effective identification of hard-to-trace sources of pollution. In Sec. 6.3, Isaacs and Donn demonstrate a means of evaluating energy efficiency, an objective consistent with minimizing occupancy costs and improving sustainability. Finally, in Sec. 6.4, Thorne analyzes the process of evaluation and describes the use of visual techniques to simplify and clarify communication between the participants and evaluation professionals involved in occupant surveys.

6.1 Rensselaer's West Bend Mutual Study: Using Advanced Office Technology to Increase Productivity

Walter Kroner, Jean Anne Stark-Martin, and Thomas Willemain
Center for Architectural Research, Rensselaer Polytechnic Institute, New York

The challenge

Many claim that an aesthetically pleasing building environment, comfortable working conditions, and control of one's own working environment will make workers more satisfied and therefore more productive. Until recently, the supporting arguments for this position were laboratory studies or subjective questionnaire results. Building owners, architects, and investors, however, were looking for quantifiable productivity data to support investments in quality design and the use of advanced technologies.

One of the most important questions in architectural design and in the case of office buildings in particular is, "How do we know whether or not an investment in qualitative improvements, the indoor environment, or design has an impact on productivity and thus a company's bottom line?" A joint team from Rensselaer's Center for Architectural Research (CAR) and the Center for Services Research and Education posed that question in their West Bend Mutual Study. Their work focused on the query, "Do environmental control technologies have an impact on office worker productivity, absentee rates, and worker response to environmental qualities?"

A number of factors make the West Bend study a unique contribution to the field of architecture. The impact of quality architectural design often has been debated, but Rensselaer's study takes a significant step toward quantifying its value. The measurement of productivity as it relates to architectural design and/or a particular environmental technology satisfies a long-standing need for a basis for decision making related to building design, innovation in environmental technology and energy, and other considerations.

The study

The study's research objectives were to analyze the impact of environmentally responsive workstations (ERWs) on office worker productivity, absentee rates, and worker response to environmental qualities. ERWs integrate and provide heating, cooling, lighting, ventilation, and other environmental qualities directly to the occupants of workstations. The key feature of an ERW is that the occupant controls, modulates, and maintains the environmental qualities (temperature, humidity, illuminance, air velocity, air directionality, etc.) and services at the workstation. ERWs are designed to operate only when the workstation is occupied and are ideally at their best if integrated with an environmentally responsive architecture.

The ERW under investigation was Johnson Controls, Inc.'s Personal Environments Module (PEM). The PEM provides the workstation occupant with individualized control of temperature, velocity, and directionality of air delivered to the desktop through two air diffuser towers; a radiant heat panel located underneath the desk surface; a desk-mounted task light; and a sound-masking device. Additionally, an occupancy sensor shuts down the unit if the workstation is not occupied for over 10 minutes and returns it to the set levels of operation when the occupant returns. Individual filters are located at each unit (Fig. 6.1). Conditioned air is delivered to the floor plenum at 15.6°C. The PEM (essentially a VAV unit) is connected to the floor plenum and mixes room air with conditioned air, filters it, and delivers it at the desired temperature at desktop level.

The West Bend Mutual Study was initiated in 1990 when the study team learned of the pending installation of 370 PEM units (the largest installation of ERWs in the world) in the new corporate headquarters of the West Bend Mutual Insurance Company (WBM) in West Bend, Wisconsin. WBM is a property/casualty insurer, providing nearly 40 kinds of property and casualty policies, both personal and commercial. This presented a rare opportunity to conduct a field study dealing with ERWs, productivity, worker comfort, and environmental satisfaction.

The old WBM building had a conventional forced air delivery system with ceiling diffusers. The new WBM building, in addition to its PEMs located in the open office plan, had a perimeter forced air conditioning system, a general ceiling diffuser system for hallways and storage rooms, and VAV units for individual office and conference rooms located in the core of the new building.

Over a 51-week period, Rensselaer conducted two concurrent studies related to worker productivity and satisfaction. The productivity study was the focal point of the team's work and had several unique strengths. It used an established employer-based productivity monitoring system, combined objective productivity data with multiple subjective assessments of worker satisfaction and comfort, included measurements of three distinct influences on productivity (a major organizational relocation, a new built environment, and a new environmental conditioning technology), and included random experimental intervention to ensure the internal validity of assessments of causal effects. A total of 295 WBM associates in the underwriting department were involved in the satisfaction study, with 116 of them also in the productivity study. Individuals in the underwriting department deal with a variety of policies. The workers accept, modify, or reject accounts based on underwriting guidelines and proper risk evaluation.

Measuring productivity

As mentioned previously, the study team used WBM's employer-based productivity monitoring system. This system, in the case of underwriters and raters, measures the length of time it takes for a file to be processed. The processing of a file requires a combination of tasks including computer use for data access and analysis, mathematical calculations related to ratings, wordprocessing, and telephone interviews. The productivity rating system differentiated between commercial and personal underwriting and whether a file was a new client or a policy renewal. West Bend Mutual Insurance Company provided the research team with productivity performance data on a weekly basis for each employee in the study.

Data collection began on January 2, 1991. For 27 weeks Rensselaer's team observed conditions and collected data at WBM's old facility until their move to their new headquarters on July 8, 1991. The timing of the move was such that the comprehensive survey of employees in their old building, which used conventional HVAC systems, was able to be compared with a similar survey in the new building with its ERW technology.

To analyze the impact of ERWs themselves, we randomly disabled worker's ERWs during the last 24 weeks of the study. We chose to selectively "disable" the ERW units by disconnecting three features: air temperature, air velocity control, and the radiant heat panel. We left all other features intact: task lighting, sound masking, and occupant sensor operation. We chose to disable each worker's ERW during 2 randomly selected weeks, with no more than 12 ERWs crippled in any given week and no ERW disabled for 2 consecutive weeks.

In addition to the productivity study we used the Tenant Questionnaire Survey Assessment Method (TQSAM) to determine the worker's attitude toward the workspace. The TQSAM was developed by Public Works Canada and is an instrument for measuring worker comfort and satisfaction based on occupant surveys using a standardized questionnaire. The questionnaire asks 22 questions, which in turn are related to 7 environmental dimensions used in the quality assessment procedure: (1) thermal comfort, (2) air quality, (3) office noise, (4) spatial comfort, (5) privacy, (6) lighting, and (7) building noise. The TQSAM also asks questions related to overall employee satisfaction and ability to do work.

Major findings

- Data analysis examining the median percentage changes in individual productivity produced the following observations:
  - The combined effect of the new building and ERWs produced a statistically significant median increase in productivity of approximately 16 percent over productivity in the old building.
  - Partial disabling of ERWs (temperature, air velocity, radiant panel) resulted in a statistically significant 13 percent median decrease in productivity level compared with productivity in the new building after the move.
- Data analysis examining the mean absolute changes in aggregate productivity produced the following observation:
  - Our best estimate is that the ERWs themselves were responsible for an increase in productivity of about 2.8 percent relative to productivity levels in the old building. The actual improvement in productivity produced by the ERWs may be greater, but given the relatively short time span (2 weeks) in which the study team was able to disable the ERWs and study the results, this can be claimed conservatively.
- The disruption caused by the move from the old to the new building created a temporary productivity drop of approximately 30 percent using both analysis methods.
- In the TQSAM study of the individual workers, the tremendous transformation of their response to the perceived quality of their environment is equally significant. The percentage of satisfied associates went from only 12.8 percent in the old building to 75.2 percent in the new building. Another TQSAM finding was that the move to the new building resulted in the removal of significant differences between male and female environmental quality and comfort ratings that had existed in the old building.

Conclusions and qualifications

The study has advanced the field of knowledge related to architecture and productivity by showing that office productivity is positively affected by architectural design. Equally important is the finding that environmentally responsive workstations, with individualized controls, increase worker productivity.

Important elements to keep in mind, given the results of this study, are the contextual features associated with the architectural design, the building owner's role in selecting advanced office technologies and making design decisions, and the participatory role of the employees. A few highlights illustrate these points:

- It was the building owner who, after learning about PEMs, insisted that the architect and mechanical engineer integrate this new technology into the design. This decision was made solely on the basis that PEMs were a good idea, even though there was no productivity data or experience with a similar large-scale installation.
- The use of PEMs was consistent with a company policy that strives to respond to individual needs and differences among its employees. Policies related to flexible hours, access to daylight and view, facilities for employees to have lunch with their families, physical fitness facilities, a cafeteria that serves breakfast and lunch, and a forever wild site with nature walks and picnic tables.
- Employees were involved in the selection of chairs, workstation partitions, desk layouts, colors and decor, and desk accessories.
- The building has won a national intelligent building design award for its excellence in architectural design and integration of advanced technology. Advanced sensor and control technologies monitor traffic, indoor and outdoor conditions, water and ice storage, heat reclamation facilities, and a host of resource management systems.

Perhaps the most significant anecdotal observation related to this particular building design is the fact that the building maintenance staff rarely receives calls complaining about temperature, stale or still air, humidity problems, or noise. Ron Lauret, senior vice president of West Bend Mutual Insurance Company, states that "by our results, productivity went up from 4 to 6 percent, and with a payroll of over $10 million a year, that's a substantial return on investment."

According to Ron Lauret, the investment made in the PEMs was repaid within 2 years.

What the study does not tell is how important selected environmental controls are in comparison with each other. For example, we do not know whether fan speed control is more important than temperature control, whether a radiant heat panel below the desk is more important than temperature control of the air coming from the diffusers at the desk level, and so on. There is, however, a strong case for continuing the work related to ERWs and buildings that give increasing control of environmental qualities to the workers.

6.2 A Guide to Evaluating Indoor Air Quality

Alan Hedge
Department of Design and Environmental Analysis, Cornell University

An evaluation of indoor air quality in a building should be conducted if any of the following situations apply:

- Workers use products that have the potential to emit hazardous air pollutants.
- Some workers have suffered an illness possibly caused by exposure to air pollutants.
- Some workers have reported persistent symptoms of headache, lethargy, eye, nose, and throat irritation, respiratory difficulties, nausea, dizziness, and skin irritation, which are alleviated when they are away from the building.

Few buildings are heavily contaminated by constant-emission sources of pollution. Consequently, blindly searching for the source of an indoor air quality problem can be more difficult than finding the proverbial "needle in a haystack." It is also unnecessarily costly and disruptive. In most buildings, an appropriate air-sampling protocol should only be designed after sufficient detective work has been undertaken and specific hypotheses have been formulated. The U.S. Environmental Protection Agency suggests the steps shown in Fig. 6.2 to help facilities managers with this process.

Evaluation method

Before starting an indoor air quality investigation, it is crucial to gather a prior *building history,* which should include knowledge of the design and operation of the building ventilation system, the work processes at various locations in the building, any temporal and/or spatial patterns in the complaints within a building, and the characteristics of occupants, including any idiosyncratic medical conditions. This knowledge ultimately is vital to defining the range of air pollutants to be assessed, how these pollutants will be assessed, the areas where these pollutants will be measured, and the time periods over which measurements will be made.

Once the building history has been gathered, hypotheses about the possible causes of the indoor air problem can be formulated. Armed with some ideas about possible cause(s), additional information to reinforce or refute these can be gathered by a walkthrough of the building, which enables the investigator to look for further clues. For an air quality investigation, a walkthrough should assess at least the factors shown in Fig. 6.3. Unless this reveals an obvious source of pollution in a specific complaint area, assessment should be made of the whole building, including the mechanical plant rooms. If the source of the problem cannot be confirmed in the walkthrough, an air-sampling protocol should be developed based on the hypothesized cause(s).

A general diagnostic indoor air-sampling protocol, using portable instruments to measure air temperature, relative humidity, carbon dioxide, and carbon monoxide, should be implemented. Air temperature and relative humidity give useful information on thermal comfort conditions, and conditions that are too warm or too dry often account for occupants' perceptions of poor indoor air quality. Studies show an optimal air temperature between 20 and 22°C and relative humidity between 40 and 60 percent for comfort, performance, and health. Carbon dioxide is exhaled by occupants and should be diluted by the ventilation system if outdoor-indoor air exchange rates are adequate. Comparison of indoor and outdoor carbon dioxide concentrations gives an approximation of the true outdoor air ventilation rate.[1]

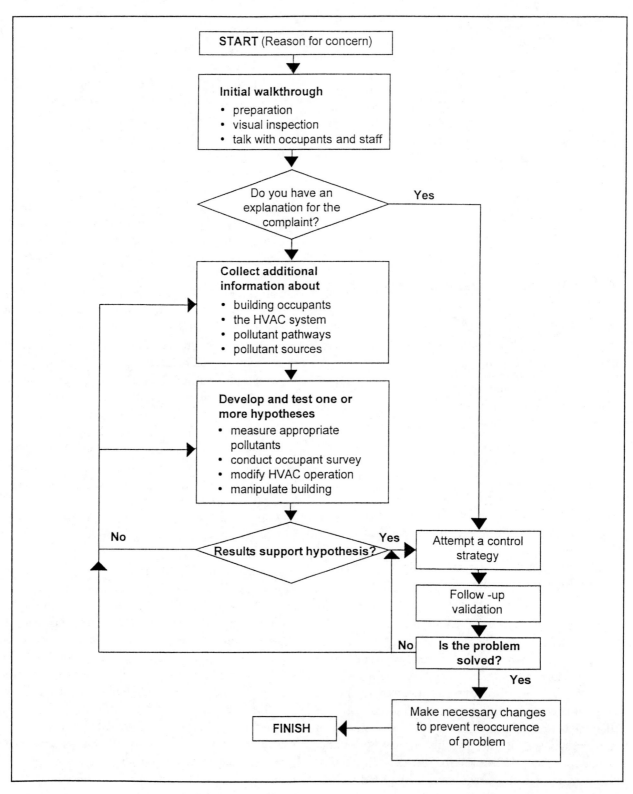

Figure 6.2 Essential steps in conducting an IAQ investigation.

Minimum information to be collected by a walk-through inspection.

1. Record conversations with staff and other occupants about IAQ concerns.

2. Look for IAQ problem indicators in occupied spaces (e.g. obvious pollutant sources; dirty ceiling registers; mould growth; odors; too warm; no air movement).

3. Look for IAQ problem indicators in air handling units (e.g. damaged filters; dirty filters; mould growth; odors; standing water).

4. Talk with operations staff about ventilation system design, maintenance, and operation.

5. Identify ventilation zones on a floor plan and areas of positive or negative pressure.

6. Check materials safety data sheets or other hazard information for products used in complaint areas.

7. Annotate a floor plan with possible pollutant sources and their locations.

8. Check for outside sources (e.g. nearby smokestack; basement garage).

9. Check space layout for barriers to air movement.

10. Collate historical information on building (e.g. design specification; maintenance problems; complaint history).

Figure 6.3 Minimum information to be collected by a walkthrough inspection.

Indoor levels should be below 1000 ppm. Carbon monoxide is a colorless, odorless, but toxic gas contained in car exhaust fumes. It can seep into buildings from basement garages via elevator shafts or through the ventilation system from outdoor automobile traffic. Indoor levels should be below 9 ppm. If this preliminary survey fails to reveal the source(s) of complaints, additional testing can be conducted for other irritant pollutants, such as formaldehyde, which should be below 0.4 ppm, or volatile organic compounds such as styrene or benzene.

Inadequate air mixing can be a source of complaints. Air mixing and air exchange in particular rooms or specific zones can be measured using an inert tracer gas such as halon or sulfur hexafluoride.

Finally, an occupant survey should be conducted. This is best performed early in the diagnostic process,

and results can be used to guide the indoor air quality investigation. This survey can use a self-report questionnaire that asks about perceptions of climate conditions and health. Looking for spatial and/or temporal patterns in the survey information can yield useful clues to the source of problems. Also an occupant survey can be conducted *after* preliminary air testing fails to uncover the source of complaints.

The case study described below illustrates how subjective and objective data can be combined to successfully resolve indoor air quality complaints.

Case study of resolving an IAQ problem

A community college in upstate New York had been receiving persistent complaints of poor indoor air quality. In the recent past, the building had been evacuated following a spill of a solvent-based organic chemical. The building is a two-story structure with some 200 classrooms and offices, laboratories, art rooms, library, cafeteria, gym, and indoor swimming pool. Inlet air is delivered from the air handling units through ceiling registers. Return air is drawn into a common ceiling plenum, where it is mixed with return air from other spaces. Return air and outdoor air then are mixed and supplied as ventilation air to the rooms.

Three diagnostic approaches were used. First, an occupant survey was undertaken to determine the nature and extent of complaints throughout the facility. Second, an indoor air quality survey was conducted, and air temperature, relative humidity, and levels of carbon monoxide, carbon dioxide, and formaldehyde were measured. Third, air exchange and air mixing was assessed using a tracer gas, because the building is a multizone ventilation system design with multiple air-handling units.

Following a series of small group interviews, a self-report questionnaire was designed. This was administered to all 230 employees in the facility. Two-thirds of the questionnaires were returned for analysis. Summary findings showed a majority were satisfied with thermal conditions, but just over half the respondents were dissatisfied with ventilation in the building. Around one-third of respondents reported work-related symptoms[2] associated with the "sick" building syndrome (headache, lethargy, eye, nose, and throat irritation). The spatial distribution of complaints was plotted over the floor plan of the building and the layout of the ventilation system zones using customized software. This revealed five areas of particular concern in the building: the print shop and surrounding offices, the biology and dining rooms, the library, and the bookstore.

Measures of indoor quality were taken in the higher complaint areas and in lower complaint areas to allow comparisons of pollutant concentrations to be made. Finally, using halon as a tracer gas, air mixing and exchange measures were taken in the high complaint areas.

Results revealed that air exchange was inadequate in the biology and dining rooms and air mixing was inadequate in the library and bookstore. The position of the air registers relative to the shelves and carrels

prevented efficient air mixing. Placing return ducts at strategic points in these areas and modifying the space layout to improve air circulation patterns resolved complaints in these areas. There was an accumulation of carbon dioxide up to 2000 ppm in some spaces, particularly in some faculty offices, indicating inadequate outdoor air ventilation. Increasing the outdoor air supply to these offices resolved complaints. Odor complaints were especially prevalent around the print shop. Subsequent interviews showed that the odor problems and complaints were most pronounced when print machines were cleaned at the start of the week with organic solvents that were then dispersed into the makeup air. Measures of indoor volatile organic compounds (VOCs) confirmed this. Cleaning the print machines at the end of the week resolved this problem.

Any one of the investigations, conducted in isolation, would have yielded an incomplete picture of events in this building. Personnel surveys had been conducted by college staff prior to this study, and they had demonstrated the presence of a problem but could not explain where, when, or why problems occurred or how to remedy them. Blindly measuring physical and chemical factors in indoor air alone might have missed crucial areas of the building and/or critical times. This information also could not describe transmission routes through the building. Simply conducting air mixing and exchange tests, without knowing the high complaint areas, would have been costly and inefficient. In short, a complete picture of events in this building and the resolution of these were only possible by combining all three methods.

Notes

1. Outdoor air ventilation can be approximated by the following formula:

$$\% \text{ Outdoor air} = C_s/C_o - C_r \times 100$$

where C_s=supply air CO_2 in ppm; C_o=outdoor air CO_2 in ppm; C_r=return air CO_2 in ppm.

2. A work-related symptom was defined as one that improved when away from work but which was experienced upon return to work.

6.3 Evaluating Energy Management

Nigel Isaacs and Michael Donn
VUW Centre for Building Performance Research,
New Zealand

Research has shown that only half the variation in energy use between commercial buildings is due to the design of the building and its services (Baird et al., 1984). The building user or operator is responsible for the rest. However, without information feedback on the consequences, the user has no opportunity to contribute in a positive manner. The following case studies show the benefits of providing information in a clearly understandable form.

Energy, fuel, and expenditure: Terminology

Energy management is commodity management rather than pure financial management. Accounts systems deal with expenditure, but energy performance is measured in terms of fuel use and service. Different fuels are measured in different "units"—electricity in kilowatthours, coal in tons, oil in gallons, etc. They are also used to provide different services—electricity for lights as well as heating, cooling, cooking, motors, and computers; gas for cooking, heating, and possibly cooling; and coal and oil for heating.

Energy use depends on many factors. Key factors for energy use in a commercial building include

- Climate—sun or shade, wind or shelter, town or country
- Use(s)—office, shops, or school
- Size—floor area, number of rooms, or number of occupants
- Heating—central air conditioning or unit heaters
- Heating controls—manual, timeclock, or computer
- Hours of use—daylight hours only or 24 hours a day
- Installed equipment—lights, computers, chillers, photocopiers, etc.

None of these factors is entirely independent. The amount of equipment will depend on the type of use—a shop will have more chillers and fewer computers than an office. The size of heating or cooling equipment required depends on the climate and the building use. To make performance comparisons between buildings or for the same building from year to year, it is necessary to make allowance for these factors.

In office buildings, energy use relates more closely to floor area than to the number of people in the building. Since the heating (and cooling) plant runs regardless of occupancy, and the number of staff can vary, the area that is conditioned is the more important factor. Although commercial buildings can differ radically in layout and construction, in modern buildings these differences have a minor effect. It is also important to recognize that there may be short- or long-term actions within the building that may increase energy use—increasing hours of work or increased use of desktop computers may increase energy use, while a new energy efficient boiler may reduce it.

Information flows

There are a number of different stakeholders in building operation. Financial managers are concerned with the collection and analysis of financial data on which to base investment decisions. Building or facility managers are concerned with the week-to-week and year-to-year operation of the building, managing repairs and maintenance and planning for the long term. Service staff or contractors implement the repairs and maintenance requirements but have a detailed knowledge of the operation of the equipment. And the key driving force is the users' desire to be provided with a comfortable environment within which they can pursue their key objectives—employment, obtaining or providing services, etc.

A key problem is that seldom are all the stakeholders provided with information on the consequences of their actions. A new model for the desirable flow of information is given in Fig. 6.4. The overlapping roles of the stakeholders are indicated by the overlapping of the defining circles. In some smaller establishments, these roles may overlap to the point where they are done by a single person. Essentially, the diagram emphasizes the importance of communication

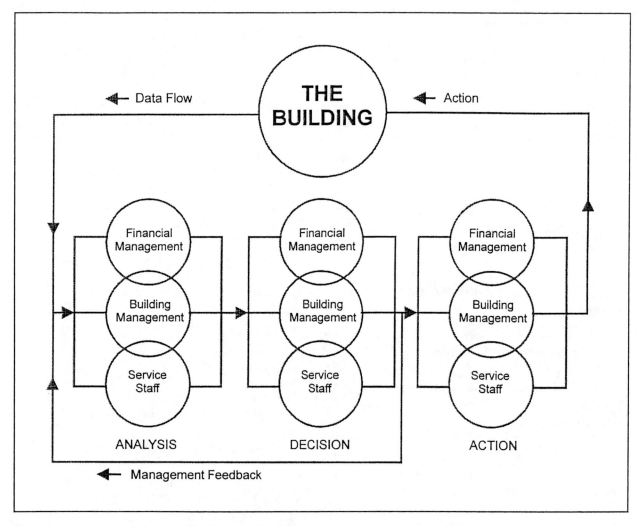

Figure 6.4 Energy management—desirable information flow.

between the stakeholders at each step in the building management process and the need for information feedback. The feedback includes not only information resulting from improvement in the operation of the building but also management feedback ensuring that all stakeholders are in a position to review any decision(s) for action. Links between capital expenditure and running costs can easily be ignored, but this must be made explicit. Without this interactive communication, the data about energy use, expenditure, etc. collected at the building never become information on which well-founded decisions can be made about energy use and maintenance. The end result is that energy-efficiency projects may not be implemented successfully.

Energy management: Information for action

The desirable information flow illustrated in Fig. 6.4 must be supported by the collection of data which, once analyzed, can be used for decisions and then to support action. The timely provision of feedback on the results of activities that affect energy use is crucial. Energy management can easily be dismissed as a technical problem that should be the sole prerogative of the technical service staff. However, unless the linkages between the financial management, building management, and service staff are robust and well-used, it is almost guaranteed that energy costs will increase.

Data collection. Energy expenditure ($) and consumption (energy unit) records should be maintained in the most appropriate location. At a minimum, these raw "data" may consist of the regular supplier accounts recorded in a manner that permits later analysis. Other data available for analysis could include

- The "production" of the building (e.g., number of person-hours worked or kilograms of widgets produced)
- The activity pattern in the building (e.g., building occupied 9 hours a day, 5 days a week including public holidays)
- Plant operation (e.g., boiler 2 has been closed down for the past 6 weeks due to lack of spare parts)
- Climate information also may be of value, particularly with buildings similar in scale to houses (under 300 m²)

If the energy data collection is a planned process executed concurrently with financial data management, the additional costs can be very small. Conversely, trying to "rescue" this information from normal financial data storage can be time-consuming. Much of our building energy management work has started with days spent in windowless archive rooms, searching through thousands of invoices for the elusive energy accounts.

Analysis. Pareto analysis is useful in deciding where to allocate scarce funding in a group of buildings. Research in schools (Donn et al., 1987), for example, found that a large proportion of the total energy consumption is used by a relatively small number of schools.

The most common energy management tool is the *area energy use index* (AUEI), which normalizes energy use by floor area (e.g., kWh/m² or BTU/ft²). A useful measure can be energy units per hour or day of work time. This means that if the energy use increases just because a new shift is using the building more this year than last, then it will not affect the AUEI.

Figure 6.5 shows a Pareto analysis on two different groups of buildings. For schools, it can be seen that

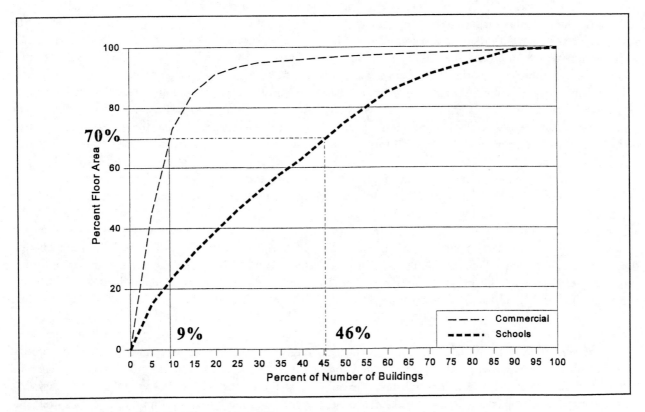

Figure 6.5 Pareto distribution of building number and floor area.

46 percent of the schools consume 70 percent of the total energy used. In commercial office buildings, the figures are even more radical: 9 percent of the buildings consume 70 percent of the energy. In terms of planning energy management investment, it is important to spend money where the total return from the investment will be highest. This is most likely when the energy management investment is made in one of the buildings that dominates the total energy picture.

When the Pareto analysis was applied to a group of 500 schools based on both total energy use and energy use per classroom (a rough measure of area), the least efficient schools were quickly identified. These were then subject to on-site physical inspection. In one school (operating 9 A.M. to 4 P.M.), monitoring found that the heating system was operating 24 hours per day, 7 days a week. The financial management system was happy because this pattern had been in place for a number of years, and no variation was detected year by year. The building management were happy because they faced no complaints from the building users. The service staff were happy because their equipment seemed to be working and they had not been informed of any complaints. The resolution was prompt and the savings paid for the work in a number of months. The change was that complaints started, since the buildings were not always warm whenever later hours were worked! This was easily resolved by the provision of after-hours controls that turned the system on for a limited period of time.

Some building types are likely to have high energy use. Buildings in use 24 hours a day or with particular climatic requirements will use more energy. Hospitals are in continuous operation and also require higher internal temperatures than many other commercial buildings. This can result in very high energy intensity—a large hospital can approach the energy use of a small town, with large energy and cost savings possible.

Decision(s). The data available to each specialist group, shown in Fig. 6.4, need to be integrated and analyzed in a form that provides whatever useful knowledge is appropriate to the particular building, use, location, management system, etc. The service staff may be interested in the energy use compared with the indoor and outdoor temperatures; the financial staff, in energy expenditure per unit of output; while the building manager may be interested in energy use per unit of floor area. All could be interested in changes since the same time last year.

The common pattern of energy use in commercial office or institutional buildings has a baseload of energy use through the year due to lighting and office equipment, with variable summer cooling and winter heating. These energy uses must be reported separately if valid comparisons are to be made. Thus an apparent leap in energy use from one month to the next could be due to equipment problems or merely due to the arrival of summer and the need for cooling.

Case study: Nelson City Library

In late 1988, the Nelson City Council (New Zealand) purchased a second-hand car sales yard to turn into a public library. A performance-oriented specification, based on the requirements of the library staff, permitted a natural energy design approach to be taken. Within the constraints of a tight budget, a low-energy design was established based on extensive daylight modeling and computer thermal simulation (Isaacs and Donn, 1992). The library was opened in February 1990 and has been monitored since that time.

Our involvement began with the architect's first inspection of the site after being awarded the contract. This included a general discussion, based on our research experience, of the opportunities for energy-efficient architecture. It was agreed that use of computer thermal simulation and daylight modeling would provide the architect with key information upon which to base design decisions. The initial budget included allowance for full air conditioning and extensive artificial lighting.

The close integration of solar and lighting modeling with building design resulted in immediate capital cost reductions. The original brief had suggested heat-pump climate control would be necessary, but very early on in the computer modeling this was shown to be unnecessary. Analysis of a number of years of weather data showed that there was very little chance of there being high air temperatures without an afternoon sea breeze. The computer thermal simulation model also showed that the peak power demand could be moderated so as to remove any need for a new electrical substation to supply the library.

The key problem identified by computer thermal modeling was that for a limited number of hours in the peak of summer, temperatures would be above 26°C. This information was provided both to the client (in the form of the relevant city council subcommittee) and to the library staff. The presentation included a description of the modeling approach and its likely accuracy in nontechnical terms and graphs illustrating likely temperatures on the worst possible days. Based on this information, a rational decision could be made, and it was decided that the risk of the building being too hot for a short period far outweighed the cost of air conditioning. The cost savings from this decision could then be put into features of greater importance to the building users and owners—including a pleasant central garden courtyard, extensive opening windows, etc.

The key to closing this information loop at the design stage was not the expenditure of large amounts of money—it was the opening of the information pathway to ensure that everyone had the knowledge they needed in a form they understood. Ongoing monitoring has found that temperatures have never reached the level suggested from the computer modeling, and discussions with staff indicate continuing satisfaction with the comfort levels in the building.

As illustrated in Fig. 6.4, the information loop must continue to provide feedback. Analysis of the first year's energy use found it was higher than the simulation had predicted. This was traced to a lack of commissioning, and the following years show a strong relationship to the levels expected.

Conclusion

The control of energy costs in buildings is not solely a technical issue. All building users can have a signif-

icant impact, whether the effect is to increase or decrease the costs. A model improving the information feedback and linkages has been proposed and illustrated by its application in the design and in-use management of a low-energy public library. Although the evaluation is based on the use of experts, the crucial role of all stakeholders reinforces the need for the use of nontechnical language.

6.4 Using Visual Methods to Focus Users' Response in Predesign and Post-occupancy Research

Ross Thorne
Department of Architecture, University of Sydney, Australia

The intellectual emphasis for architects is on vision. Gardner (1991) in his theory of multiple intelligences suggests a minimum of seven, one of them being "visual intelligence." He also points out that a person with an emphasis on one kind of intelligence may be poor at another. For example, the person with the intelligence necessary to be a superb ballet dancer may not be erudite in abstract verbal concepts. Similarly, a visually oriented design architect may not be able to conceptualize easily in verbal constructs. But the social sciences have relied on the intelligence of words. Social science methodologies, now adapted for predesign research and post-occupancy evaluation, were originally developed through verbal constructs for the design of survey instrumentation and numerical constructs for the processing of data.

The use of different intelligences by different disciplines may result in one having difficulty understanding the discipline environment of the other, and vice versa. For example, some early social science evaluations of buildings produced information in a form that was quite useless for designers, although in a form quite consistent with the original discipline's methodologies (Thorne, 1981/84).

Designers are likely to have difficulty interpreting the verbal constructs embodied in the methodologies and discussion of results derived from the use of those methodologies. In other words, designers and social science—oriented researchers are like two communities (Purcell and Heath, 1982) between which conscious attempts at understanding need to be made.

Having enjoyed an elementary and largely visual predesign investigation of clients' needs and wishes as part of the design process in architectural practice, it seemed a logical step for me to investigate what they thought of it after the buildings were complete. But also, what did other users of the building think of them? The work by Canter, the psychologist at the Building Performance Research Unit (BPRU), University of Strathclyde, was my first and major influence. I undertook studies at first with him (Canter and Thorne, 1972) and then other psychologists (Purcell et al., 1972), using methods (including survey instruments) developed for the BPRU by Canter (Markus et al., 1972).

From one evaluation of an office, it was realized that the type of statistics used to document results in sample survey methods may at times be inappropriate. Having results that state, for instance, that 70 percent are satisfied with the noise levels should not be accepted like a political poll; i.e., the remaining 30 percent are irrelevant. It was found by a free comment on the questionnaires that one person was having an excruciating noise experience in an office where noise was generally not considered a problem (see Thorne, 1981/84). This alerted us as researchers to the fact that office workers (and users of other building types) do not necessarily experience the same building environment in a similar way. They have different rooms with perhaps different furniture and different orientation, etc. Therefore, they cannot be considered to be a homogeneous group, except for the most general questions about the building.

Accordingly, a post-occupancy evaluation process needs to be designed so as to "find" individuals who are experiencing problems that are building-oriented or caused by problems within the interior environment. In a walkthrough type of POE (described in Daish et al., 1982) in a small building, this is relatively easy. But in a large organization wishing to retain confidentiality between the employees and the researchers, it is more difficult. The case study shows one method of finding the problems experienced by individuals.

The importance of incorporating visual information in evaluations came through a focused study of noise and noise-causing interruptions to office workers in a large open office leased by a government department (Purcell and Thorne, 1977). It became apparent after the research that some form of visual mapping of noise sources, as experienced by individuals, would have been helpful, but it was not critical to the study. The idea is suggested in Thorne (1981/84), where the study is described in relation to other evaluative office studies.

Using visual mapping techniques in POE questionnaires can be most helpful in precisely locating problems if the POE is being used as a means of identifying remedial work required for a new design. Other uses of visual material may be in both predesign research and post-occupancy evaluation. Illustrations may be used in predesign surveys to discover community acceptability of different housing design types (Thorne, 1992), for example, or in a POE to allow users to identify, say, the furniture that has been allocated to them to comment on its efficacy. The visual mapping technique and questionnaire illustrations of furniture were both used in the following case study (a full report is provided in Thorne and Turnbull, 1991).

Case study: POE as a fine-tuning device for newly designed office space

A large corporate client had recently had two of its divisions move into newly designed office space on two floors leased a couple of blocks away from its central Sydney head office. Some individuals had made complaints to supervisors in the new offices; the company was concerned, since it was considering refitting all the floors of its head office (a multistory mid-1960s building) with a design similar to the two new floors. A considerable investment was involved, since the partitioning was armor-plated tinted frameless glass ceiling to floor between offices and corridor and plasterboard between offices, while a whole range of specially designed furniture had been manufactured.

The company requested a self-completion questionnaire providing respondent anonymity to the firm and confidentiality to the independent researchers who located everyone on each floor by number only. The company wished to discover their employees' attitudes toward a large number of items: whether the new design suited the company image, the internal appearance generally, individual offices and their furniture in particular; the new centralized filing system; visual and aural privacy; access to both the company's and external services; lighting glare and air conditioning; wayfinding/location, security, and confidentiality in the building; the elevators; management policies on work space and restrictions on modifying or personalizing work spaces; efficiency and courtesy of the company's building services in making repairs; and the degree of user participation in the design of the new offices.

The information required was, of necessity, fine-grained. Bipolar scaled questions, scaled attitudinal statements, and scaled satisfaction questions comprised most of the instrument, the design of the whole questionnaire being influenced by the methodologic direction of Weidemann and Anderson (1985). Wineman (1986) also was scanned for possible issues to address in the questionnaire.

As a comparison and kind of control group, several respondents also were selected from the older head office building, and those questions from the new office's questionnaire which were appropriate to the older offices also were included in this group's survey instrument. This would show that while having some complaints, the staff in the new offices were more satisfied than the staff in the older offices.

The two visual components of the questionnaire for the new offices were a plan of their whole office floor and a picture of each piece of the newly designed and/or selected piece of furniture available to office staff. Following traditional questions on how noise reduced concentration, interfered with telephone conversations, created distraction, etc., the respondents were asked to note down the sources of noises that affected them and mark their location on the floor plan on the adjacent page. The illustrated plan (Fig. 6.6) provides locations and sources and the number of complaints for those sources; for example, five people complained about equipment noise from the computer room. Having code numbers for the individual respondents allowed the researchers to ascertain the transmission distance of noises. It also allowed them to notify the building services section of the company, bypassing floor supervisors or managers and making it known that "there appears to be a noise problem with the air-conditioning registers in the drafting room" or "there are a number of offices at the eastern end of the floor where the phone bell is left on loud while the occupants are out." Advice was given about enclosing computer printers, which also were a problem. Providing this information verbally would have forced the respondent to make the embarrassing statement that "The conversations in Mr. Smith's office annoy me" or "the phone in Mr. Smith's office is too loud." By using the plan, however, a building services person could go to the office and say, "There have been complaints about the loudness of the phone in this office." This approach is perceived as being a little more anonymous and less threatening.

The second visual component (Fig. 6.7) was an isometric drawing and brief description of every piece of furniture available—37 pieces in all. Beside each was a box to tick if the respondent possessed that piece in his or her office, followed by a three-point scale of satisfaction. What the researchers had not foreseen was the need for space to comment about what was wrong with the piece of furniture. However, comments were volunteered that indicated some poor design and selection and an inability to operate ergonomic chairs. To overcome this lack, the furniture section of the questionnaire was recirculated to staff members asking them to indicate what the design fault was if they were dissatisfied. They also were asked, if they wished, to sign a card giving the researchers permission to break confidentiality to the building services section of the company so that someone could show them how to adjust ergonomic furniture or repair other items.

With 37 pieces of furniture, some appearing quite similar to others, reliance on word descriptors would have created uncertainty for both the respondents and the researchers.

The outcome was that the cost of repairs to one type of table was debited to its designer, the manufacturer was "black listed" by the company and did

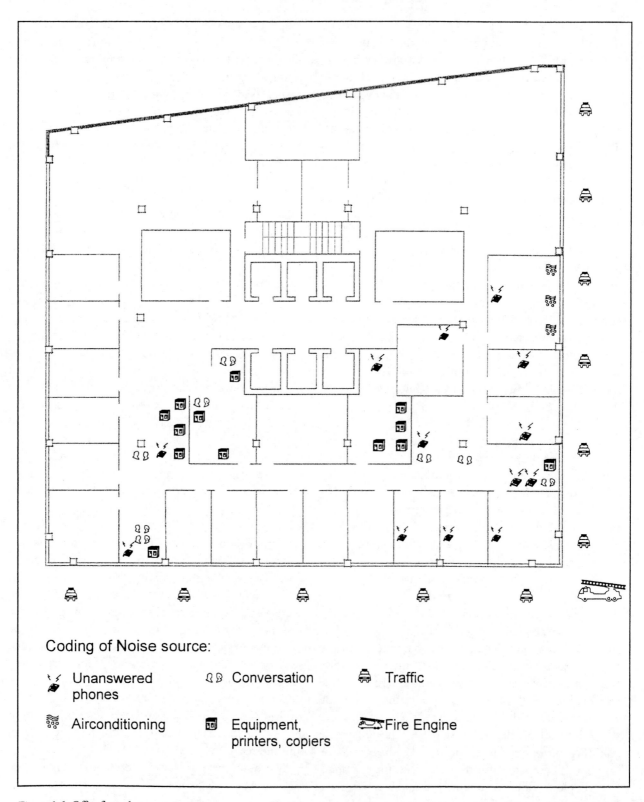

Figure 6.6 Office floor plan: mapping noise sources.

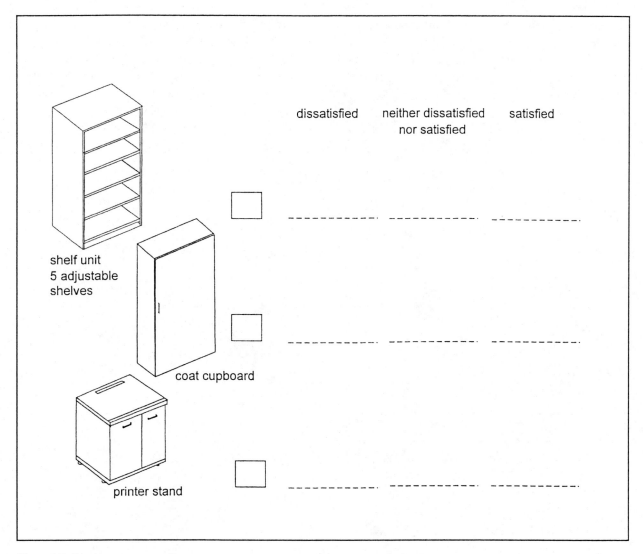

dissatisfied   neither dissatisfied   satisfied
nor satisfied

shelf unit
5 adjustable
shelves

coat cupboard

printer stand

Figure 6.7 Furniture assessment sheet.

not supply further furniture, and the office workers had a number of frustrations eliminated.

Concluding comment

The "problem" of the multitude of interacting aspects of a design being brought together to develop a "solution" remains an intriguing central issue for architects. Quizzing the clients not only on their functional needs (even down to the types and quantity of items they had to store or place around themselves) but also about the visual quality or essence of what they would like their building to possess was always as important as developing the three-dimensional jigsaw of spaces into a coherent, buildable whole.

The quizzing of the client was a form of elementary predesign research into functional needs and "image of the future" design. Although the information was written down, it also was retained in the designer's mind as a series of visual images. Ideally, the designer would like to actually see the items to be rehoused in the new design; observe how the person or persons currently lived, worked, or performed;

and make a mental picture of how they wanted this changed. This mentally pictured database would be constantly referred to during the design process of drawing, evaluating the drawing, changing it, redrawing, reevaluating, etc.

Finally, a design would be produced that, to the designer, seemed to optimize (rather than satisfy) the stated functional needs, with the building budget and the image having been translated from the client's language into the visual language of the architect. Introducing visual mapping techniques into questionnaires for building evaluation purposes is one means of addressing issues raised by the different intelligences of the different interests and disciplines involved.

CHAPTER 7

Cost Evaluation

Underlying all evaluations is a desire to achieve performance improvements. At some stage these must be measured in financial terms. Helen Tippett's section on life costing brings forward well-known procedures for evaluating the economic consequences of building-related decisions so that real and sustainable performance improvements are achieved. She describes how the technique can be used for evaluating the economic consequences of design, building, and maintenance decisions.

Life-cycle costing allows present and future costs and benefits to be considered from a common baseline. Tippett stresses that "life costing is not the mechanics of calculating costs." Building quality assessment and user evaluations are necessary prerequisites to any economic evaluation. The significance of life costing is not that it determines design, building, or maintenance decisions but rather that it provides the opportunity to assess alternate financial strategies and building options that take account of all the significant costs of building ownership and operation over a building's lifetime. Building evaluation makes good financial sense.

7.1 Life Costing

Helen Tippett
VUW School of Architecture, New Zealand, and School of Architecture and Building, Deakin University, Australia

Providing accommodations for an organization requires the commitment of funds to procure a facility that may be in service for a long period of time. How long that period may be and how well the accommodations serve the needs of the users depend on the initial investment decisions and the continued allocation of funds to operate, maintain, and modify the facility as and when required.

In any assessment of accommodation needs, questions about present and future costs very soon arise: "Can we afford to do this or that?" "Now or later?" Then comes the key question: "Can we afford not to?"

Basis of the technique

Life costing, or *life-cycle cost analysis,* helps to answer these questions. It is neither a decision-making process nor a set of economic guidelines. It is simply a technique to relate present and future costs by discounting them all to a common baseline. It provides a method of assessing alternatives by bringing together all the significant costs of ownership over a period of time (or "life cycle" of the building).

Life costing allows us to consider the economic consequences of design, building, and maintenance decisions in terms of the dollars spent today and the dollars required tomorrow.

A "today" dollar is not the same as a "tomorrow" dollar because money invested in any form earns, or has the capacity to earn, interest. As a simple example, ignoring a number of other issues for the moment, consider these alternatives:

Wall surface A costs $100 per square meter. The other, B, costs $70 now and another $30 refinishing 5 years from now. Which is preferable? If B is selected, the *owner spends $70 now and may place a sum of money in the bank which can grow with interest into $30 in 5 years when it is needed. If the going interest rate is 7 percent compounded annually, then only $21.40 must be deposited now, and we say that the "present worth" or "present value" of alternative B is $91.40 compared with alternative A at $100.*

This method of reducing (discounting) the value of future dollars is central to assessing the life costs of a building over a given period chosen by the owner.

When the decision is made to build a new facility, it is necessary to deal with hundreds of related decisions regarding the level of amenity and required building qualities—the image, configuration of spaces, access and security, mechanical and electrical systems, materials and finishes—that will provide a suitable facility that the organization can afford.

In an existing building or in the purchase of a new building, these decisions may have been made some time ago by others. Each decision has economic consequences. Surfaces must be cleaned and refinished, environmental control systems must be fueled and maintained, and individual components must be repaired and replaced from time to time. All the while, dollars are committed to supporting user activities and doing whatever is done in the building.

Sharpening the tools

The concept of life costing is not new. There is no lack of detailed reference material on the topic. What is new is wider recognition that every organization needs to bring together the management of its property as a physical, economic, and operational resource.

The starting point for economic evaluation of a building is not its cost but its physical qualities and performance to suit the operations of the organization. As a physical resource, the location, condition, and expected life of the building and services must be assessed. From an operational viewpoint, functional suitability and user satisfaction must be considered. The issue is whether or not that resource is providing value for money.

Today, monitoring of building performance and issues of energy efficiency, space utilization, and required level of service are gaining more attention from owners and senior management Economic analysis of building decisions on a "life-cycle" basis has been formalized by some large property owners for years. Engineers routinely consider life-cycle costs in the initial choice of heating and cooling systems. Legislation in many American states requires the use of life-cycle cost analysis in the awarding of contracts for public projects (GSA, 1976). Consideration of life-cycle costing is part of recommended practice in tendering and selection of suppliers (CIDA, 1993).

Buildings constructed in the 1970s are beginning to show their age. Chillers are near the end of their expected 20 to 25 years of life. Technological advances must be built in to existing buildings. Internal working environments no longer meet the needs or match the expectations of occupants. More recent buildings, speculative projects of the inflationary booms of the 1980s, are neither wearing nor working well.

The restructuring of government agencies has significantly changed accommodation needs. At the same time, premises occupied by these agencies have been valued as a corporate asset, not as a "sunk cost" of previous administrations, and management performance is now linked to the use of these resources.

Consider a management decision where an extra $10,000 investment in the lighting installation will reduce annual energy costs by $1000. If the organization expects to use the facility for 20 years, would the extra investment be worth it? If the extra $10,000 is borrowed at 10 percent, constant annual interest and principal repayments will be $1175 yearly. If internal funds are used, there will be no interest cost, but the organization foregoes the opportunity to invest that $10,000 elsewhere to earn $1175 yearly. In either case, the cost of the decision is $1175, which is more than the projected energy savings.

Taking this example further, if this installation will improve general and task lighting for the users, the benefit of this improved performance may be difficult to judge directly, but the assessment of the cost at $175 yearly enables management to decide. If the installation encourages more awareness of saving energy by other means, the cost may indeed be less.

Decisions on what, when, and where money should be spent on facilities should not be made without considering the costs and benefits of present decisions and future actions to implement them. Building quality assessment and user evaluations are prerequisites to economic evaluation. The users are frequently in the best position to assess the need for and benefits of improved serviceability of facilities. Their expertise must be brought in to the number crunching and technical appraisal of maintaining a building (Bromilow, 1992; Gray and Tippett, 1993).

The process of life costing

In the mid-1970s, the concerns of clients and architects at the rapid increase in the costs of operating buildings led the American Institute of Architects to produce a guide for architects on life-cycle cost analysis. This described the fundamentals of the technique and its place in the processes of facility planning and designing buildings (AIA, 1977). The guide lays the critical groundwork for use of the technique in practice. The AIA task force then consulted with various federal agencies, drawing on their combined experience in a second publication on the use of life costing in practice (Haviland, 1978).

A number of state and federal agencies in Australia have produced guides on life costing and costs in use, with detailed recommendations on information systems for building maintenance management and performance monitoring. (Bromilow, 1992; NCRB, 1991).

The conclusion of a 1989 study on managing operational property assets in the United Kingdom was that *property was underconsidered and poorly managed by most* (Avis et al, 1989). Avis and his research team found that pertinent questions were not asked until the organization was under severe cost or profit pressure on their main activities.

In an updated text on the theory and practice of life-cycle costing, Flanagan and coauthors (1989) debunk some of the myths that have grown up

around life costing: It is not concerned only with present and equivalent values that have no real meaning to everyday financial decisions; future running and replacement costs are not too uncertain; it is appropriate for buildings as a whole as well as individual components like HVAC systems, claddings, and wall and floor finishes.

The important part of a life-costing study is not the mechanics of calculating costs but rather establishing the parameters for the analysis itself. Of course, future costs are not certain. The end figures in a life-cost study are not precise estimates despite those decimal places in the discount factors. They are simply indicators of relative value to enable more informed decision making. Haviland outlined the critical tasks in undertaking such a study:

- Clarify the intended use of the analysis.
- Identify the alternatives to be analyzed.
- Select the time frame and a discount rate appropriate to the organization.
- Establish the cost factors to be considered and available data.
- Consider the life-cost measures to be used.
- Report the findings carefully, explain the assumptions and uncertainties underlying the analysis, and qualify the apparent precision of this mathematical technique.

Objectives and outcomes

While life-costing studies follow a common procedure, the objectives and desired outcomes are determined by the organization. The purpose may be

- To establish expected life of components in an assessment for ongoing maintenance versus replacement, taking account of current operating and maintenance costs, projected savings in operating costs, energy efficiency, and improved performance.
- To assess timing of substantial refurbishment by identifying trigger factors, such as pending obsolescence of major components, operating and maintenance costs reaching a predetermined level, or significant changes in user space needs.
- Where more than one trigger factor occurs, further analysis is required to assess refurbishment, disposal,

and replacement options with respect to the total investment in the facility, subject to current and future appropriateness of location and property market conditions.

The outcome desired may be to develop a project maintenance budget for the next 5 to 10 years, taking account of optimal life costs for one facility compared with another. The scope of the study may be limited to a few building elements that are expected to have a significant impact on future costs or an overall assessment of all future costs.

Where the objective is to make a choice among alternatives, such as whether to upgrade passenger elevators now or later, only differential information on costs that are different for each option need to be considered (after the physical condition, performance, and expected life of the present elevator system have been assessed). This is familiar grist to the mill of economic analysts in lease or buy decisions on general-purpose office accommodations.

Where the objective is to assess the consequences of a given decision, more comprehensive cost information is required for the analysis. Examples would be assessing the total life cost of maintaining a particular facility for a given period, examining options for relocation and rebuilding, or assessing the net savings from passive solar design where that decision affects the initial cost of the whole building and many operating and maintenance costs in addition to energy used.

Critical factors in life costing

The time frame and discount rate are critical factors that depend on many considerations unique to individual organizations: the importance of property to their operations in one or more locations, the period of analysis appropriate to their planning strategies, the baseline date, the expected useful lives of their facilities, and external factors likely to influence their decisions.

The timescale for analysis is not necessarily the same as the expected physical life of the building or individual components. For most building life-cycle cost studies, the economic life of a building and a particular building component is defined as the period of time after which it becomes more economical to replace rather than to continue to maintain it. There can be a tendency to maintain building and service elements that are becoming obsolete, to the point where their good condition does not warrant replacement, even though this may preclude replacing them with more efficient elements that will improve the space functionality and operation of the facility as a whole.

Individual property owners tend to base maintenance programs on their own experience and management priorities rather than on published guidelines on the likely economic life of building components.

Selecting a discount rate

The discount rate should be selected to suit the individual organization and the objectives of the study. Typically, it may be the actual cost of borrowing funds for the project plus related charges or a rate of return set by the organization for any of its investments or a rate reflecting a missed opportunity in not being able to use the funds for some other use.

The higher the discount rate, the less important future costs are relative to initial or present costs and the less worthwhile it becomes to try and avoid future expenditure by increasing initial costs. As the life cycle becomes longer, the annual savings to justify an extra initial expenditure flatten out, approaching the discount rate itself.

Figure 7.1 shows the annual savings or other benefits required to justify an extra initial cost of $1 over a selected number of years. This lies behind many short-term investment decisions to limit initial costs. For example, with a 7 percent discount rate, a savings in operating or salary costs equivalent to $24,000 per year for 5 years would justify spending $100,000 initially to improve the performance of the facility. If the savings continue for a proposed 25-year life, spending nearly three times that amount would result in a net benefit to the organization.

Many institutions and government agencies adopt a rate of 10 percent for financial planning as the typical average rate of return on private investment before taxes and after inflation. However, in common with the policy for U.S. federal agencies, a 7

Number of years	5	10	15	20	25	30	35	40
15% discount rate	30c	20c	17c	16c	15c	15c	15c	15c
10% discount rate	26c	16c	13c	12c	11c	11c	10c	10c
7% discount rate	24c	14c	11c	9c	9c	8c	8c	7c

Figure 7.1 Annual saving required to justify an extra $1 initial expenditure.

percent discount rate is often adopted for decisions on building procurement or upgrading of operational property. This rate represents an estimate of internal rate of return on general-purpose property leased from the private sector, exclusive of property taxes and expected inflation.

Deferred maintenance action has the effect of reducing the total life-cost calculation. For example, if maintenance action costing $20,000 is put off for 5 years from year 5 to year 10, the present worth of that future cost item at the 7 percent discount rate is reduced to some $9800 compared with the present worth from that expenditure in year 5 of about $5700. Unless there is some penalty with a greater present value than $4000, such as foregoing potential savings or high risk of accident or breakdown, the total life cost is reduced by deferring maintenance.

Progressive maintenance is a soft target for budget cuts. Many items are subject to gradual decay, and the effects of undermaintenance are not noticeable. The most immediate concern to the organization is usually avoiding disruption of operations through building or component failure. The tightness of maintenance budgets necessitates careful prioritization of work.

Management is frequently under pressure to demonstrate short-term gains. But buildings are long-term, durable assets in the main. Readily quantified measures such as initial acquisition cost and ongoing area costs per staff person may be very misleading. It is better to face up to the future costs of building ownership. Better performance indicators can be defined using available information about routine operating and maintenance costs and likely refurbishment upgrades over the planned occupancy period.

Cost categories and information available

The cost categories and level of detail in a life-costing study should highlight the items the owners consider most relevant to making decisions about their premises over the selected "life" period. Many research studies have found that two conditions inhibit wider use of life costing:

- Multiple systems of data recording, some custom-designed to suit individual parts of the organizations and operations, that may not be consistent or comparable with other data.
- Difficulty in establishing cost components and relationships from historic records without reference to management information that has influenced past design and operating cost decisions.

To manage operational property in a proactive sense, it is necessary to track financial, physical, and operational data. Often the data are held by different groups in the organization and used for different purposes.

Benchmarks are necessary to assess and prioritize further capital works required to maintain the facility. Most organizations lack the data required to set benchmarks but recognize the benefits of adopting guidelines from other commercial property and public-sector studies as a starting point to develop internal measures of economic performance.

Research by the Centre for Building Performance Research in 1986–1987 on government and commercial office buildings in New Zealand found that operating costs, including routine maintenance, energy, cleaning, and other regular recurring expenses, ranged from 2.0 to 3.7 percent of the estimated value of the building construction brought to the common base year 1986 (Tippett and Sterios, 1987a, 1987b).

A similar range from 2.5 to 3.5 percent was noted by Bromilow in the 1992 NCRB guidelines on building property asset management information: "annual building maintenance averages about 0.5 to 1.5 percent of building replacement value, with energy and cleaning costs each about 1 percent" (Bromilow, 1992). A U.K. study in 1993 by the Oxford Brookes School of Real Estate Management noted that "maintenance costs and energy expenditure can each typically form about 20 percent of an organization's total annual expenditure on property" (Avis et al., 1993).

Benchmarks for major refurbishment and upgrading expenditure are harder to identify. Bromilow suggests that in the long term, the average seems to be a little less than expenditure on maintenance, i.e., equivalent to 0.5 to 1.5 percent of capital cost per year. The wide range of expenditure found in individual case studies highlights the reality that maintenance is a soft target for budget cuts. When deterioration and obsolescence are gradual and there is no obvious penalty in loss of staff time, lower business activity, or higher operating costs, progressive preventive maintenance is likely to be deferred.

Total life-cycle costs

Two measures are commonly used to express total life-cycle cost over a particular period:

- *Total present worth*, otherwise called *net present value*, brings all present and future costs to their value in the baseline year, summed to a single figure.

- The second measure, *equivalent uniform annual cost*, or *charge rate*, expresses all present and future costs as an equivalent annual rate over each of the years in the life cycle. This annualized figure is an average number that does not indicate the actual number of dollars that will be incurred in each year but indicates the order of a sinking fund to be reserved each year to maintain the facility to the desired levels of quality and serviceability throughout occupancy.

Computers have now made the use of discounting formulas to move sums of money backward and forward in time ridiculously easy. However, the fact that such tools exist does not necessarily mean that they are widely understood or appropriately used.

Reporting the outcomes of life costing should identify the magnitude of future costs in a context that suits the policies and decision-making processes within the organization. Life costing should help owners and senior management, as well as those who must implement the decisions, to consider cost tradeoffs that are not obvious. The people involved in managing these resources must still make many judgments. The object of life costing is to ensure that the judgments are well-informed, "to make that collection of decisions that will provide the benefits required within the cost constraints identified" (AIA, 1977).

In the early stages of facility planning and design of a new building, life-costing studies of key elements may have a dramatic impact on the physical form and cost of the end product. For an existing building, life-costing studies first establish *if*, and then *where* and *when*, money should be spent that is consistent with the capacity of the building to provide an appropriate facility for the organization now and in the future.

Case study: An exploratory life-costing study of a national office

In 1993, the property group of a government organization commissioned a life-cycle cost study of one of its national offices. The study was to provide a basis for planning future capital outlays and ongoing costs to maintain the facility for its present use over a period to be determined.

The building was designed and constructed in the mid-1970s as a prestige, high-specification, purpose-built facility with an expected long life and relatively low intensity of use. The ground floor is primarily reception and public spaces with two office floors above and basement carparking, The structural design allowed for two more stories if required. Sited on reserved land in a pleasant garden suburb adjacent to the central business district, the location is well regarded for corporate head offices and institutional buildings. The area is a mixed-use precinct of commercial and medium-density residential developments with clear urban planning requirements to preserve the character and density of the precinct.

The first stage of the study was a physical condition survey of the facility by inspection of the building documentation, the exterior envelope, interior construction, and services, gathering of information on current energy, cleaning, and routine maintenance costs. Historical data were not available, but no recent items of significance were noted by the building manager other than carpet replacement to the upper floors.

The report to the head office property group on the first stage confirmed that after 17 years there were no major defects in the concrete structure or building envelope. Some maintenance and repair work was required to remedy minor cladding defects and avoid further deterioration. The quality of the building shell and interior fit-out was such that with appropriate management, a much longer life could be expected than the period of 30 years specified later in the study in consultation with the property group.

From the initial inspection of services plant and equipment, a number of options for maintenance, replacement, or upgrading were identified, which indicated opportunities for significant energy savings. This was the starting point for detailed study of the services options to determine estimates of costs and their potential to improve energy efficiency and performance.

The cost estimates to implement all the proposed services options were about seven times the current annual maintenance costs with potential annual savings of up to 40 percent in energy but little effect on maintenance expenditure.

User evaluation. At this stage, a user evaluation of the premises involving two staff groups was conducted by the Centre for Building Performance Research at Victoria University using their well-tested "touring interview" procedure, which draws on the users' experience of the facility. Following an introductory meeting, the two groups selected as representative of the occupants toured various parts of the facility to identify and discuss whatever building features and qualities they considered to be important. In the final review meeting, the participants discussed the topics raised during the tour, starting with the ones considered most important. For some issues, staff made recommendations on what might usefully be done to improve or better utilize the facility, which were incorporated in the final report of the whole study.

The staff considered that the building was in good physical condition and well maintained, apart from the items specified in the report to the owners. The location was highly regarded, and the design also was considered appropriate, the most important exceptions being security and safety aspects.

There was extensive discussion about possible actions to improve the situation. Ideas ranged from relatively minor adjustments to substantial rearrangement of the secure areas of the site and public access zones within the building. Some physical features of the building had caused accidents, mostly from slipping on marble floors, tripping, or missing a step on stairs. Staff members reported that the arrangement of glazed windlock and doors at the main entrance was confusing for visitors and potentially dangerous.

During the touring interviews and group discussion, staff members made reference to many of the internal and finish defects noted earlier in the consultants' inspection, adding insights from the user viewpoint on the patterns of use, cleaning, and their own operations. These comments ranged from difficulties in changing light bulbs in the high public spaces to problems of distraction and/or noise readily resolved by partitioning.

In view of the concerns raised by staff, additional building works to address the safety and security issues were included in the life-costing analysis. The building modifications were expected to cost about half the estimated sum for the services options.

Time frame and economic life of components. The period for analysis in this case study was set by the property group at 30 years from 1995 as year 1 to end year 2025. It is often hard to think of a building as having a discrete predictable "life." Through periodic renewal of its constituent elements, it would be possible to prolong the physical life of this building for centuries, as is done for many national treasures. In general, "the economic life" of a building or component is defined as the period of time after which it becomes more economical for the organization to replace rather than to continue to maintain a building or component (where economic obsolescence is often triggered by external market conditions).

The estimated remaining life of the services elements investigated in the first stages of the study ranged from 5 to 30 years. For other facility elements, the remaining life of components prior to replacement or upgrade was assessed using typical life spans for similar national offices spaced at intervals over the next 30 years (NPWC, 1989).

Where the economic life of a component exceeded the analysis period, a residual or salvage value, proportional to the estimated remaining life, was included in the life-costing analysis.

A discount rate of 7 percent exclusive of taxes and inflation for the life-cycle costing analysis was adopted in consultation with the head office property group.

Cost categories and data availability. As a member of the AIA task force observed in 1977: "Establishing cost categories is a bit like slicing a number of identical pies. There are many ways to slice the cost pie. Any system of cost categories is simply a filing system—a series of pigeonholes designed to accumulate and compare data in that category."

Many large property owners have a computerized database with basic information on their property assets. The message from the 1993 follow-up study by Oxford Brookes University on the pitfalls of unwieldy information systems for property management is "limit the size and/or scope of the systems being implemented and build incrementally on small successes." (Avis et al., 1993)

Both the Uniformat II classification for building elements and related work, developed by the National Institute of Standards and Technology, and its counterpart recommended by the National Committee of Rationalised Building (NCRB) for use in Australia, where the main categories may be subdivided to the detail of technical specifications when required (Bowen et al., 1992; Bromilow, 1992, 1994), were considered.

To develop an indicative program for maintaining the whole facility in this case, the NCRB classification of elements was adopted with simplified cost categories. The cost categories used in this exploratory study were

- Initial capital cost of upgrade or replacement (including installation but excluding fees and tax).
- Operating and maintenance costs (O&M) recurring annually for ongoing use of the facility or component, including energy costs where applicable. (Other recurring costs-in-use such as rates and insurances were not included.)
- Cost of next upgrade or replacement at end of estimated economic life.
- Functional use costs associated with the intended functions within the facility where appropriate (primarily salaries of personnel).
- Salvage cost or residual value where remaining life of components exceeds the analysis period.

From the life costing of options for services maintenance or replacement and building works arising from the user evaluation, an indicative program for maintaining the facility over the period 1995 to 2025 was compiled. All costs were presented in "today" dollars, not future inflated dollars, and then discounted back to the baseline year using the 7 percent discount rate.

Where improved facility performance was not thought to be critical to operations or anticipated energy/other savings did not offset costs, action was deferred until near the estimated economic life of the components, thereby reducing the total life cost for the analysis period.

Putting the analysis in context. The sum of future costs for 30 years, in present day dollars, does not directly answer the question, "How much should we plan to spend on this building?" Life-cost analysis produces numbers that do not mean very much until they are related to investment decisions already made, operational policies of the organization, and internal or external benchmarks for maintaining comparable facilities.

In this study, the estimated future costs of this national office to the year 2025 were first related to the capital investment it represented in the 1994 baseline year. The "initial capital cost" was taken as the replacement cost of an identical building in 1994 less depreciation for one-fifth of the very long life intended in the original 1974 design. Present worth of future costs was some 35 percent of that notional initial cost. Total present worth of initial and ongoing costs less sale value in 2025 were then compared with the total life cost of a new building and found to be very similar.

A different outcome emerged when capital investment in the present property was rated at the low commercial market valuation obtained during the study (due to reservations on other uses). Present worth of future costs was over 70 percent of that valuation, but comparison with the new building option showed a substantial economic advantage in continued occupancy in the location of first choice for the next 30 years—provided the facility continues to meet user requirements and property markets do not skyrocket.

Ongoing facility costs. While total present worth provides a basis for considering alternate property and premises strategies, the second life-cost measure of equivalent uniform annual cost of various ongoing facility costs allows comparison with historic data, planned budget levels, or other benchmarks. The annualized future costs in this case, using the 7 percent discount factor, were 2.8% of the "initial capital cost" in the same 1994 dollars for each year in the 30-year analysis period. This averaged cost was well within the range of 2.0 to 3.7 percent for corporate and government head offices in New Zealand and Australia found in previous life-costing studies (Tippett and Sterios, 1987a, 1987b; Bromilow, 1992). However, annualized future costs would be over 5 percent per year if current market valuation was taken as the actual present value of the facility to the organization.

Whether owned or leased, buildings are a vital resource in every organization. Annual accounts present the asset valuation "in the books" and record past expenditure on operating and maintenance. Market valuations establish what they are worth to other organizations. Neither provide the answers on how much an organization should invest and continue to spend on a particular building.

In this study, the original objective of the building evaluation was to identify elements requiring significant expenditure in the near and not so near future to continue the present use of a facility. That outcome could not be achieved until the different perspectives of property as a physical, financial, and operational resource were brought together.

Life costing produced no future costs with certainty for the organization's property group. It simply exposed the economic consequences of past decisions, present options, and possible tradeoffs over the next 30 years of the building's life in present-day terms. The group is now in a better position to make informed decisions on an appropriate maintenance program for this national office—and to review that program as those future costs become present certainties.

evaluation resources

CHAPTER 8

CPBR Checklist

Compiled by Harry Bruhns
Formerly at VUW Centre for Building Performance Research,
New Zealand

8.1 A Framework for Checking Building Performance

This chapter is devoted largely to a checklist of the factors that can influence building performance. The checklist was first developed by the Centre for Building Performance Research for a project involving the evaluation of a corporate head office and the preparation of a brief for new accommodation (see Sec. 5.1). Subsequently, the CBPR extended the checklist and made it applicable for more general use in building evaluation.

Generally speaking, checklists are useful in situations where it is important to think of everything that could be important to building quality. Specifically, we suggest that the CBPR checklist can be used in four ways:

1. For design or design audit work
2. For briefing and programming work
3. For planning and evaluation
4. As a framework for a database

There are three points to make about the use of this checklist. First, we expect that users will wish to adapt it to their own purposes, possibly adding, deleting, or changing its content. Second, the checklist is not intended to be prescriptive; it is not mandatory to take account of all the factors in the checklist. Third, by its nature, the checklist cannot deal with interactions between its contents at any level of detail.

At its broadest level, the checklist is structured into six attributes:

1. Corporate
2. Site
3. Construction
4. Space
5. Internal environment
6. Building services

Each of these attributes is divided into a set of factors. Each factor is described and examples given of items that may be investigated. As examples, these are wide-ranging and illustrative rather than comprehensive.

8.2 Attribute and Factor Descriptions

1. Corporate attribute

The requirements summarized under the *corporate* attribute are the overall requirements of an organization purchasing or renting a facility. They are the broadest level of requirements and are concerned with *what* the building achieves or is intended to achieve rather than *how*. They are requirements of those to whom the building is a means for achieving organizational objectives. Hence corporate requirements are concerned with the procurement of the building and its broad functions rather than with the details of physical building design.

Factors	Description	Items
Corporate objectives	Awareness of corporate objectives, what the building's contribution is expected to be, and any implications they may have had on decisions made about the building. For example, corporate goals might include a 50 percent increase in turnover in the next 5 years and affect accommodation requirements.	Corporate mission statement Anticipated growth Production and sales targets Corporate culture Likelihood of changes Acquisitions
Serviceability	In general terms the building's capability to support the broad functions for which it is required now and in the future.	Location Total area and cost Space for people Space for other functions Adaptability if requirements change
Image	The impression the building creates for people and the extent to which the building signals its status and identity may be the influence of location, neighboring buildings, and the building itself, e.g., the color, shape, architectural features. Any particular image may be required to complement the corporate image and the activities to be carried out in the building, and by the organization, particularly where those activities involve marketing.	Status and image of location Future local development Planning developments Name, height, shape, color Details of cultural symbolism External and internal ambience Parking adjacent to entrance Entry welcoming or imposing Foyer reception area Visitors parking areas
Tenure	Contractual and legal arrangements—how well the building conforms to requirements (e.g., will it be ready when expected). This requires lease negotiation and checking, knowledge of the parties, risk analysis, etc. The reputation, financial status, reliability of other parties.	Contractors, subcontractors Owner, agent, leasing tenant Other parties Lease type (net/gross, etc.) Special conditions in lease Rental holiday or fit-out assistance may be negotiable Termination of lease conditions/restrictions
Code compliance	Compliance with a variety of laws and codes and specifications. District schemes may assist or impede corporate objectives or building plans. Not being aware of these at the stage of checking and deciding may cause later delays and additional costs.	National law and codes Local government by-laws District schemes In-house codes Is a change of use planned

Factors	Description	Items
Time	Will the building be ready when needed and remain available for the duration it is required? Construction may take longer than expected, or parts may not be vacated in time to allow fit-out and move-in at the required date. Legal processes may delay use of the building. The uncertainty in all these needs to be within predetermined acceptable levels. The move itself must be planned in this context.	Uncertainty of move-in date Rental review period Time for own needs assessment Time for permits and approvals Time to plan and do fit-out Useful life of building
Initial cost	The costs before the building comes into regular use. For renting, it is the cost of procurement, moving, etc. For purchase, procurement and moving must be added as part of the purchase cost. Costs of moving may vary with location and ease of access.	Land and construction cost Holding and finance charges Professional fees Naming rights Costs, preletting income, etc. Fit-out costs Moving costs
Life cost	The life cost is the full cost of a building over the term of the organization's investment in or use of a building. A building with lower initial costs may load a greater life cost on the organization. A life-cost analysis, taking account of all immediate and future costs and income, will calculate the cost of a specific option or compare the costs of different options.	Initial costs Annual income Annual cost Refurbishment costs Disposal costs Reliability of cost estimates Risk evaluation
Rent	Income may be derived from renting the whole building, or subletting portions of it. For a tenant, rents may be the main ongoing cost of a building. The level and security of those income/costs needs to be taken account of. Consideration should be given to foreseeable future changes. Risk analyses can help calculate the likely outcomes of various scenarios, booms, busts, etc.	Rental for zones Gross income Subletting income Future changes in property market Likelihood of location-based changes
Operating cost	Annual operating costs may account for a major part of the total cost of a building over its life, or the term of use by an owner or tenant. Energy and maintenance costs vary widely among buildings, and may be a substantial part of the total annual costs of a building. Whether directly charged (net lease) or incorporated (gross lease) the building occupier (owner or tenant) is liable.	Central/whole building energy costs Energy costs for tenant Current and future maintenance costs Facility management costs Insurance and taxes Any other future costs

Factors	Description	Items
Refurbishment	New or existing buildings may need refurbishment during the expected period of use by an organization. Given the organization's requirements and anticipated length of tenure, what kind of interior and exterior refurbishments will be required, and how much will they cost and when? Who will pay for predictable refurbishments and those resulting from building failure?	Structural reinforcement Roof, cladding, repainting HVAC systems, plant, ducts Fit-out, partitions Drapes, lining, carpets Building failure (leaks, collapses, etc.) Legal and contractual responsibilities
Disposal	What is to be done with the building at the end of its use by the organization? What is the magnitude of income or costs at the end of the tenure or investment period. Are they to be discounted to present costs? Can time of disposal be changed to meet changed circumstances?	Relettability Future contractual obligations Sale price Demolition costs Contract termination conditions Fit-out ownership
Security	If the functions to be carried out in the building are critical, account may need to be taken of unlikely but possible catastrophes in the provision of energy, water, sewerage, staff support, etc.	Earthquake, flood, landslip National/international conflicts Civil disobedience Electricity, gas, coal, oil Potable water Sewerage Emergency food and accommodation

2. Site attribute

This includes those items concerned with the site, regardless of the building that is on it; the location of the site and the environment (built and climatic) in which the building is located or will be constructed.

Factors	Description	Items
Access	How accessible is the building for all those who are expected to use it, including occupants, employees of the tenants, clients, consultants, representatives, and visitors of various kinds?	Ease of locating building Visitor parking available Proximity to public transport Walking distance from train Distance to key organizations Taxi stand in vicinity Delivery parking

Factors	Description	Items
Built environment	Does the surrounding built environment affect the performance of the building with respect to owners and users? Is the built environment likely to change in important ways in the future?	High-rise in vicinity Likelihood of rezoning Current and future levels of construction activity Effect of sun and wind on site
Microclimate	The climate in and around a building site affects pedestrian comfort, use of grounds, energy use for heating and lighting and potential for natural ventilation. Exposure to wind and sea may affect maintenance costs and degradation of materials. The microclimate also may be modified by hills, trees, and nearby buildings. Neighboring buildings may provide useful sun, obstruct desired sun, or create unpleasant solar reflections. They may provide wind shelter or accentuate wind gusts. Analyze meteorologic records or on-site monitoring.	Solar orientation Morning and afternoon sun Exposure to wind Wind test results Rain exposure/protection Condition of nearby buildings (corrosion of materials, etc.) Air pollution due to nearby traffic, industry, chimneys, etc. External noise sources On-site climatic data available
Local services	The distance to, accessibility of, various services not specifically related to work, that tend to be used by people, en route to and from work and during the work day are important to perceptions about a building's convenience. The well-being of occupants, time lost for shopping, etc., ease of finding staff may be dependent on local services.	Nearby takeaways, restaurants, etc. Household shopping Personal services (hairdressers, doctor, dentist, etc.) Proximity to shopping center Sports and recreation facilities
Site	The nature of the site may affect the well-being of occupants, staff satisfaction, ease of finding staff, etc. For buildings of specific function (e.g., care, entertainment) there may be specifically required functions of the site.	Has its own grounds Condition of grounds Recreational areas Exposure/privacy of grounds Sheltered/sunny lunch space Space for children/day care Security (e.g., throughways, dark spots, hiding places)
Conditions	Flooding, groundwater, subsidence, earthquake risk, access to water, phone, gas, electric mains, and planning regulations with respect to these may all affect the proper functioning of a building on site.	Groundwater/flooding Stability of site Geologic analysis Engineering analysis Local authority records check External sources of dust, Smells, pollutants, noise Access to water, phone, gas, electricity

Factors	Description	Items

3. Construction attribute

Construction includes all those items which make up the physical building, that support it and define its shape, spaces, and materials. It includes the foundations, skeleton, fabric, internal walls, fit-out, fittings, furnishings, and furniture but excludes the building services, which are dealt with as a distinct attribute. Depending on the extent of refurbishment and fit-out options available, the construction factors provide the basis and ultimately the limitations on the performance that can be obtained from a building.

Factors	Description	Items
Structure safety	Structural soundness is concerned with the capacity of the overall building to absorb and respond to shocks and forces of various kinds, such as earthquake, wind, and the loads resulting from its use. The effects of unsuitable structure may range from undue vibration or swaying in wind, through such things as foundation settlement, to total collapse of the building. The overall safety of the structure needs qualified engineering analysis. An earthquake engineering analysis may be required to determine likely earthquake performance.	Age of building and codes in force at date of construction Type and stability of foundation system Type and stability of skeleton Condition of the structure Corrosion of reinforcing steel Earthquake stability Wind stability Floor vibrations Compliance with safety codes Cost of strengthening
Structural adaptability	Is the structure able to be modified for additions and alterations that may be required (e.g., a mezzanine floor or extra floor)? Can the building bear the loads that may be required in its intended use?	Maximum allowable loads on existing foundations Maximum loads on skeleton Floors can bear required loads
Overall dimensions	Does the overall structure provide for the requirements of the client? What restrictions or limitations does it introduce? E.g., organizational communications might be affected if functional groups are split over too many floors.	Number of floors Floor-to-ceiling height Building height acceptable Useful area of single floors
Shell geometry	Building shape affects various aspects of the current and potential performance of the building. The overall structure (the size and shape of the building, and its immovable parts) places constraints on layouts. The shape and solar orientation also can affect the building's response to climatic conditions, e.g., equal quantities of unshaded glass	External form Dimensions of perimeters, surfaces, volumes Window and wall areas Solar gains, shading, and wind exposure in each direction Effects on image/ambience

Factors	Description	Items
	on north and south faces can cause heating and cooling problems.	Shelter for pedestrians
Structural layout	For a given external shape, the uses and layouts to which a building can be put are further constrained by the positions of the major internal support structures. Trial layouts can be used here. See "Space attribute."	Position of core and supports Positions of fixed internal structural walls Suitability for desired modular layout Size(s) of internal modules
Cladding materials	The materials used in the construction of the shell cladding may affect building performance and occupant functions. Badly chosen materials may lead to functional problems and increased maintenance costs. Materials can be checked by observation and chemical analysis of drilled samples.	External finishing materials Condition of external finishes Signs of corrosion Condition of windows Air infiltration Evidence of water leaks Age and condition of sealants
Access	How well suited is the building design for accessibility, in terms of building function, client, and user requirements? Does it facilitate the entry and exit of people, materials, and goods and supplies as required.	Disabled access to main entry Disabled access throughout Materials/goods entrance Goods loading bay Goods lift (check also size) Location of car park access
Security	Security requirements affect the safety of building users, the hours of work, and access to information and products/goods. How well does the structure of the building assist or inhibit making it secure? Parts of the building may require particular security.	Work areas during/after hours Internal recreational areas Service and car parking areas Grounds and site security Is blast resistance required

Factors	Description	Items

4. Space attribute

Space includes those factors and items which ensure that the building provides spaces for all the functions required of it and can be adapted with a reasonable flexibility to changing requirements in the future.

Factors	Description	Items
Major zones	Does the building or premises provide appropriate space for the major functions that are required of it?	Office space Basement and carparking Amenities and services Other space (e.g., retail)
Office spaces	Is there adequate provision of the main work spaces required for the occupant's activities? As well as office spaces, requirements may include spaces for secretarial, clerical, and client activity as well as for dealing with the public, photocopying, and so on.	Fixed offices (1–2 persons) Fixed offices (3–6 persons) Open/partitionable space Quiet work spaces Executive offices Other work space types
Other personnel space requirements	Space may be required for other functions. This is organization-dependent. An organization needs to have a good knowledge of its needs. Some form of requirements analysis is recommended. This usually requires layout tests by an office designer.	Consultants work space Visitor space Meeting spaces Reception—main entrance Reception—each floor Display areas Informal rest/discussion areas
Keeping the building functioning	An often forgotten but practical necessity is to provide space for those who will keep the building functioning, e.g., building managers, maintenance people, cleaners.	Office for caretaker Office for building manager Cleaner's office Storage of cleaning and maintenance materials Storage for window cleaning units
Storage	Most offices need significant amounts of space for storage of working materials, including paper, books, files, diskettes and tapes, archival materials. Equipment storage (computers, display equipment, etc.) also may be required. How much of what types of paper, other working materials and equipment needs to be stored near	Working materials Records storage for groups and divisions Accessibility of storage Local versus centralized storage requirements Location of library or libraries

Factors	Description	Items
	which people? What security is required? How critical is it?	Security against access by unauthorized persons Fire protected storage
Circulation space	It is essential that space be allowed for movement of people and goods. Circulation space in office buildings usually constitutes 25 to 40 percent of available internal space. As well as the amount of circulation space, the width and length of various parts of it affects the size of equipment that may be moved, traffic density, and time to get to other parts of the building.	Permanent corridors Space for partitioned corridors Relationship to lifts, stairwells Circulation between worksta-tions and among groups Potential bottlenecks Width of barriers
Stairs	The location and accessibility of stairs are impor-tant to wayfinding and can significantly affect the time required for communications and ease of interaction among different groups. Stair locations and design also affect the safety of moving around in the building.	Location(s) and locatability Maximum internal distance to stairs from any point Stair surface material Age and condition and safety Width and slope of stairs Ambience of stairwells Emergency exits
Social	How does the building affect interpersonal com-munication? Does the space suit your organiza-tional culture, and does it assist or impede the required contact and communications between various groups and individuals in the organization? Can groups be placed to allow ready access to each other as required?	Personal privacy as required Line of sight within groups Access between groups Access around building Access to main entrance Access to other entries/exits Corridor/zone meeting places Size of floors
Wayfinding	How does the building affect finding your way around it? Does signage take account of visitors, clients, those unfamiliar with the building, as well as regular staff? Wayfinding is also affected by the positions of entrances, lifts, and stairs and major parts of the structure or external objects which may be used to find one's bearings. Are the spaces used by visitors near entrances or other easily located places?	Inherent limitations of fixed building structure Ease of finding main entrance Ease of wayfinding within existing building Quality of current signposting Wayfinding within possible new layouts Ease of finding carpark, and from there, locating the main building areas

Factors	Description	Items
Staff amenities	It is important that space is provided for the well-being of staff. It is part of attracting staff to work there, promoting an organizational culture, and showing management commitment to staff/occupants. Do the internal amenities provide adequate services for the numbers that will use them, without overcrowding and maintenance problems? Are external amenities sheltered or exposed?	Kitchen/cafeteria Gymnasium and/or other recreation amenities Location and quality of toilets, showers, sick bays, etc. Accessibility of the amenities Away from public spaces Cleanliness and cleanability HWS can be supplied, cost Balconies, courtyards, etc.
Space use flexibility and quality	Growth and change are continuous in buildings. It is important to ascertain how flexible are the building's shell and internal constructions. How many options are there for partitioning? How easily can the building be repartitioned in the future? How flexible are the services? How easy is it to move computers and other electronic equipment?	Percentage of useful space limited by permanent walls Modular integration/flexibility Is adequate space use now possible (without new fit-out) Bldg factors/efficiency of space use
	For layout design and alterations identify whether the location of window mullions, lights, etc. define a consistent modular unit. How many workstations can be fitted in the unit? Will required desks, filing cabinets, etc. fit in these workstations? How many rows of people can be fitted between windows and the first barrier wall or corridor? Is the resulting "window depth" (distance from windows) acceptable to the people in the innermost rows? See also "Construction attribute: Structural layout."	Minimum and maximum numbers of people per floor Space can accommodate groups of different sizes Ease of rearrangement of workstations within group spaces Ease of rearrangement of group spaces within the building as a whole Groups can be positioned with appropriate status
Sublettable space	Is there excess space in the building for current organizational needs? Is excess space desirable? Are the organization's needs variable? Is subletting a viable option? If so, does the building allow it conveniently, or can it be made to do so?	Area of sublettable space Marketability (likely income) Appropriate tenants available Separate access and amenities Separate energy metering Separate lighting controls
Fit-up elements	Fixed partitions, raised floors, suspended ceilings, floor finishes, and segregated ducting and trunking for power, data, and telecommunications may all be fit-up elements. These elements may have a life span as short as 5 years and are often extensively modified or replaced on change of ownership or	Age and condition of ceilings, walls, windows, floors, carpet Years before replacement of elements is needed Presence of dangerous materials (e.g., asbestos)

Factors	Description	Items
	lease. If existing elements are to be used, access may be necessary to fit additional cabling, lights, power points, etc.	Internal sources of dust Access for cabling, power points, etc.
Finishes, furnishings, and fittings	The provision of desks, chairs, decor, cable handling, furniture, mobile/movable/demountable partitions, storage, acoustical separation, and task lighting all need careful consideration in terms of usability, flexibility, and image. Workplaces in offices are regularly moved, and the effective management of change is an important organizational responsibility.	Color and decor Drapes and wall hangings Furniture, equipment Ergonomics

5. Internal environment attribute

Internal environment includes those items whose main function is to modify the environment and to provide an enclosed or semienclosed space for particular activities and materials. For office buildings, the principal requirement is to provide an environment that enhances occupants' well-being and facilitates their productivity. The quality of the internal environment is both objective and subjective. Instrumental measurement can provide accurate and useful information on environmental conditions, but the subjective experience of the building users should always be the final arbiter in the evaluation of those conditions.

Factors	Description	Items
Air quality	Poor air quality affects the health of building users, resulting in higher rates of absenteeism and lower productivity. Three main aspects should be checked, viz., air circulation in individual spaces, air transfer between spaces, and specific air pollutants. Air quality can be negatively affected by pollutants, by inadequate flow, by the location of exhausts and inlets, and by short-circuited transfer within the building.	Building users comments Overall ventilation rate Internal odors/pollutants External odors/pollutants Main building exhausts and inlets well separated to prevent exhaust recirculation Inlets away from refuse bins, carparks, loading bays, etc. Air transfer within building
Ventilation	The method of ventilation (whether natural or mechanical) has implications for the air quality issues listed above. The general characteristics of the method employed, in particular the extent of control available to the building user, and the interaction with other environmental factors should be checked. For ventilation to be effective, good air must	NATURAL Opening windows Extent of adjustment available Adequacy of windows in wind Adequacy in warm, calm conditions External wind protection Circulation to core areas

Factors	Description	Items
	reach the breathing space of the building occupants. All links and air-handling processes between the main air supply inlets and the "occupants' noses" must be fully functional for this to be achieved.	MECHANICAL Positions of internal grilles (inlets and outlets) Local control zones Air circulation to core areas System noise Adjustment of air volume and direction
Thermal comfort	Frequently the focus of complaints, conditions that are judged too hot, cold, or stuffy by building users, have a detrimental effect on performance (see also "Building services attribute: HVAC systems"). Spot checks should be carried out and an assessment made of conditions likely during different times of the year	Air and radiant temperature Humidity and air speed Thermal zoning Location and control of terminal units Solar overheating Potential underheated areas Downdrafts and air leakage Heating and drafts in foyers
Noise	Noise levels can affect concentration, ease of communication between staff, and privacy of communications. From the user viewpoint and especially the 30 percent of the population who are particularly sensitive to noise, the key performance requirements are the avoidance of annoyance, irritation, or discomfort due to noise; the prevention of speech interference; and the creation of acoustic privacy where appropriate. By contrast, a building that is too quiet may be felt to be "dead" by many occupants. "Spot" subjective measurement is feasible here, but a quantitative evaluation of background noise, speech privacy, and reverberation time can provide useful information for more detailed evaluations.	Exterior noise climate Noise with windows closed Noise with windows open External noise sources (e.g., traffic, construction activity now or in the future) Internal noise sources Interior background noise levels Isolation of current or future noise sources Reverberation times Surface sound absorption Sound transmission of walls, partitions, floors, ceilings
Lighting	Inadequate illuminance levels, poor color rendering, inappropriate directional effects, and lighting systems that result in glare problems can lead to deterioration of visual acuity. Both natural and artificial lighting (as well as combined effects) should be assessed, bearing in mind that both are	GENERAL Average illuminance levels Uniformity ratio Relative task visibility Internal surface reflectances Cost and energy efficiency

Factors	Description	Items
	potential sources of heat gain and that the energy costs of running artificial lights can be significant. Natural daylight in the working spaces of office buildings is widely considered to enhance working conditions. Solar glare needs to be prevented, and special lighting requirements may need to be considered, e.g., for extensive use of computer terminals, drafting and graphics work. The levels of natural lighting and the quantity and quality of artificial lighting also affect the ambience of the internal environment.	**NATURAL** Window types and location Daylight factors and distribution Glare from sky and low-angle sun, reflections from neighboring buildings Glazing type **ARTIFICIAL** Luminaire types and locations Illuminance levels Color rendering Glare from luminaires Directional effects Lighting distribution Switching systems/zones Automatic controls Heat gain recovery potential Emergency lighting External lighting (for access and security)
Special areas	While most of the above is addressed to the general needs of the individual user, some activities will have special environmental requirements, possibly independent of the general systems. These should be noted and the building evaluated with them in mind.	Provision for air-conditioned computer suites Provision for environment sensitive chemicals Provision for special use zones, e.g., wet process copier ammonia
Ambience	Ambience is a product of a variety of factors and items to do with the layout and design of the spaces in a building. Ambience is commonly described by such terms as welcoming, calm, relaxing, oppressive, depressing, claustrophobic, exciting, boring. It is affected by items such as the interior colors, condition of interior constructions, internal dimensions, and views to the exterior, as well as lighting, noise, and other environmental factors described above. Evaluation of the ambience is necessarily a judgment made in the light of organization culture, occupant preferences, current fashions, and the building itself.	General look and feel of the building interior Exterior views Views likely to be built out Appearance of walls and ceiling Appearance of floor coverings Appearance of blinds, etc. Size and height of windows Fittings and furnishings Room sizes and ceiling height Pleasantness of lighting Nature and quantity of noise Feeling of warmth

Factors	Description	Items

6. Building services attribute

This attribute includes those items which play an essential part in the quality of the internal environment created by the building. They facilitate communications within the building and with the external world and support the functionality of the building as a whole. It is vital to ensure that all building services have the capacity to handle expected user requirements (or can be readily modified to do so) and that they are able to cope with likely changes of user requirements in the future. Inadequate capacity in any of the services and inability of those services to be adapted to needs are likely to lead to increased operating costs and may result in major costs or the need to move to another building. In all areas of building services, an assessment of current and likely future needs is essential. Checking and evaluating services for an existing or proposed building will usually require the input of one or more professionals familiar with each of the range of services used in a given building.

Factors	Description	Items
All systems **Capacity and flexibility**	Inadequacies in services will have major implications for building performance, at best necessitating disruption as plant is fitted or replaced, at worst forcing a move to another building. All necessary building services should be available, have the capacity to handle expected user requirements (or can be readily modified to do so), and be able to cope with predicted future changes in user needs. Modern offices may generate considerable heat through lighting and equipment, although with technology changes these are decreasing. Can the systems handle this as well as the basic climatic load?	Locate all existing plant Identify age, brand, model, type Capacity of each system Capacity of each plant item Obtain as-fitted drawings Check that drawings are true Check system specifications Type/adaptability of controls Zones of the building served Is system capacity adjustable Previous users' comments
Maintenance	Productivity and costs are influenced by the maintainability of the building services. Are all systems reliable and can they be maintained at reasonable cost with the minimum interruption to the operation of the organization? For example, can air filters only be reached through the office areas. Also consider preventative maintenance. E.g., are systems restrained against earthquake forces, can dangerous gas leaks occur?	Past maintenance records Maintenance manual exists Commissioning records Availability of spare parts Accessibility in plant rooms and occupied spaces Disruption of occupants when carrying out maintenance
HVAC systems	The heating, ventilating, and air-conditioning (HVAC) system. A knowledge of these systems is needed to gauge the extent of control of thermal	Types of systems (general) Fuels used (gas, oil, electricity, LPG, etc.)

Factors	Description	Items
	conditions and ventilation available to building management and to individual users and the likely operating costs. Is it heating-only with natural ventilation, mechanical ventilation with heating, or mechanical ventilation with heating, cooling, and humidity control? Does it comprise a fully centralized system, a number of zoned systems, or individual units, or some combination of all these? An overall appraisal requires qualified engineering analysis	Major plant items (boiler, chiller, pump, fan, controls) Terminal units (radiators, convectors, air supply/extract grilles) Overall zoning and control Are control zones consistent with building shape and climatic influences Individual user controls
HVAC distribution	Centralized HVAC systems need to provide heating and cooling and move air in, out of, and around the building. The efficacy with which this is done depends as much on the distribution systems as the plant. Air may be brought into the interior spaces but not reach the occupants. Heat may be inadequately distributed to some parts of the building. Some parts may be overheated. Cooling systems may not be able to remove high levels of solar or equipment heat gains. Poorly designed distribution systems may cause inconvenience in other ways.	Media used (water, air, other) Identify zone subdivisions Age/condition of fans, pumps Age/condition ducts, pipes Cleanliness of ducts, presence of mold, fungi, dust Short-circuited airflows within building (redistribute stale air) Access/maintenance to ducts Space for added ducts/piping Distribution system noise
Electrical services	Electrical services with inadequate capacity, distribution systems design, and control will severely limit organizational activities. If these services cannot cope with the load imposed by the building and organizational needs, then upgrading, additional wiring, and metering will be required. As well as capacity, various aspects of the quality of supply may be important. Are the correct voltages, phases, supply reliability, etc. available in the parts of the buildings in which they will be required? Transformers can cause electrical interference affecting other equipment.	Mains reserve capacity Method of cable distribution Metering subdivisions Do meters measure electricity use in specific zones/areas Power points to workstations Power points to other areas Computer supply protection Switching of lighting systems Emergency generator Substation in building Freedom from radio/electrical interference where required
Information technology	Effective electronic communications systems are now vital facilities in most office buildings. Increasing use of information technology is placing rapidly increasing requirements on these systems and will continue to do so for the foreseeable future. Communications systems need to	Corporate information technology policy and equipment objectives Phone/data lines into building Phone/data lines to floors/zones

Factors	Description	Items
	reach most points within the building and between most workstations and the outside world. They include phone conversation, facsimile transmission, local area networks, voice, electronic and document mail, access to external computers and databases. Future requirements will include video transmission.	Phone/data lines to workstations Current and future transmission needs Current load, capacity for expansion, and flexibility of existing data lines
	Given the pace of increase in communications requirements, the ease with which additional cabling may be installed is frequently more important than existing cabling. Check that the building can provide cabling adequate to current and future needs.	Ease to install phone/data lines Ceiling space cabling options Cabling access between floors Underfloor cabling options Space for PABX, file servers, patch panels, other central/zonal devices Trial layouts of networks Maximum distance between workstations to be connected
Vertical transport	The availability of adequate vertical transportation services (lifts, escalators) affects productivity and image; e.g., in terms of the total time spent by people making trips between floors, inadequate systems can lead to a significant proportion of salaried time spent waiting for lifts. This aspect of building performance is often given insufficient attention in spite of the fact that people's time is the major expenditure of very many organizations, especially those which occupy high-rise office buildings.	Number of lifts/escalators Location(s) with respect to staff sections Maximum distance to lifts/escalators Locatability for visitors Speed for high-rise locations Overall transport capacity Maximum carrying capacity Inspection and service records available Condition of controls, shaft, motors, etc.
	Inadequate vertical transportation may be difficult and/or expensive to remedy. Lifts and escalators have inherently less flexibility to cope with future changes. Their capacity and control should therefore be checked thoroughly. Techniques are available to calculate lift numbers, speed, and size for a given organization.	Condition and appearance of surfaces, quality of design Opening width of lift doors Is a goods lift needed/present Time before next refit (years)
	Lift foyers and the lifts themselves create an important first impression for visitors and clients. Undue delays, slow traveling times, and gloomy	

Factors	Description	Items
	appearance create a poor impression. Lack of signs can cause wayfinding difficulty.	
Water services	The provision of hot and cold water to support cleaning, hygiene, and catering needs is an essential service. The overall water capacity within a building, and the method of supply and distribution contributes to the quality of staff facilities. It can limit the introduction of new production or service facilities such as kitchens. Hot water services (HWS) costs are sometimes significant—on occasion, complex heating systems need to be run to supply small quantities of hot water. Significant increases in HWS supply or distribution may require additional plant or electrical wiring; hence it is useful to check that it is supplied to all required locations, or can readily be supplied to them. Hygiene and health may be affected by inadequate or polluted systems.	Local or central HWS supply Fuel used to provide HWS Reserve capacity Is HWS supplied to all required points (or can it be readily supplied) HWS linked to overall heating system Hot and cold water for toilets, washrooms, etc. Hot and cold water for kitchens, cafeteria, etc. Cleanliness of holding tanks Source of water
Fire protection	The consequences of fire can be disastrous, with loss of personnel, equipment, documents, the building itself. Has the building been evaluated professionally? Check fire fighting equipment, escape procedures, and exit routes. What is the flammability of construction materials? Are dangerous goods stored in or near building? What are insurance provisions? Critical facilities such as computer systems and records storage may have special fire protection requirements.	Location of fire detectors (smoke, heat) Dry risers, hoses, extinguishers Distribution of sprinklers, links to firefighting equipment Pressurization of exit routes Emergency exits/procedures Smoke stop doors Requirements of special areas
Costs of services	All services incur running and maintenance costs, which together constitute the major component of the annual operating costs of a building. These costs vary considerably with the types of services installed. Their apportionment between building owner and tenant(s) depends on the design of the services and the terms of the lease (see also "Corporate attribute: Life cost").	Unit costs for each fuel How is energy metered, zones Alternative electrical tariffs Plant costs, operation, labor Quality of past maintenance, implication for future costs Ease and frequency of systems maintenance Timing of refurbishments needed, costs Terms of lease

8.3 Developing Your Own Checklist

Checklists can be used in most situations in which buildings and facilities are being evaluated. They are useful primarily because of the sheer number of things that have to be right for a building to work well. However, because people and organizations have different functional requirements, the CBPR checklist will not be relevant to every organization's accommodation requirements. We now describe an approach to developing your own checklist.

The need for your own checklist

Four uses of a checklist were listed earlier:

1. For design or design audit work
2. For briefing and programming
3. For planning and evaluation
4. As a framework for a database

In this section, we are concerned mainly with the situation in which compiling your own checklist is most useful in evaluating a building or buildings for a specific accommodation requirement. To begin, it is worthwhile to briefly review the key functions of checklists:

Memory jogger	It would be virtually impossible to remember the literally hundreds of items that may need to be checked in a complex commercial building. Checklists provide a thinking aid, a design aid, and a tool to assist the evaluator and ensure a comprehensive approach to the evaluation task.
Efficiency	An effective checklist saves going back for more information or to check things that were missed out first time.
Recording	Checklists provide a place or a category against which to record observations, notes, and measurements.
Team work	Checklists help communication. They group items together in a common framework using consistent terminology, thereby reducing misunderstandings about meaning when given parts of the building are being discussed.
Prompter	A checklist is not the last word in this type of building evaluation but can act as a prompt for identifying and dealing with other things that may be important to the organization's activities.

The effectiveness of a checklist may be measured by how well it fulfills these five functions.

Assessment of needs

The key requirement for developing an effective checklist is an accurate and comprehensive knowledge of your needs. We list here some activities useful in making an assessment of your needs:

- The checklist itself may be used, for example, to draw attention to an issue that has not yet been identified. However, in assessing your needs, it is almost always worthwhile to adopt an exploratory approach for at least some part of the assessment process.
- Open-ended discussions with staff at various levels may identify key building issues that are seen as particularly good or particularly bad. The first category provides useful things to look for in new accommodation; the second highlights things that one should make a particular effort to avoid. These issues may not have been on any previous checklist, or if they were, the extent of their priority may not have been realized.
- More formal evaluation activities such as general performance assessment may be used to identify important issues. These activities also may assist reaching a consensus when there are conflicting requirements.

Characteristics of a good checklist

When a good knowledge of requirements has been obtained, the checklist can be compiled. We have identified four important general characteristics or design rules for checklists:

Compre-
hensive

It must be comprehensive because it will be used to ensure that all important factors are included in the evaluation. This may ultimately make the difference between an inadequate building and one that significantly enhances the functioning of the organization that is to occupy it. It is therefore vital that the checklist be examined with the client group to ensure that everything is covered.

Convenient

It needs to be conveniently organized so as to minimize the amount of page turning and searching that people have to do when using it.

Legible

It needs to be well laid out and legible. Remember that it will often be used by people walking around a building in difficult conditions.

Balanced

If the checklist is to be used as part of the procedure for a scored comparison of buildings, it needs to be balanced so that particular aspects of performance are given neither too much nor too little emphasis.

Putting it together

For users developing their own checklists, considerable time and effort can be saved by using the CBPR checklist as a base. It provides a framework in which to group the myriad of factors that may need to be checked, a terminology to cover most aspects of building performance, and a trial list of items that need to be checked.

We repeat our belief that checklists should always be referred back to the groups of users involved in assessing the set of needs incorporated in the checklist. It is difficult for one person to "think of everything," and the final checklist will almost always be improved by group input.

CHAPTER 9

CPBR List of Techniques

The purpose of the CBPR list of techniques is to alert the reader to the wide range of methods that are now available for the evaluation of buildings. It fulfills a similar function to the CBPR checklist. Whereas the checklist identifies the wide range of topics and features that may be important in a building or facility evaluation, the list of techniques indicates the many methods available to assist the evaluation process.

Approximately 120 concepts, techniques, and tools that may be called on in the process of evaluating buildings and facilities are listed and briefly described. The list of techniques will be especially useful for those who have identified a building issue or problem and want to know what techniques are available.

The list of techniques is a comprehensive listing of evaluation concepts, techniques, and tools. As such, it provides a first-level source of information about what can be done in building evaluation. A broad mixture of items is listed, including disciplines in the field of evaluation, specific procedures and processes, and equipment that can be used. It may therefore be used to obtain more detailed information on techniques referred to here and in other parts of the book or used directly in its own right.

The list is arranged in alphabetical order of keyword, as follows:

Column 1   *Keyword*—so that techniques of possible interest may be located readily.

Column 2   *Summary*—a brief outline of the technique so that the reader may judge quickly whether or not it is applicable.

Column 3   *Description*—providing further information and cross-referencing to other items within the list itself and to the Bibliography.

Applicable standards for measurement and required levels will vary from country to country, as well as for different building uses. The reader should refer to relevant standards or professional organizations for further local information.

Keyword	Summary	Description
Acoustics	Evaluation of the acoustic environment of a building, inside and outside	High noise levels can be unpleasant, interfere with verbal communication, and affect occupants' concentration. Various techniques can be used to evaluate the acoustic quality of a space. The level of background noise due to exterior (e.g., traffic, construction) and interior sound sources (e.g., HVAC equipment) determine acoustic privacy and speech interference. Acoustic factors can be evaluated just by going into a building and listening, as well as by instrumental measurement. *See also Background noise and Reverberation time.*
Activity logging	Observation and recording of the use of spaces over a period of time	Recordings are used to compare the actual use of spaces with the intended use, and identify changes that may be useful. Observations are made at regular predetermined times over a specified number of days. Results show relationships between people, places, activities, and time durations and can indicate the quality of fit between requirements and designed space.
Air circulation	Movement of air within a space	Air circulation patterns may be evaluated using smoke tubes to trace the pattern from air inlet to air outlet in a given space. A hand-held anemometer may be used to measure high air speeds (say > 1 m/s) and for checking the airflow at grills; the amount of fresh air also may be checked in this way, but a knowledge of the air-handling plant and air distribution system is essential. *See also Smoke methods.*
Air movement	The speed of the air	Air movement evaluation may be carried out using a Kata thermometer. In use, the Kata is heated and the time for the temperature to fall from 38 to 35°C is measured; in conjunction with a calibration factor and knowledge of the air-temperature, the speed of air movement may be estimated in the range 0 to 1 m/s. Smoke tubes may be used to check the direction of air movement or even its speed if the smoke movement can be timed.

Keyword	Summary	Description
Air pollutants	Measurement of chemical, physical, and biologic contaminants in the air	Air pollutants may be measured by a variety of chemical and physical sampling techniques. In the context of building evaluation by the user, sampling tubes—analogous in concept to the breathalyzer—can be used to measure the concentration of most of the common gaseous pollutants, such as carbon dioxide, carbon monoxide, formaldehyde, and a range of volatile organic compounds. For particulate matter, the presence of dust may be observable; relatively long-term sampling through screens and filters is required for quantitative assessment. For biologic contaminants, sampling followed by incubation on agar is the conventional (and relatively specialist) procedure.
Air quality	Covers matters such as air circulation, air transfer, and pollutants	*See Air circulation, Air transfer, Air pollutants, Air movement, and Smoke tubes.*
Air temperature	The temperature of the air	Air temperature may be measured using a simple mercury-in-glass or electronic thermometer—this is known as the dry-bulb temperature. *See also Temperature.*
Air transfer	Movement of air between spaces	Air transfer between spaces may be checked using the instruments noted in *Air circulation* and *Air movement* above. More sophisticated techniques using tracer gases such as nitrous oxide and sulfur hexafluoride are available. Given that many air-transfer problems manifest themselves in the form of odors, it is possible to utilize distinctive odors for qualitative studies of air transfer.
Archival research		*See Document search*
Artificial sky		*See Effulger*
Assessment of needs		*See Requirements analysis*

Keyword	Summary	Description
Background noise	Determination of background noise levels on a space	Background noise should be measured using a portable sound level meter fitted with octave filtering. This enables the levels to be compared with noise rating curves appropriate to the occupants' requirements. A single reading of the total sound (in dBA, say) might obscure potentially important information on its spectral characteristics and, while useful, should be taken as indicative only. With an appropriate sound source in an adjacent space, the same technique may be used to assess the speech privacy of a given space. It may sometimes also be necessary to evaluate how well sound is transmitted in the space. In such cases, sound propagation tests may be undertaken and the results used to determine available indices where appropriate.
Behavior mapping	Manual: recording what people are doing and when and where they are doing it	A short-hand method of describing from observations how a space is used at different times, and the numbers of people using it. Results of observations at predetermined time intervals and at different locations are usually recorded on plans of the space.
Behavior mapping	Instrumental: the use of instruments to record occupant activities in a building	Mechanical or electronic support devices may be used to acquire data about occupants' activities and behavior in a particular setting. They may be used in most forms of behavioral observation, particularly for behavioral mapping and tracking studies. Instruments include hodometers (to map movement of people and preference patterns) time-lapse film, still photography, and video techniques.
Behavior tracking	Recording the movement of individuals within a space	Movements and associated activities of individuals are recorded from observation to describe the general behavior patterns in the environment, e.g., by superimposing a number of tracks on maps.
Building appraisal	Generic term for performance evaluation of buildings and facilities	*See Building diagnostics and Participatory evaluation.*
Building diagnostics	Generic term for performance evaluation of buildings and facilities	U.S. National Research Council's Building Research Board defines building diagnostics as "a set of practices that are used to assess the current

Keyword	Summary	Description
		performance capability of a building and its likely performance in the future." Building diagnostics is a broad term and covers the many investigative and evaluative activities used for evaluating building and facility performance and identifying whether or not building related problems exist in a facility.
Building factors	Influences on the effective space provided by a building	A number of features concerned with the shape, size and placement of parts of buildings can severely limit their effectiveness, e.g., the shape of the floor plan, the dimensions of workspaces, the layout of the ceiling grid and its relation to light fittings, air supply and extract grills, window mullions, and so on. These can reduce the effective floor space by from 5 to 25 percent.
Checklists, general	General description	Checklists may be used to guide and record information about behavior or behavior settings, building or facility performance, or the building itself. They are used to check the existence of specific objects, conditions, or events and may provide a systematic recording format. Often used to record physical conditions and factors, e.g., maintenance or user activity. The primary function of a checklist is to assist completeness of evaluation. Some examples of typical checklists follow.
Checklists, building	For a general building survey	An item's checklist, divided for instance into client data, general description, roof, walls, floors and staircases, internal finishes, drainage, services, external works. Identified within each of these are groups and subgroups of items to be checked. A checklist may include spaces for entering specific information, e.g., area, condition, materials, etc.
Checklists, energy	Of features of a building likely to affect energy use	A checklist designed to assist in the walkthrough evaluation of the energy performance of a building is a tool commonly used in energy audits. Such checks are normally intended to identify likely causes of energy waste and opportunities for energy savings. *Ref: Baird and Brander, 1982.*

Keyword	Summary	Description
Checklists, failures	Of systems, components, and materials to identify potential failure areas	Comprehensive checklist for detailed check of buildings, systems, components, and materials, designed in particular to identify likely areas of failure in the future. The checklist is usually divided into systems (e.g., roofs, walls, floors and staircases, internal finishes, painting defects, drainage, services) and numerous items within each system. Each item comprises the element (e.g., eaves, pipework), symptoms of problems, and defects that might cause those symptoms.
Climatic monitoring	Instrumented monitoring of microclimate	Instrumentation can be used to record temperature, humidity, direct sunshine, and diffuse solar radiation, wind, rain, etc. at the site of an existing or proposed building. The information can be useful in evaluating the energy and environmental performance of buildings. *See Meteorological records*.
CO_2 levels	Measurement of CO_2 levels	*See Air pollutants*
Cognitive mapping	Mental maps	Cognitive maps are the mental pictures we carry of our surroundings. They structure the way we look at, react to, and act in the environment. Expressing them graphically as sketches or diagrams can often assist those involved with facility evaluation to better understand people's responses to and use of buildings. *Ref: Zeisel, 1984.*
Computer-aided facilities management	Integrated computer software for facilities management	Programs within CAFM software packages address such issues as inventory management, requirements programming, location and layout planning, purchasing coordination, maintenance planning, administration, energy use, and cost accounting, among others. Usually the packages work as an integrated system so that information in one module is accessible to other modules. *Ref: Hamer, 1988.*
Construction feasibility	Estimation of short-term economic yield of a proposed building	Construction feasibility techniques use the construction cost, inflation over construction period, finance costs, and income in the year after occupancy begins to establish short-term costs and benefits for a proposed building. The techniques

Keyword	Summary	Description
		are applicable to the economic evaluation of projects and refurbishments.
Cost-benefit analysis	General term for analysis of the benefits versus the costs of activities	Cost-benefit analysis takes all the known costs of an activity (e.g., implementing the recommendations of a building evaluation) and compares them to the benefits of that activity. The analysis may be carried out for all or any part of a building or facility. Some cost-benefit analysis usually needs to accompany most forms of building and facility evaluation. *See also Construction feasibility, Life-cost analysis, Quantity surveying.*
Daylight factor		*See Lighting, daylight*
Delphi technique	A method for eliciting expert opinion	A forecasting methodology for generating expert opinion on any given subject based on a series of related questionnaires. The technique uses written answers rather than placing experts together in face to face meetings. Writing anonymously prevents domination by certain individuals in the group setting. *Ref: Allen, 1978*
Diagnostics		*See Building diagnostics*
Document search	Gathering information from the plans and contract documentation for a facility to be evaluated	A systematic search through records to retrieve existing information relevant to a facility to be evaluated. A document search is likely to include a search of planning and policy documents, conceptual design and working drawings, estimated and actual capital and operating costs, maintenance records, organizational and staffing statistics, engineering reports, and production records. The search allows history, context, and policy to be identified for comparison with performance or to establish trends within or across building types. *See Literature search.*
Drager tubes		*See Smoke methods*
Duct inspection	Checking ducts for dirt, biologic growths, and leakage	Contamination of the air inside a building may result from dirt, dust, mold, fungal growths, bac-

Keyword	Summary	Description
		terial contamination, etc. inside ducts. A visual inspection may identify some of the causes of air quality and building sickness problems. More complex methods include incubation of samples taken from duct surfaces and the use of smoke or tracer gases.
Earthquake engineering	Analysis of structural frame to estimate earthquake resistance	Analysis of structural integrity to estimate earthquake resistance of building. *See Engineering analysis.*
Effective floor space		*See Building factors*
Effulger	Simulation of daylighting conditions using models	A device (frequently an illuminated, room-sized space with highly reflective walls) designed to simulate the distribution of light outdoors. Model tests are used to predict the likely levels of natural illuminance in a building. Also termed *artificial sky.*
Energy audit	An evaluation of the overall energy performance of a building, with a view to identifying areas of energy waste and likely cost savings	An energy audit involves a comprehensive overview and analysis of energy use and energy flows within a building. It is likely to call upon a variety of individual techniques for the analysis of energy performance. *See Energy invoices, Walkthrough, energy audit.*
Energy invoices	Analysis of past years' energy supplier invoices	Various forms of analysis of energy use and energy cost information, from electricity, gas, coal, and other fuel invoices, can be used to evaluate the energy performance of existing buildings. For a single building, the analysis provides information on characteristics of energy performance such as seasonal patterns, end uses, and base loads. The information from invoices also can be summarized to monitor and compare the energy performance of each building in an organization's building stock. *See also Load profiles, Performance line analysis, Energy management programs, Energy management software. Ref: Baird and Pool, 1985*
Energy management programs	The organized evaluation and optimization of energy performance	Setting up and operating an energy management program involves various forms of energy performance evaluation as part of allocating resources

Keyword	Summary	Description
		within the program and monitoring the overall program effectiveness. The results of evaluations are likely to be put to better use as part of an energy management program, or better, as part of an overall building management program. *Ref: Baird et al., 1984*
Energy management software	Computer programs for analysis and management of energy costs and use in buildings	Many microcomputer programs exist for the collection, storage, and analysis of energy use and costs for a building or groups of buildings and for modeling energy use for specific conditions in a given building. They can be used to monitor energy use, manage investment in energy management, and alert management to energy problems.
Energy monitoring	Use of monitoring equipment for in situ measurement of energy use in a building	Instruments can be used to obtain regular and detailed measurements of energy use for particular functions in the building. They are often more convenient than methods which require people to be in regular attendance. They also can be used to identify the energy used in particular parts of a building or for specific end uses, e.g., heating, cooling, lighting, equipment, hot water services. Instrumentation can obtain data at much more frequent intervals than by manual recording or from suppliers' invoices. Two important issues requiring consideration are setting the appropriate frequency of measurement and avoiding obtaining too much data to analyze. *See also Load profiles. Ref: Baird and Pool, 1985*
Energy simulation software	Modeling of energy use, cost, and thermal environmental conditions for a building	Can be used to test energy and environmental performance of a building still in design stages. Information from modelling existing buildings may be compared with actual energy use data to see if the energy use is within expected levels. A range of programs is available.
Energy targets	Use of calculated energy use and cost targets to evaluate energy performance	Evaluation of energy performance by calculating an energy demand (according to the building and system design) and comparing to an energy target for buildings of that type/function. *Ref: CIBS, 1977*

Keyword	Summary	Description
Engineering analysis	Analysis of structural stability and safety	Engineering analysis requires professional skills, and specialists should be called in if there is any doubt as to a building's structural soundness.
Environmental impact	The impact of the building on the surrounding environment	This can range from the effect the building has on the surrounding microclimate, e.g., wind effects, shading, blocking of views, pollution from vents, flues and bioeffluents, etc. to consideration of its use of material and energy resources.
Environmental measurement	Quantitative information on spatial and sensory aspects of the building and its internal environment	Various dimensions of the environment are measured and recorded and later rated, generally by experts, as to their acceptability in the situation. These may be correlated with a user satisfaction measure. Measurements may include visual, aural, thermal, and dimensional parameters.
Environmental questionnaire	Users' responses to environmental conditions	A questionnaire may be used to obtain ratings and narrative descriptions of the internal environment. The information thus obtained can be used to assess overall environmental quality. *See also Interviews, Questionnaires, Participatory evaluation. Ref: Vischer, 1989*
Environmental temperature		*See Temperature*
Ergonomics	Matching the physical aspects of the work place to the those of the user	Ensuring that the static and dynamic characteristics of the physical working environment mesh with those of the user—in terms of workstation layout, design of seating, equipment, etc. For the case of VDUs, see *Cuttle, 1980*
Expert walkthrough		*See Walkthrough, expert*
Failure diagnosis	Classification of building failures	Enables the classification of building failures in terms of three basic causes, *viz.*, dampness, movements, and chemical/biologic changes. These may be further categorized in terms of the source of the cause and the type of human error involved (if any) in the resulting defect. There are many potential sources of building failures relevant to each of the basic causes. *Ref: Porteous, 1989*

Keyword	Summary	Description
Flue gas analysis	Measurement of CO_2 and O_2 levels in flue gas	The measurement of carbon dioxide and oxygen levels shows the efficiency with which boiler plant is operating.
Focus groups	A skilled moderator facilitates a discussion among selected individuals assessing, programming, planning, evaluating issues related to planned, renovating, or existing facilities	Focus groups consist of 8 to 12 individuals who freely discuss an issue among themselves. A skilled moderator keeps the discussion focused on the issues, makes sure all participants speak and none dominate, and keeps track of time. Used to assess user reactions to existing facilities, to elicit evaluation comments about slides of comparable facilities, to help raise issues of interest to different user groups. Also useful to determine concept structure and specific language used by different groups to describe their experience of place. Focus groups are not designed to reach consensus, make group recommendations, or make decisions.
Focused evaluation	Generic term for evaluation of specified issues	A focused evaluation will be carried out usually to investigate causes and find remedies for problems that have already been identified in a built facility. The problems may have been highlighted by some aspect of unsatisfactory performance previously noted in the facility, by users' complaints or by an earlier exploratory evaluation.
Focused study		*See Focused evaluation*
General performance assessment		*See Participatory evaluation*
Geologic analysis	Analysis of geology of a building site	Geologic analyses require professional expertise.
Glare		*See Lighting, visual quality*
Heliodon	Used for prediction of sun effects on buildings	This device, when used in conjunction with a model of a building or space, enables complete and rapid visualization of sun penetration and shading at any time of the day or year for a wide range of latitudes. The results may be sketched, photographed or videorecorded as required.

Keyword	Summary	Description
Hodometer	Instrument for the measurement of travel distances	Used in conjunction with *Behavior mapping studies*.
Illuminance levels		*See Lighting*
Infrared thermography	Direct measurement of radiant temperature to detect "hot spots"	Infrared thermography uses infrared-sensitive devices to identify faults in the thermal insulation of building fabric, pipes, ducts, etc. and leaks in piping. It can be applied to a range of situations, from detecting heat losses and energy waste in single buildings and components (using hand held devices) to aerial photographic surveys of whole communities using infrared-sensitive film.
Inspection	Observations by experts of (usually) previously identified issues	Although observations by users are a vital part of building evaluation observation needs to be carried out on occasion by people with specialist knowledge of the factors and items being evaluated. *See Duct inspection,* for example.
Instrumental measurement	The general use of instruments for measuring building and facility performance	Instruments can be used to obtain more detailed data on building performance than is generally convenient by observation and to measure phenomena that are not amenable to direct observation. Instrumental measurement can be used to obtain information about a wide range of building and facility performance parameters such as air quality, energy use, behavior tracking and mapping, and many other items listed in the evaluation file.
Interview, general	Obtaining verbal descriptions of users' responses to a facility	Interviews are normally used to obtain information about user attitudes toward their environment. The technique consists of asking people questions and recording their answers as faithfully as possible, such that they can be conveniently analyzed later. Interviews vary in location, type, questions asked, depth, methods of recording, and analysis. Unstructured interviews are useful for exploratory studies, structured interviews for causal hypotheses.

Keyword	Summary	Description
Interview, focused	For information on specified issues	As with focused investigations in general, focused interviews are designed to elicit information about specific issues. In contrast to open-ended interviews, which may elicit general perceptions of satisfaction or dissatisfaction with a facility, focused interviews address issues whose importance has already been determined.
Interview, structured	Interview with predefined questions	The structured interview is used to obtain information about particular attitudes and activities. Usually these will be issues already found or believed to be important to the users of a facility. It involves using prescribed sets of questions about specific areas to be investigated to develop hypotheses, structure experiments, or validate the implied meanings discovered by other techniques. The type and order of questions are decided in advance for the interviewer.
Interview, unstructured	Interviews where users direct the content	In an unstructured interview the users are asked to provide comment on what they see as important issues in or about a building or facility. The technique is used to obtain information possibly beyond the limitations of observations, questionnaires, and interviews with a predefined structure. It can gather information on reasons for major actions, normal and abnormal patterns of activity, information on areas of uncertainty, perceived successes and failures of systems, adaptations made, etc. It is also used to identify and test questions worth including in a questionnaire.
Interview, touring	A range of techniques, involving a walkthrough of the building by users and/or evaluation consultants.	Touring interviews usually involve a systematic walkthrough of a facility with interest groups (users and others with an interest in the building) and a task group (the consultants assisting and facilitating the evaluation). Different organizations have developed various methods for carrying out the walkthrough. Differences may be in the participants included in the walkthrough group and the degree to which the consultants and interest groups contribute to the form of the walkthrough. As with other unstructured techniques, the tour-

Keyword	Summary	Description
		ing interview is used in an exploratory fashion, with open-ended questions, to gather information from interest groups on their perceptions of and levels of satisfaction with a building. *See also Task group.*
Investment analysis	Analysis before investment to ensure its viability	Can be carried out prior to design and construction, or prepurchase, or before a major refit, to estimate the financial viability or feasibility of a project or purchase. The technique involves analysis of market conditions and financial trends as well as building performance.
Large-scale mock-ups		*See Modeling*
Life-cost analysis	Analysis of income and costs over the life of a building or term of investment in a facility	Life-cost analysis is a method of economic performance evaluation designed to take account of the long-term costs and benefits of a given building or activity. Inflation, the escalation of costs and income, and the disposal value of the building are also incorporated, with future costs and income being discounted to their present value. *Ref: Tippett and Sterios, 1987a,b; Haviland, 1978; see Sec. 7.1*
Lighting, artificial	Lighting levels and visibility provided by electric lighting system	Includes measurement of the average illuminance levels and their uniformity (ratio) on the horizontal working plane, together with the relative task visibility at locations of interest. *Ref: SANZ, 1984*
		Average illuminance levels and uniformity ratio on the horizontal working plane may be assessed using a photometer (or a luxmeter). As well as ensuring that the average illuminance meets the requirements of the occupants, a check should be made that the uniformity ratio (of minimum illuminance to average) is not less than 80 percent of the average.
		While the above measurements will indicate the illuminance on a working plane, they do not indicate how visible the task is likely to be. The rela-

Keyword	Summary	Description
		tive task visibility may be quantified using an illuminance contrast meter which assesses how task visibility is affected by veiling reflections. It can be used to check out clerical workstations, VDU screens, etc.
Lighting, daylight	Level of natural light available in a space	Usually quantified as the ratio of the interior to exterior illuminance levels and expressed as a percentage to give the daylight factor, its measurement is a relatively specialist task whether in the field, in the laboratory using models in an artificial sky, or using specialized computer software to simulate daylighting in a space. Daylight evaluation techniques can be applied in the design stage (using information from plans) or in existing buildings. *See also Lighting, artificial. Ref: Hopkinson et al., 1966; Cuttle, 1980.*
Lighting, visual quality	General quality of the visual environment	The visual quality of work spaces in a building is dependent on such factors as glare, colors, surface reflectances, positions of workstations, as well as levels of natural and artificial lighting. Some can be evaluated by simple visual observation (e.g., by building users); others may need a trained eye or require the use of technical equipment or methods and a knowledge of lighting technology. *Ref: Hopkinson et al., 1966.*
Literature search	Collection of research and practice information to aid an evaluation	The planned gathering of published information on building and facility performance and methods of evaluation. The information may be used to assist planning an evaluation and to provide comparative data. A number of methods may be used to increase the efficiency of a literature search, both in retrieval and documentation. Efficient searching requires identifying the purposes for which published information is being sought and the likely reliable publications, journals and libraries. Published bibliographies relating to specialist areas can be a time saving starting point. It is important to reevaluate regularly the choice of literature sources and to keep accurate records of useful documents.

Keyword	Summary	Description
Load profiles	Annual, monthly, daily, hourly, or higher frequency profiles of loads (e.g., energy use)	A graphic representation of the quantity of fuels, electricity, water, specialist gases, and other substances used in buildings, over regular time intervals, can provide information on end use, base and peak loads, out-of-hours consumption, and opportunities for cost savings. For example, energy use can be charted for each hour of the day or for each season to see if it follows a predictable pattern. *Ref: Baird and Pool, 1985.*
Maintenance management	Planning and monitoring maintenance activity	Buildings require regular observation and maintenance to minimize the overall maintenance costs. The use of organized procedures such as planned preventative maintenance will assist this. Setting up and operating a maintenance management program involves monitoring the cost-effectiveness of maintenance as part of allocating resources within the program and monitoring the overall program effectiveness.
Mean radiant temperature		*See Temperature, mean radiant*
Meteorologic records	Use of meteorologic station climatic records	Meteorologic records obtained from the station nearest to a building can provide quantitative data on the climatic influences to which a building is or will be subjected. Depending on the station, available data may range from daily maximum and minimum temperatures and rainfall, through to hourly records of temperature, humidity, sunshine, diffuse radiation, rainfall, and wind speed and direction. This information may be used to predict and/or evaluate energy performance, HVAC system performance, and the environmental conditions in a building.
Modeling, physical	Construction of small-scale models of the building	Small-scale models may be used in the simulation of various aspects of part or all of a building to obtain performance information that is difficult or time consuming to gather from plans or from existing buildings. For example, a model may be used with a heliodon to examine the penetration

Keyword	Summary	Description
		of sunlight into a building and likely glare or over-heating problems or with scaled-down models of equipment to test whether a building provides the required space functionality. *See also Sunshine and shade, Simulation.*
Modularity analysis	Identification of internal design modules.	The shape of a building and positions of entrances, window mullions, poles, lights, power points, air inlet and exhaust grills control where partitions can and cannot be placed and hence define the size and locations of workstations and offices. A building may thus provide regular modules appropriate to an organization's space needs, a variety of sizes, or no regular modules at all. Analysis involves the identification of all the elements that limit layout and thus define modules and measurement of the size and positions of modules. *See also Effective floor space*
Narrative	Written narrative of user behavior	The technique involves recording ongoing activities, events, and other behavior of the building users in narrative or written format and in the manner and sequence in which it occurs. This technique is perhaps the simplest method of observation. It can only be used in limited situations involving a small number of people and can be useful for exploratory studies.
Needs assessment		*See Requirements analysis*
Noise levels		*See Background noise*
Observation	Visual observation of what people are doing in a facility	Observation is used to study and record what people do in the designed environment/facility. Observation may be of activities or the traces of activities. Recorded data may indicate the influence of a space or simply record the existing environment or areas. Observation may be obtrusive or unobtrusive, using simple means or tools such as videotapes, hodometer, etc. *See also Behavior mapping, Behavior tracking, Physical trace, Checklists*

Keyword	Summary	Description
Olf method	Used to quantify human perception of air pollution	This method makes use of units termed the *olf* and the *decipol* to quantify air pollution as perceived by humans. Sources of pollution are quantified in terms of the olf, which is the air pollution due to a standard person; the perceived air pollution is quantified in terms of the decipol, which is the pollution caused by a standard person ventilated at a rate of 10 liters/s. The measurement of olf values and perceived air pollution in decipols requires a panel of judges. *Ref: Fanger, 1988; see also Air pollutants*
Participant group	Evaluation group representing a particular group of users	A participant group comprises a representative sample of members of a particular group of users or others with an interest in a facility. A participant group may, for example, represent the views and interests of office staff, management, clients, cleaners, or visitors, among others. One participant group may be used to represent each of the groups identified as having an interest in, and/or useful information to contribute to, the evaluation. *See also Participatory evaluation, review*
Participatory evaluation, general	Generic term for evaluation methods that involve users and other interest groups	Participatory evaluation covers the broad range of programs, procedures, and techniques that involve user groups and others with an interest in a building. Participatory evaluation usually involves group activities that make use of each group's insight, experience, and knowledge of its own requirements.
Participatory evaluation, review	With negotiated review	This technique of participatory evaluation comprises a series of stages to obtain a comprehensive evaluation of a facility. Key stages are 1. The touring interview by task group (facilitators) and participant group (evaluators) 2. The review meeting, in which the information gathered during each touring interview is discussed and a negotiated set of recommendations for the facility is elicited by consensus.
Performance line analysis	Analysis of the relationship between energy use and other factors	Performance line analysis is based on the correlation of energy use with factors thought to influence it (e.g., degree days, operating hours, prod-

Keyword	Summary	Description
		uct output). The aim is to identify which factors influence energy use and quantify the relationship. The technique also can indicate plant inefficiencies and problems with controls. *Ref: Baird et al., 1984*
Physical trace	Use of traces left on building by the users	This technique is used to obtain information about how people interact with their environment. It involves observing and recording physical traces left as a result of behavioral and environmental actions on the building, for instance, actual circulation patterns and frequencies. Physical traces are suitable for use in both exploratory and focused evaluations. *See also Behavior mapping, Behavior tracking*
Planned preventive maintenance	Forward scheduling of maintenance activities	Planned preventative maintenance is a management technique in which evaluation of technical and historical data is used to predict likely rates of failure. Maintenance is scheduled accordingly to minimize the expenditure required to keep a building functioning well. For example, it is cheaper to replace all fluorescent tubes at the appropriate interval than to replace individual tubes when they fail. *See also Maintenance management Ref: Lee, 1976; RAIA 1983*
Plus 3, minus 3 questionnaire		*See Questionnaire, +3, −3*
POE		*See Post-occupancy evaluation*
Pollutants	Levels of pollutants in the external and internal air	Measurements of the levels of chemical, particulate, and biologic pollutants in the air. Can be used to establish if air pollution is causing health or comfort problems within a building. *See also Air pollutants*
Post-occupancy evaluation, POE	A generic term for evaluation of existing buildings and facilities	A variety of general programs and procedures and specific techniques of existing building and facility evaluation have become known as post-occupancy evaluation. Most of the techniques listed in this book may be used as part of a POE. Recently,

Keyword	Summary	Description
		POE has been defined more narrowly by some specialists as a check of whether or not a building fulfills the requirements specified in its brief. *See also Building diagnostics, Participatory evaluation*
Preoccupancy evaluation	Evaluation of a building for future occupancy	A preoccupancy evaluation can include a standard POE on the existing organization, checking prospective accommodations, scoring procedures to compare accommodations. The whole evaluation procedure is designed to check and evaluate the fit between an organization's requirements and the potential accommodations. *See Scoring*
Predicted service life	An estimate of the service life of a building, predicted from records or tests	Predicting the service life of a building can be done at the design stage. It will assess the life expected to be achieved without major problems, if the building is maintained according to the proposed maintenance management plan.
Quality assurance	Managing a service or project to provide a high probability that its objectives will be fulfilled	Quality assurance is based on planned and systematic management activity to provide adequate confidence that a product or service will satisfy given requirements for quality. It demands planning, organizing, direction, and control of work to ensure that quality requirements are met.
Quantity surveying	Measurement of quantities and estimation of construction cost	Quantity surveying involves the application of standard methods of measuring quantities and estimating cost and the use of cost planning and control techniques. This discipline is well established in the building industry, and the techniques are not discussed further here.
Questionnaire, general	General technique for requesting responses to a facility, in written form	Questionnaires consist of presenting people with written questions to answer in written form. They may be used to obtain information on users' attitudes to a facility, activities in the facility, and about the users themselves. They can be used to gather information on users' perceptions of their environment and problems or positive features of buildings. Use may range from open-ended (exploratory) to the very specific (focused).

Keyword	Summary	Description
Questionnaire, +3, −3	Request three best and three worst aspects of facility, as seen by users	A questionnaire that requests from the respondents what they see as the three best and three worst features of the facility in which they work or visit. Some biographic information is also requested to assist identification of the part of the facility that is being rated. The method is intended to counter the tendency of unstructured questionnaires and interviews to identify the faults rather than successes of a facility. While faults may have a more immediate priority in that they are causing someone problems, the successes of a building also can furnish useful information. *Ref: DHC, 1986a,b*
Radiant temperature	The temperature of the surfaces in a space	An important component of thermal comfort. Radiant temperature can be quantified using globe thermometers, infrared level heat detectors, etc. *Ref: Vischer, 1989; see also Temperature, mean radiant*
Rating scale	Ordering or prioritizing of issues or items in an evaluation	Rating scales are comparatively precise techniques for assessing user satisfaction with specific aspects of the physical environment. They can be used to record in a measurable way people's feelings and judgments by having them respond to questions or statements about a facility in a series of semantic scales (e.g., The building is comfortable to work in: strongly agree, strongly disagree). Users can express opinions which collectively indicate the acceptability of an environment or various alternatives. Suitable for exploratory studies, they also may be used with observations to investigate causal hypotheses. *Ref: Vischer, 1989*
Relative humidity	Ratio of actual weight of moisture in air to amount it could hold at a given temperature (strictly speaking, this is the percentage saturation; it has the same value as relative humidity)	Relative humidity may be estimated by comparing the dry-bulb temperature with the wet-bulb temperature, the latter being measured on a mercury-in-glass thermometer, the bulb of which is surrounded by a moist fabric wick. Measurement of both dry- and wet-bulb temperatures may be made conveniently using a whirling hygrometer, which is sensitive and reasonably robust.

Keyword	Summary	Description
Requirements analysis	Generic term for finding out what users need	The investigation and analysis of user requirements, with the objective of finding out what is really needed of a building or facility and to establish priorities for use when requirements may conflict. A wide variety of techniques may be used to establish requirements relevant to different aspects of building performance. Frequently, evaluation of facility performance is a process of finding out more about requirements—a participatory evaluation may be more concerned with requirements that were previously unknown to those who could initiate changes in the building. Exploratory techniques may be used first, followed by more specialized (focused) techniques as required.
Residual values	Where costs and benefits are difficult to quantify	A method for the analysis of alternative investment options for use when there are a number of factors that are difficult to quantify (e.g., value of the image or social benefits of a given building strategy). *Ref: Scott, 1984*
Resultant temperature		*See Temperature*
Reverberation time	Quantifies a key acoustic parameter with major implications for speech and music	Reverberation is a measure of the length of time sound persists in a room and has a major effect on sound quality. It is specified as the length of time it takes for a sound to decay by 60 dB after it has been stopped, and this is capable of both subjective and objective measurement. A subjective impression may be gained simply by listening to the sound decay following a single hard clap or similar noise. Instrumentation is available which will measure the reverberation time over a range of frequencies, so that its balance may be assessed.
Review meeting	Arriving at recommendations by a consensus process	The review meeting plays a key part in the *negotiated review participatory evaluation*. It is used to explore and discuss the information and comments gathered in a touring interview and to frame recommendations for action. It is valuable because evaluation is usually a multigroup activity involving both several groups of users and several

Keyword	Summary	Description
		disciplines. The review meeting serves to provide a negotiating arena both within and between interest groups and a forum for reaching consensus on recommendations for action.
Risk analysis	Identification and analysis of the distribution and probability of risk	Risk analysis predicts the probability of an investment having a less favorable outcome than expected. The techniques are based on the analysis of uncertainty in the input data (e.g., uncertainty in future rents, property values, fuel prices, costs of materials, etc.) to predict the probability of various outcomes. *Ref: Marshall, 1988*
Satisfaction scale	Measurement of user satisfaction	Measures user satisfaction with various parts of a building. The satisfaction scale comprises ten questions in the form of bipolar adjectives, e.g., good, bad; adequate, inadequate; depressing, stimulating. The results may be pooled to generate a rating that allows comparison of user satisfaction with different parts of a facility or to compare responses in different facilities. The technique can provide a useful and economical method of identifying which facilities, or parts of facilities, require further attention. *See also Rating scale*
Scoring, general	General technique for assigning an overall performance rating to a facility	Scoring techniques are generally used for evaluating potential accommodation (existing or in planning stages) or selecting among a range of alternative buildings. A scoring technique will usually begin by identifying what aspects of a building are important to the organization and assigning numerical priorities (e.g., 1 to 10) that measure the perceived importance of each of these. In each of the proposed options these same factors will be evaluated as to how well they are provided (e.g., poor to excellent). Each aspect is then given a score that reflects both its priority and the degree to which a given building met that priority. Overall scores are obtained by combining all the individual scores, usually by simply adding them together, though more complex methods may be used. *Ref: Duffy et al., 1983; Baird et al., 1989*

Keyword	Summary	Description
Sick building syndrome	Investigative procedures for health problems associated with a building	Where a building condition is suspected as being the cause of one or more persons' illness. The investigator will go through a systematic series of checks with a view to identifying and correcting the problem. The checks should be carried out by an experienced investigator and include obtaining a history of the complaints, the building, and its systems; a chronology of events leading to the complaint (including medical histories); recent renovations and changes to system operation; and an inspection of the services. These steps may be followed by more detailed testing phases.
Simulation, general	General technique for facility evaluation by abstract or physical modeling	Simulation is a general term for methods of analysis and evaluation using abstract or theoretical models (e.g., mathematically or using computer software) or physical models (full-scale mock-ups, scale models, plans, flowcharts, etc.). The techniques are based on the assumption that the model accurately represents the building to be evaluated, and the behavior of, or results from, the model can be used to predict the behavior of the actual facility. Examples of simulation follow.
Simulation, building performance	Analyzing performance by calculating what the building will do	Simulation is used to predict the behavior of a building through analysis of physical parameters describing the building. A wide range of performance parameters may be simulated with computer and software technology, e.g., structural performance, energy use, and HVAC system and components operation. Simulation of building performance can be used in design stages to predict how a building will behave. With an existing building a simulation can indicate how the building was expected to perform—discrepancy between this and actual performance can suggest system breakdowns and other problem areas. *See also Energy simulation*
Simulation, user environment	Use of simulations of building to elicit user responses	Simulation of the user environment is used to discover attitudes held through a reconstruction or modelling of the spaces and/or environment. It allows respondents to project themselves into the

Keyword	Summary	Description
		environment. Reconstruction and questionnaire measurement techniques are used to tap attitudes to the simulations. Comments are evoked from representations of the settings rather than the settings themselves. Slides, movies, video, models, mock-ups, model rooms, computer graphics, photographs, verbal descriptions, and drawings may be used to prompt the respondent.
Smoke methods	Use of visible gases to make air movement within a space directly visible	Various methods of producing smoke may be used, depending on the scale of the test being carried out. To trace the direction of particular air movements, or even check their speed, tubes containing stannic chloride or glass rods dipped in titanium tetrachloride (both of which smoke when exposed to the air) may be used. In large spaces, smoke "bombs" may used in the space or air supply ducts.
Social mapping	Effects of the building on interactions between people	A social map is used to explore and identify relationships between people in designed environments, e.g., the influence of physical settings on social interactions. The methods consist of recording preferences and rejections expressed by individuals in terms of how they perceive themselves in relation to others. Social maps can reveal which members of a group interrelate and what these relationships mean in terms of spatial organization or communication networking.
Solar access	Effect of neighboring buildings and landforms on availability of sun	Techniques exist to estimate the degree to which neighboring structures will obstruct the sun on a building or site at various times of the day and year. These techniques range from simple geometric calculations of obstruction angles and sun position, through modeling the site on a heliodon, to sophisticated computer packages.
Solar orientation	How well does design of building relate to climate	Climatic influences vary with direction, an obvious example being that the equatorial side of a building gets more sun. Buildings designed without regard to compass directions often overheat on one side and can be unpleasantly cold on the

Keyword	Summary	Description
		other. Simple observation can establish whether a building attempts to take this into account, and a range of techniques exist for more sophisticated analysis of solar orientation. *See Sunshine and shade.*
Sound absorption		*See Reverberation time*
Sound transmission		*See Background noise*
Space provision	Evaluation of quality and quantity of space provided by a building	The evaluation of space provision requires both a careful analysis of the space requirements of an organization and of the building under consideration. *See Trial layouts, Modularity analysis*
Stated objective	Establishment of criteria for performance evaluation	A form of requirements analysis to establish criteria against which outcomes can be measured and evaluated. It is used to determine a current statement of objectives, as opposed to the original brief, to identify in overview the areas of consistent opinion as to organizational objectives and building function. *See also Requirements analysis*
Subjective measurement	Use of people to evaluate	The majority of the factors that influence building performance can be evaluated to some extent by people; indeed many factors (e.g., the nuisance value of otherwise harmless odors) can only be evaluated subjectively. In general, it is the subjective experience of conditions in or around a building that is the final arbiter of most aspects of its performance. Usually building and facility evaluation involves subjective and objective measurements used in a complementary fashion. *See Observation, Instrumental measurement*
Sunshine and shade	Assessment of sunshine and shade on building exteriors and interiors	Sunpath diagrams (plots of the sun's altitude and azimuth) enable an evaluation to be made of the time of the year and time of day that sunshine may fall on a given site, allowing for any surrounding obstructions. They also enable graphic prediction of the shadows cast by a building and the sunlight penetration to its interior. Models on a heliodon

Keyword	Summary	Description
		also may be used for this purpose. *See also Heliodon. Ref: Turner, 1969*
Surveys	Generic term for gathering information on users' responses	Surveys can be used to assess attitudes, preferences, and opinions about the physical environment. Methods may include questionnaires, structured and unstructured interviews, activity logs, rating scales, social and cognitive maps. Surveys involve direct interaction with participants and as such they are reactive or obtrusive.
Taguchi methods	Methods of profiling assessments and requirements of a product on a single integrated diagram	Questionnaires are used to assess user/manager requirements and technical assessments are made of the physical/space (design) requirements by ratings or measurements made by design professionals. The technique has been claimed to reduce development time and improve quality by significant amounts. *Ref: Meredith, 1992*
Tariff analysis	Analysis of electricity tariffs	Electrical tariffs may be analyzed to evaluate energy cost performance. The evaluation may lead to the user changing tariffs and significant cost savings. *See Yuill, 1985*
Task group	Neutral group of people to organize and facilitate an evaluation	The task group has the particular role of organizing and facilitating a participatory evaluation of a facility. Typically consisting of three people, it may comprise experts or laypersons, depending on the requirements of a given evaluation. The group usually does not include users, visitors, and others with a direct involvement in the facility or the results of the evaluation. As well as administering the evaluation, the task group takes notes during walkthroughs, records the results of interviews, gathers other data and facilitates, and coordinates meetings. *See also Participant group*
Task visibility		*See Lighting, artificial*
Temperature	Air, resultant, and environmental temperatures are important parameters in the evaluation of thermal comfort	For many purposes, air temperature is sufficient indication of thermal comfort, but if a strong radiant component is likely, say, from a window or a poorly insulated roof (hot in summer, cold in

Keyword	Summary	Description
		winter), then mean radiant temperature also should be measured. This can be used independently or combined with air temperature (50:50) to give the "resultant temperature" or (67:33) to give the "environmental temperature." *Ref: CIBSE, 1986*
Temperature, mean radiant	The average temperature of the surfaces of a space relative to a position within that space	Mean radiant temperature can be estimated simply by using a mercury-in-glass thermometer, the bulb of which is located in the center of a 150-mm black sphere. The reading is called the *globe thermometer temperature*; from a knowledge of this plus the dry-bulb temperature of the air and its speed of movement, the mean radiant temperature of the surrounding surfaces may be estimated. Having measured the thermal environment conditions, it then remains to evaluate these against the user's needs, which will depend on the activity to be accommodated and the clothing levels of the occupants.
Tenant questionnaire survey assessment method (TQSAM)	Determine workers' attitude toward the workspace	TQSAM was developed by Public Works Canada. It is an instrument for measuring worker comfort and satisfaction based on occupant surveys using a standardized questionnaire *Ref: Kroner et al., Sec. 6.1; Dillon and Vischer, 1987*
Thermal comfort	Conditions under which users experience satisfaction with the thermal environment of a space	Can involve measurement of temperature and relative humidity of the air in a space, the speed of air movement within the space, and the mean radiant temperature of the internal surfaces. Assessment of thermal comfort also depends on the level of activity of the users and the amount of clothing worn by them. *See Air temperature, Relative humidity, Air movement, and Mean radiant temperature. Ref: ASHRAE, 1993*
Thermography		*See Infrared thermography*
Thermohygrographs, temperature/ humidity	Continuous measurement of temperature and humidity	Typically taken over a 1-week period on a chart recorder and collated with outside conditions, continuous temperature, and humidity measure-

Keyword	Summary	Description
		ments within a space give a useful indication of internal environmental conditions. They also can show the speed at which a building responds to changes in external climate and HVAC operation and the quality of environmental control within the building. *Ref: Baird and Brander, 1982*
Thermohygrographs, systems	For monitoring HVAC systems operation	Chart recorders used to continuously monitor temperature and humidity over daily or weekly periods to provide information on the energy performance of buildings, e.g., spaces being heated or cooled outside normal hours of use, overheating, and significant occupant behavior.
Tracer gas	Use of tracer gases to measure rates of air movement within spaces and rates of transfer between spaces	Various gases, such as nitrous oxide (NO_2), and sulfur hexafluoride (SF_6) may be used in conjunction with the appropriate measuring equipment to evaluate the movement of air within a building. The tracer gas is released in a space and sampled both within the space and in adjacent spaces to measure air transfer rates, ventilation rates and air leakage. These techniques require the use of specialist gas chromatographs or infrared analyzers. *Ref: Charlesworth, 1988*
Trial layouts	Evaluation of the capacity of a building to provide for an organization's space needs	The area or volume of space in which a particular set of activities is to be carried out may be only a rough indicator of the useful space in a building. Such factors as the shape of the building, location of entrances and fixed constructions, module sizes, location of lights and windows, along with requirements such as required group, office and workstation sizes, determine the amount of useful space provided by a building. Trial layouts are necessary to determine if a building will perform as required for space provision. *See also Building factors, Space provision*
Uniformity ratio		*See Lighting, artificial*
Unstructured interviews		*See Interviews, unstructured*

Keyword	Summary	Description
Urban simulator	Use of models to see proposed buildings in urban context	Involves the use of miniature TV cameras and models of the urban built environment. The view from the TV camera eye is displayed on a video screen, simulating, for example, the view seen by a person walking down the full size street. Used to evaluate the visual impact of proposed buildings on the urban environment. *Ref: Reed et al., 1981*
User	Any person with an interest in a building or facility	For building and facility evaluation, the term *user* is given a wide definition to include all those who live/work in a building or are affected in some way by its performance. User groups may include office workers, management, investors, visitors, cleaners, clients, consultants, and neighbors, among many other groups. Identifying the user groups relevant to a particular evaluation of a given facility is a key part of that evaluation.
Value management	Generic term for analysis involving finding lower cost alternatives of equal value	Value management (also known as *value analysis* or *value engineering* includes a broad range of techniques for evaluating products to find those which fulfill user requirements at lesser cost. *See also Construction feasibility, Investment analysis, Life-cost analysis*
Walkthrough, general	A group of techniques based around a walkthrough of the building to be evaluated	The walkthrough is an important technique that can be used in a variety of ways in a building or facility evaluation. The technique can involve users or other interest groups, experts, or both. It makes use of the physical environment as a prompt to help respondents articulate their reactions to a building. Typical purposes include eliciting information from walkthrough participants and from other occupants, and carrying out physical checks of the building. Walkthroughs may form the basis for a questionnaire or other later more focused observations. Descriptions of specific techniques follow:
Walkthrough, energy audit	Energy audit	A walkthrough of a building with the specific purpose of evaluating its energy performance and identifying opportunities for energy management and conservation measures. *Ref: Min. of Energy, 1988.*

Keyword	Summary	Description
Walkthrough, expert	Expert walkthrough	Checking and evaluating a building using a group of specialists. May be open ended or designed to examine predefined aspects of a building or facility, e.g., physical condition, factors that affect energy use, serviceability for a given purpose. Checklists are often used in expert walkthroughs and may involve formal or informal interviews with users on site.
Walkthrough, touring	Touring interview	The touring interview is based on the use of the physical environment as a prompt to help respondents articulate their reactions to a building.
Wayfinding	The ease of navigation in a building	Wayfinding is concerned with the ease with which staff, clients, and other visitors can find their way to specific parts of the building and out again. Various methods may be used to learn, first, whether wayfinding problems exist and, second, how they may be remedied. *See also Behavior tracking, Behavior mapping*
Wind tunnel	Testing the effects of wind on a building using a scale model in a wind tunnel	Usually carried out by expert consultants. Some local authorities have predesign tests in their ordinances that can be done by nonexpert users with access to wind-tunnels. *Ref: Wade et al., 1987a,b*

CHAPTER 10

Definitions

In this chapter we have reproduced an abridged version of the *Standard Terminology of Facility Management (Building Related)* promulgated by the American Society for Testing and Materials (ASTM, 1992). This standard has been the result of a worldwide consensus process and represents the clearest and most consistent set of terms and definitions available. Consistency of terminology is vital in the building evaluation process so that everyone operates from a common basis of understanding in what can be both a trans- and inter-disciplinary process.

The definitions that follow have been extracted, with permission, from the *Annual Book of ASTM Standards,* copyright American Society for Testing and Materials, 1916 Race Street, Philadelphia, PA 19103. To quote from the scope of the standard:

This terminology consists of terms and definitions pertaining to the description, measurement, prediction, improvement, and management of buildings and building-related facilities and, in particular, terms related to the standards generated by ASTM Committee E-6 on Performance of Buildings. The purpose of this terminology is to provide meanings and explanations of technical terms, written for both the technical expert and the nonexpert user. Terms are listed in alphabetical sequence. Compound terms appear in the natural spoken order.

Base building A general-purpose office building intended, but not yet adapted, to suit the operational requirements of a specific tenant.

Building A shelter comprising a partially or totally enclosed space, erected by means of a planned process of forming and combining materials.

Building component A building element using industrial products that are manufactured as independent units capable of being joined with other elements.

Building construction (1) The act or process of making or forming a building by assembly or combining elements, components, or systems; (2) The structure or part thereof so formed.

Building envelope Perimeter elements of a building, both above and below ground, that divide the external from the internal environment.

Building performance The behavior in service of a construction as a whole or of the building components.

Durability The capability of a building, assembly, component, product, or construction to maintain serviceability for at least a specified period of time.

Serviceability The capability of a building, assembly, component, product, or construction to perform the function(s) for which it is designed or used, or both.

Building projection Pilaster, convector, baseboard heating unit, radiator, or other building element located in the interior of a building wall that prevents the use of that space for furniture, equipment, circulation, or other functions.

Building subsystem Complete, integrated set of parts that functions as a unit within the finished building.

Building system Collection of equipment, facilities, and software designated to perform a specific function.

Capital cost Costs of acquiring, substantially improving, expanding, changing the functional use of, or replacing a building or building system.

Classes of buildings Buildings categorized by selected attributes concerning facility serviceability and performance.

Drawing

Record set drawing (as-built drawing) Construction drawing revised to show changes made during the construction process, usually based on marked-up prints, drawings, and other data furnished by the contractor.

Working drawing Detail drawing, usually produced by a draftsperson under direction of an architect, engineer, or other designer, showing the form, quantity, and relationship of construction elements and materials and indicating their location, identification, grades, dimensions, and connections.

Dwelling Building designed or occupied as the living quarters for one or more families or households

Engineering economics Application of engineering, mathematical, and economic techniques to the economic evaluation of engineering alternatives.

Evaluate To assess the capability of a facility to perform the function(s) for which it is designed, used, or required to be used.

Fabric All the elements, components, parts, and materials of a building, at any scale and of any age.

Historic fabric Those portions of the building fabric that have historic significance.

Facility A physical setting used to serve a specific purpose.

Facility durability The capability of a facility to maintain serviceability for at least a specified period of time.

Facility evaluation Comparison of the qualitative and quantitative results of judgments, observations, measurements, analyses, or other tests against performance criteria established for a specified purpose and to a specified precision and reliability.

Facility-in-service Facility as completed and operational.

Facility operator Organization or agency having a contract with the owner or investor to operate a facility.

Facility performance Behavior in service of a facility for a specified use.

Facility program

Design program (design brief) Document specifying what facilities will be provided to the occupants and confirming to the owner the requirements for the facility.

Functional program Document that specifies functional facility serviceability requirements of occupants and owner.

Project brief Document describing the required facility serviceability in detail sufficient for the project to proceed.

Facility project brief (statement of work) Document describing services to be provided by the design consultant (architect, engineer, or interior designer) for a facility in detail sufficient for the design to proceed.

Facility serviceability Capability of a facility to perform the function(s) for which it is designed, used, or required to be used.

Facility serviceability profile Graphic display, usually as a bar chart, of the set of rating scores for aspects of the serviceability of a facility.

Facility use Functions and activities that take place in a facility.

Feasibility study Study of a planned scheme or development, the practicality of its achievement, and its projected financial outcome.

Feature Of a facility, a building element, building component, building subsystem, unit of furnishing or equipment, or aspects of design, arrangement, form or color, which helps or hinders the satisfaction of a requirement for serviceability.

Combination of features Features which, when present together in a facility, affect satisfying a requirement for serviceability.

Fit-up Alterations and improvements to the base building and to the building systems including demolition, where required, to prepare the accommodation for occupancy.

Floor In a building, supporting structure (general horizontal) constituting the bottom level of each story.

Floor area

Gross floor area Entire area within the inside perimeter of the exterior walls.

Net floor area The part of the gross floor area located within occupiable space.

Function The action for which a person or thing is specially fitted or used or for which a thing exists.

Functional Performing or able to perform a regular function; designed or developed chiefly from the point of view of use.

Functionality Being suitable for a particular use or function.

Guide for rating A document that explains how to rate the serviceability of an existing or planned facility for a specific purpose. A guide identifies typical requirements and provides a rating scale for comparison with the relevant combinations of features present in the facility.

Hours of operation

Active hours Times when a facility is normally fully occupied and operational.

Silent hours Period when a facility is essentially unoccupied and only security and building operations staff are present.

Transitional hours Times in the morning after the first workers normally arrive, until a facility if fully operational, and in the evening from the end of normal work until the occupants have left.

House Building intended in its entirety as a dwelling.

Lease Contract between the owner of real property (lessor) and another party (lessee) for the possession and use of the property for a specified term in return for rent or other income.

Lighting

Ambient light Surrounding light, such as that reaching an object in a room from all light sources in the room.

Glare Effect of brightness or brightness differences within the visual field sufficiently high to cause annoyance, discomfort, or loss of visual performance.

Task lighting Localized lighting system consisting of a functional arrangement of luminaries to accommodate the specific visual task or work area needs.

Maintainability Capability of a system or facility to be maintained to a specified level of reliability at a specified measure of cost or economy.

Occupancy Discouraged term, to be used only in connection with building codes, where the term refers to the number of occupants in a space or other specific classification of use.

Occupancy instrument (OI) Agreement between a prospective or current occupant and the manager or owner of a facility concerning occupancy in that facility.

Occupant (1) Department, agency, corporation, or other organization, or a part thereof, that is or will be occupying space in a particular facility; (2) individual or family living in a housing dwelling.

Building occupant One who has certain rights to possession of or control over the premises occupied, such as tenant or owner.

Physical protection Barriers that will delay or deter someone attempting unauthorized physical access to assets at a specific location.

Portfolio Group of securities, building, or other properties held by an individual or institutional investor.

Project Resources and activities used to achieve a specific set of objectives within a specified time schedule.

Rating process The process of determining the serviceability of a facility for a specified purpose.

Rating scale Set of descriptions of combinations of features in which each combination has been selected to indicate a specific level of serviceability on a scale from the lowest to the highest level likely to be encountered.

Rating score Result (expressed as a number) of finding the combination of features described in a specified rating scale (for one aspect of serviceability) that matches most closely the attributes present in a facility.

Regulation Rule prescribing a set of conditions and requirements that has been made mandatory for those under its control by an executive (administrative) authority.

Reliability The probability of performing without failure a specified function under normal conditions for a specified period of time.

Requirement statement The serviceability requirements for a facility, together with applicable performance criteria, performance test methods, and optional explanatory comments.

Space categories

Assignable area Floor area of a facility assigned to or available for assignment to occupant groups or functions, including interior walls, building columns, and building projections and excluding circulation.

Basement Space partly below average grade having less than one-half of its clear height (measured from floor level to ceiling level) below average grade.

Building core and service area Floor area of a facility necessary for the general operation of a building that is not available for general occupancy, including: primary circulation areas, mechanical, electrical, telephone, and custodial rooms serving individual floors; toilet rooms, building lobbies and atria, stairways, elevators, vertical shafts and chases, loading docks; and also central, mechanical, electrical, telephone, and custodial spaces and penthouses but excluding interstitial area.

Building gross area Sum of the floor areas of a building included within the outside face of outer building walls for all stories.

Cellar Space wholly or partly below average grade having more than one-half of its clear height (measured from floor level to ceiling level) below average grade.

Primary circulation area Portion of a building that is a public corridor, lobby, or atrium or is required for access by all occupants on a floor to stairs, elevators, toilet rooms, or building entrances.

Secondary circulation area Portion of a building required for access to some subdivision of space, whether bounded by walls or not, that does not serve all occupants on a floor and that is not defined as primary circulation area.

Support space In offices, part of usable area not assigned or dedicated to a specific task or function. Support space includes meeting rooms, waiting areas, storage, lounges, operational equipment (e.g., computer rooms), copy areas, libraries, and similar areas.

Usable area Floor area of a facility assigned to or available for assignment to occupant groups or functions, including interior walls, building columns and projections, and secondary circulation.

Workplace Part of a usable area, intended for an individual or group to work in.

Workspace Part of a usable area, intended for a specific function or type of work.

Workstation All or part of a workplace, suitable for carrying out one function or type of work.

Specification Precise statement of a set of requirements to be satisfied by a material, product, system or service.

Tenant Organization that has rights and obligations of occupancy in a facility, as specified in a lease or occupancy agreement.

Visitor Person present who is not an occupant of that facility.

CHAPTER 11

Bibliography

Advisory Group on Estate Management, Department of Health (1989), *Guidance on the Strategy for Estate Information and Computer Technology: Part of Estatecode Level 2,* London, HMSO.

Albrecht, J., and Lim, G. (1986), "A search for alternative planning theory: use of critical theory," *Journal of Architecture and Planning Research* 3(2):117–131.

Allen, T. H. (1978), *New Methods of Social Science,* New York, Praeger, pp. 119–131.

American Institute of Architects (AIA) (1977), *Life Cycle Cost Analysis: A Guide for Architects,* ed. by D. Haviland, Washington, D.C., The American Institute of Architects.

American Society of Heating, Refrigerating and Air Conditioning Engineers, Inc. (ASHRAE) (1993), *1993 ASHRAE Handbook of Fundamentals,* SI edition, Atlanta, Georgia, ASHRAE.

Argyris, C., and Schon, D. (1974), *Theory in Practice: Increasing Professional Effectiveness,* Washington, D.C., Jossey Bass.

ASTM E1480-92 *(1992) Standard Terminology of Facility Management (Building Related),* Philadelphia, American Society for Testing and Materials.

Avis, M., Gibson, V., and Watts, J. (1989), *Managing Operational Property Assets,* U.K., Department of Land Management and Development, University of Reading.

Avis, M., et al. (1993), *Property Management Performance Monitoring,* UK School of Estate Management, Oxford Brookes University and Department of Land Management and Development, University of Reading.

Baird, G., and Brander, W. D. S. (1982), *Building Energy Management Methods for Government Buildings,* CRP18, Wellington, Victoria University of Wellington, New Zealand.

Baird, G., Donn, M., Pool, F., Brander, B., and Chan, S. A. (1984), *Energy Performance of Buildings,* Boca Raton, Fla., CRC Press.

Baird, G., and Pool, F. (1985), *Energy Use and Performance Monitoring of Commercial Sector Buildings,* report 123, Auckland, New Zealand Energy Research and Development Committee.

Baird, G., Bruhns, H., Gray, J., and Percival, R. (1989), *Proceedings of a Seminar on Total Performance of Buildings,* Wellington, N.Z., Centre for

Building Performance Research, Victoria University of Wellington.

Baird, G., and Isaacs, N. (1994), "A checklist for the performance evaluation of buildings and building services," in *Engineering for Better Building Performance,* CIBSE Australia and N.Z. Third Regional Conference, Melbourne Australia, 16–18 Feb. 1994.

Baldwin, R., Leach, S. J., Doggart, J., and Attenborough, M. (1990), *BREEAM 1/90: An Environmental Assessment for New Office Designs,* Garston, U.K., Building Research Establishment.

Bassett, M. (1990), *ALF Design Manual: Aid to Thermal Design of Buildings* (technical paper p. 28), Judgeford, Building Research Association of New Zealand.

Becker, F. D. (1974), *Design for Living: The Resident's View of Multi-Family Housing,* Ithaca, N.Y., Center for Urban Development Research, Cornell University.

Becker, F. (1982), *The Successful Office: How to Create a Workspace that's Right for You,* Rending, Mass., Addison-Wesley.

Becker, F., Davis, G., Duffy, F., and Sims, W. (1984), *ORBIT-2: Organizations, Buildings, and Information Technology,* Norwalk, Conn., Harbinger.

Becker, F., Davis, G., and Duffy, F. (1985), *ORBIT-2 Summary Report,* Norwalk, Conn., Harbinger.

Becker, F., Davis, B., and Sims, W. (1991), *Managing Space Efficiently,* Ithaca, N.Y., Cornell University International Facility Management Program.

Becker, F., and Quinn, K. (1994), *Worksmart: Organizational Workplace Analysis,* Ithaca, N.Y., Cornell University International Facility Management Program.

Beddek, P. J. H., and Kernohan, D. (1990), "The measurement of quality in buildings" in *Proceedings of the New Zealand Institute of Building National Conference,* Auckland, N.Z., November 1990.

Bedford, T. (1948), *Basic Principles of Ventilation and Heating,* London, H. K. Lewis.

Blach, K., and Christensen, G. (1976), "The performance concept: Why and how?" in *Building Research and Practice,* May/June (International Council for Building Research Studies and Documentation).

Blachere, G. (1966), *Saviour batir: habitabilite-durabilite economie des batîments,* Paris, Editions Eyrolles.

Bordass, B., and Leaman, A. (1993), *Control Strategies for Building Services,* Advanced Systems of Passive and Active Climatisation, Barcelona, Institut Catala d'Energia (ICAEN) Thermie programme.

Bordass, B., Leaman, A., and Willis, S. (16–20 May, 1994), *Control Strategies for Building Services: The Role of the User,* Watford, U.K., Building Research Establishment.

Boudon, P., (1972), *Lived in Architecture* (English edition), London, Lund Humphries.

Bowden, B. (1984), *Proceedings of the Senior Architects' Conference,* Commonwealth of Australia, April 4–6, 1984, Canberra, Department of Housing and Construction.

Bowen, B., Charette, R. P., and Marshall, H. E. (1992), *Uniformat II: A Recommended Classification for Building Elements and Related Site Work,* Washington, D.C., National Institute of Standards and Technology.

Building Performance Research Unit (BPRU) (1972), *Building Performance,* London, Applied Science Publishers.

Brand, S. (1994), *How Buildings Learn,* New York, Viking Penguin.

Brass, A. E., and Jaeggin, K. W. (1967), *A Study of the Performance of Buildings: Technical Paper No. 247,* Ottawa, Ontario, Canada, Division of Building Research, National Research Council.

Brauer, R. (1985), *Facilities Planning,* New York, ANACOM.

Brill, M., Margulis, S., and Konar, E. (1984, 1985), *Using Office Design to Increase Productivity,* Vols. I and II, Buffalo, N.Y., Workplace Design and Productivity, Inc.

Bromilow, F. J. (1992), *Building Property Asset Management Information Guidelines,* Highett, Victoria, Australia, National Committee on Rationalised Building.

Bromilow, F. J. (1994), *Building Life Cycle Costs: A National System for Recording Performance Data* (revised edition), Highett, Victoria, Australia, National Committee on Rationalised Building.

Bruhns, H. R., and Isaacs, N. P. (1991) "The quality assessment of office buildings," in *Proceedings of the European Symposium on Management, Quality and Economics in Housing and Other Building Sectors: State of the Art,* ed. by A. Bezelga and P. S. Brandon, Portugal, Technical University of Lisbon, pp. 63–68.

Bruhns, H. R., and Isaacs, N. P. (1992), "The role of quality assessment in facilities management," in *Facilities Management: Research Directions: Proceedings of 2nd International Symposium on Facilities Management,* ed. by P. Barrett, London, Association of Facilities Managers, pp. 105–115.

Burt, Hill, Kosar, and Rittleman Associates/Min Kantrowitz Associates (1987), *Commercial Building Design: Integrating Climate, Comfort, and Cost,* New York, Van Nostrand Reinhold.

Bycroft, P., Thompson, V., and Batman, G. (1987), *Post Occupancy Evaluation in an Australian Context,* Canberra, Department of Housing and Construction.

Campbell, D. T., and Stanley, J. C. (1963), *Experimental and Quasi-Experimental Designs for Research,* Chicago, Rand McNally.

Canter, D., and Thorne, R. (1972), "Attitudes to housing: A cross-cultural comparison," in *Environment and Behaviour,* 4(1)3–32.

Canter, D. (1977), *The Psychology of Place,* United Kingdom, Architectural Press.

Charlesworth, P. S. (1988), "Air exchange rates and airtightness measurements: An applications guide," in *AIVC Document,* AIC-AG-2-88, Warwick, U.K., Air Infiltration and Ventilation Centre.

Chartered Institute of Building Services (CIBS) (1977) CIBS Energy Code: Part 1 (1977); Part 2 (1981); Part 3 (1979); Part 4 (1982). London, Chartered Institution of Building Services Engineers.

Chartered Institute of Building Services (CIBS) (1977) Design Data. (1986), CIBSE Guide, Vol. A., London: The Chartered Instituion of Building Services Engineers.

Construction Industry Development Agency (CIDA) (1993), *Best Practice in Building and Construction,* Sydney, Australia, Construction Industry Development Agency.

Cotts, D. G., and Lee, M. (1992), *The Facility Management Handbook,* New York, ANACOM, a division of American Management Association.

Crisp, V., Duffy, F., and Laing, A. (1993), *The Responsible Workplace: The redesign of work and offices,* London, Butterworth Architecture, chap. 2.

Crosby, P. B. (1980), *Quality is Free: The Art of Making Quality Certain,* New York, Mentor/Penguin Books.

Cuff, D. (1991), *Architecture: The Story of Practice,* Cambridge, Mass., MIT Press.

Cuttle, C. (1980), *Lighting for Good Visual Conditions in Workplaces,* Wellington, New Zealand, Accident Compensation Commission.

Daish, J., Gray, J., and Kernohan, D. (1986), "A touring interview method of building evaluation: The place of evaluation in building rehabilitation," in *Special Technical Publication 901,* Philadelphia, American Society for Testing and Materials, pp. 46–68.

Daish, J., Gray, J., Kernohan, D., and Salmond, A. (April 1982), "Post-occupancy evaluation in New Zealand," *Design Studies,* 3(2)77–83.

Daish, J., Gray, J., and Kernohan, D. (1988), "Post occupancy evaluation," *Architecture New Zealand,* July/August, pp. 20–21.

Davies, C. (1983), *Underused and Surplus Property in the National Health Service: Report of the Enquiry,* London, Department of Health and Social Security.

Davis, G., et al. (1993), *Serviceability of Buildings: Serviceability Tools,* Vol 1: *Methods for Setting Occupant Requirements and Rating Buildings*; Vol. 2: *Scales for Setting Occupant Requirements and Rating Buildings*; Vol. 3: *Generic Requirement Packages* (in progress); Vol. 4: *Requirement Scales for Office Buildings* (excerpt from Vol. 2); Vol. 5: *Rating Scales for Office Buildings* (excerpt from Vol. 2), Ottawa, Canada, The International Centre for Facilities.

Davis, G. (ed) (1986), *Building Performance: Function, Preservation and Rehabilitation,* STP 901, Philadelphia, ASTM.

Davis, G., Gray, J., and Sinclair, D. (1990) *Buildings that Work: How to Get Places that Meet Your Needs,* Ottawa, International Centre for Facilities for Public Works Canada.

Davis. G., Gray, J., and Sinclair, D. (1991), *Occupants' Requirements and the Serviceability of Office Facilities,* Ottawa, International Centre for Facilities for Public Works Canada.

Davis, G., Schley, M., and Meyer, W. (1992), "How to get the building you need," *ASTM Standardization News,* November 1992, pp. 42–47.

Davis, G., and Ventre, F. (eds.) (1990), *Performance of Buildings and Serviceability of Facilities,* STP 1029, Philadelphia, American Society for Testing and Materials.

DEGW (1986), *Eleven Contemporary Office Buildings*, London, DEGW.

Department of Housing and Construction, Australia (DHC) (1986), *Post-occupancy Evaluation: Field Manual* (draft).

Department of Housing and Construction, Australia (DHC) (1986), *Post-occupancy Evaluation: Explanatory Manual* (draft).

Design Data. (1986), CIBSE Guide, Vol. A., London: The Chartered Instituion of Building Services Engineers.

Dillon, R., and Vischer, J. (November 1987), *Derivation of the Tenant Survey Assessment Method: Office Building Occupant Survey Data Analysis*, Canada, Public Works Canada.

Donn, M., Isaacs, N., and Bruhns, H. "A National Energy Programme for Schools," *Third International Congress on Building Energy Management*, Vol. III, A. Faist, E. Fernandes, and R. Sagelsdorff, eds. École Polytechnique Fédérale de Lausanne, October 1987, pp. 348–355.

Dorman, G. (1981), *Middle Grades Assessment Program: User Manual*, Chapel Hill, N.C., Center for Early Adolescence, University of North Carolina.

Duffy, F., Cave, C., and Worthington, J. (1976), *Planning Office Space*, London, Architectural Press.

Duffy, F., Eley, P., Giffone, L., and Worthington, J. (1983), *ORBIT: Information Technology and Office Design*, London, DEGW.

Duffy, F., and Chandler. (1984), *ORBIT Summary Report*, London, DEGW/EOSYS.

Duffy, F. (1989), "Building appraisal and office design," *Architecture New Zealand*, September/October, pp. 106-107.

Duffy, F., and Henney, A. (1989), *The Changing City*, London, Bulstrode Press.

Duffy, F. (1992), *The Changing Workplace*, London, Phaidon.

Duffy, F. (July 1993), *Inaugural Address at the Royal Institute of British Architects*, London, text published in Building Design.

Duffy, F., Laing, A., and Crisp, V. (1993), *The Responsible Workplace*, Oxford, Butterworth Architecture.

Duffy, F., and Tanis, J. (1993), "A vision of the new workplace," *Site Selection*, April, pp. 427–432.

Energy Publications (1982/86), *Energy Managers Workbook*, Vol. 1 (1982) and Vol. 2 (1986), Cambridge, England, Energy Publications.

Engineering Interface Limited (1988), *Healthy Building Manual: Systems, Parameters, Problems and Solutions*, Ottawa, Ontario, Engineering Interface Limited for Coordinating Council of Commercial, Institutional and Agricultural Energy Management Task Forces, p. 122.

U.S. Environmental Protection Agency (EPA) (1991), *Building Air Quality: A Guide for Building Owners and Facility Managers*, Washington, D.C., U.S. Government Printing Office.

Fanger, O. P. (1988), "The olf and the decipol," *ASHRAE Journal*, October, pp. 35–38.

Farbstein, J., Archea, J., Kantrowitz, M., Shibley, R., Wineman, J., and Zimring, C. (1986), "Designing and building with rehabilitation in mind," in *Building Performance: Function, Preservation and Rehabilitation*, ed. G. Davis, Philadelphia, American Society for Testing and Materials.

Flanagan, R., Norman, G., Meadows, J., and Robinson, G. (1989), *Life Cycle Costing: Theory and Practice*, Oxford, U.K., Blackwell.

Friedmann, A., Zimring, C., and Zube, E. (1978), *Environmental Design Evaluation*, New York, Plenum Press, pp. 213–222.

Gardner, H. (1991), *The Unschooled Mind: How Children Think and How Schools Should Teach*, New York, Basic Books.

Gold, R. (1973), "Urban violence and contemporary defensive cities" in *Geography and Contemporary Issues*, ed. by M. Albaum, New York, Wiley.

Gray, J., Bruhns, H., and Baird, G. (1990), "The building performance approach to new accommodation," in *Proceedings of Facilities Management International Conference*, Glasgow, Facilities Management International.

Gray, J., and Tippett, H. (June 1992), *Office Space: A Primer for Managers* for the N.Z. Government Office Accommodation Task Force, Wellington, VUW Centre for Building Performance Research.

Gray, J., and Tippett, H. (1993), "Building quality assessment: A prerequisite to economic analysis," in *Building Economics and the Built Environment, CIB International Symposium*, Lisbon, September, Conseil International du Batiment.

General Services Administration (GSA) (1976), *Life Cycle Costing in the Public Building Service*, Washington, D.C., General Services Administration.

Gump, P. V. (1987), "School and classroom environments," in *Handbook of Environmental Psychology*, ed. by I. Altman and D. Stokols, Vol. 1, New York, Wiley.

Habermas, J. (1984), *The Theory of Communicative Action*, trans. by T. McCarthy, Boston, Beacon Press.

Hair, I., Isaacs, N., McDonald, C., and Milne, F. (October 1990), *A Practical Approach to Estate Performance Analysis: The Lanarkshire Experience*, Edinburgh, Scottish Health Management Efficiency Group.

Hamer, J. M. (1988), *Facilities Management Systems*, New York, Van Nostrand Reinhold.

Haviland, D. S. (1978), *Life Cycle Cost Analysis: Using It in Practice*, Washington, D. C., American Institute of Architects.

Hedge, A., and Wilson, S. (1987), *The Office Environment Survey*, London, Building Use Studies.

Hopkinson, R. G., Petherbridge, P., and Longmore, J. (1966). *Daylighting*, London: Heinemann, Chapter 13.

Isaacs, N. P., and Trethowen, H. A. (1985), *A Survey of House Insulation*, research report R46, New Zealand, Building Research Association of New Zealand.

Isaacs, N. (1988), "Energy in buildings: Four rules for better management," *Accountant's Journal (NZ)*, 67(3)36–37.

Isaacs, N. (1991), "Building in energy efficiency," *Terra Nova*, 10:20–22.

Isaacs, N., Donn, M., Davies, K., and Turner, L. (1991), "Energy efficient architecture," *Architecture New Zealand*, May/June, pp. 94–98.

Isaacs N. and Donn M. (1992), "Natural energy public library: Design to reality, in *American Council for Energy Efficient Economy (ACEEE) 1992 Summer Study on Energy Efficiency in Buildings*, Pacific Grove, Calif., Vol 1, pp 1.123–1.132.

Isaacs, N., Bruhns, H., Gray, J., and Tippett, H. (1993), *Building Quality Assessment: Research, Development and Analysis for Office and Retail Buildings*, Wellington, N.Z., Centre for Building Performance Research, Victoria University of Wellington.

International Organization for Standardization (ISO) (1980), *Performance Standards in Building: Contents and Presentation, ISO 6240-1980(E)*, Geneva, Switzerland, ISO Central Secretariat.

International Organization for Standardization (ISO) (1984), *Performance Standards in Building: Principles for Their Preparation and Factors to be Considered, ISO 6241-1984(E)*, Geneva, Switzerland, ISO Central Secretariat.

International Organization for Standardization (ISO) (1991), *ISO Compendium, 4th ed., ISO 9004-2:1991(E)*, Geneva, Switzerland, ISO Central Secretariat, p. 312.

International Organization for Standardization (1994), *ISO 9000 Compendium: International Standards for Quality Management*, 4th ed., Geneva, Switzerland, ISO Central Secretariat.

Joiner, D. A. (1983), "A case for appraisal in architecture," in *Proceedings of the Conference on People and Physical Environment Research*, ed. by Duncan Joiner et al., Ministry of Works and Development, Wellington, New Zealand.

Joiner, D. A., and Ellis, H. P. (1985), "Design quality is negotiable," in *Place and Place-Making: Proceedings of the People and Physical Environment Research Association Conference*, Melbourne, PAPER.

Joiner, D. A., Daish, J., and Thorne, R. (1987), "Getting knowledge into public design," in *Environmental Design Research Association Conference 1987*, Ottawa, EDRA.

Joiner, D. A., and Ellis, H. P. (1989), *Making POE Work in an Organisation in Building Evaluation*, ed. by W. Preiser, New York, Plenum Press, Chap. 22, pp. 299–306.

Kernohan, D., Gray, J., and Daish, J., with Joiner, D. (1992), *User Participation in Building Design and Management*, London, Butterworth-Heinemann.

Kleeman, W. (1985), "Increased productivity through participatory office design," in *Unveiling a Strategic Resource: Proceedings of the Sixth Annual Conference of the International Facilities Management Association*, Houston, IFMA, pp. 82–96.

Leaman, A. (1991–1993), "Data sheets on office occupants comfort, productivity and satisfaction," *Facilities J.*

Leaman, A. (1993), "The importance of response time," *Hong Kong Building Journal*, June.

Leaman, A., and Borden, I. (1993), *The Responsible Workplace: User Expectations*, London, Butterworth Architecture.

Lee, R. (1976), *Building Maintenance Management*, London: Granada Publishing Ltd., Student Edition, pp. ix, 291.

Lipsitz, J. (1977), *Growing Up Forgotten: A Review of Research and Programs Concerning Early Adolescence*, Lexington, Mass., D.C. Health.

Markus, T. A., Whyman, P., Morgan, J., Whitton, D., Maver, T., Canter, D., and Fleming, J. (1972), *Building Performance:* London, Applied Science Publishers.

Marshall, H. E., and Ruegg, R. T. (1980), "Energy conservation in buildings: An economics guidebook for investment decisions," in *NBS Handbook 132*, Washington, D. C., U.S. Department of Commerce, National Bureau of Standards.

Marshall, H. E. (1988), *Techniques for Treating Uncertainty and Risk in the Economic Evaluation of Building Investments*, NIST special publication 757, National Institute of Standards and Technology, U.S. Department of Commerce.

Meridith, J. (1992), *The Management of Operations: a Conceptual Emphasis*, 4th ed., New York, Wiley.

Ministry of Energy, Energy Management Group (1988), *Public Organisation Energy Audit Manual*, Wellington, N.Z., Ministry of Energy.

Moore, G. T., and Zube, E. (1986–90), *Advances in Environment, Behaviour and Design*, Vols. 1 to 3, New York, Plenum Press.

National Committee on Rationalised Building (NCRB) (1991), "Asset management in tough times", in *Proceedings of the NCRB Facilities Management '91 Conference*, ed. by S. N. Tucker, Victoria, Australia, National Committee on Rationalised Building.

National Research Council (NRC) (1967), *Building Check List*, Ottawa, Ontario, Canada, Division of Building Research, National Research Council, NRC no. 9364.

National Public Works Conference (NPWC) (1989), *Life Cycle Costing*, Commonwealth of Australia, NPCW.

Nagda, N. L., Rector, H. E., and Koontz, M. D. (1987), *Guidelines for Monitoring Indoor Air Quality*, New York, Springer-Verlag.

Oxford Regional Health Authority: Regional Architect (ORHA) (1985), *Functional Suitability Assessment: Pilot Study Report* (revised version of April 1984 report), Oxford, U.K., Oxford Regional Health Authority.

Palmer, M. A. (1981), *The Architect's Guide to Facility Programming*, Washington, American Institute of Architects.

Parkin, P. H., Humphreys, H. R., and Cowell, J. R. (1979), *Acoustics, Noise, and Buildings*, 4th ed., London, Faber and Faber.

Passini, R. (1984), "Wayfinding in architecture," in *Environmental Design Series*, Vol. 4, New York, Van Nostrand Reinhold.

Perin, C. (1970), *With Man in Mind*, Cambridge, Mass., MIT Press.

Porteous, W. A. (1994), "Learning from aggregated building failures," in *Proceedings of the CIB W86 Internation Symposium Dealing with Defects in Building*, Varenna, pp 65–74, Conseil International de Batiment.

Porteous, W. A. (1989), A Proposal for the Classification and Minimisation of Building Failures in *XIth International Congress of the International Council for Building Research Studies and Documentation*. Theme II. Volume 1 page 177.

Preiser, W. F. E. (ed.) (1978), *Facility Programming: Methods and Applications*, Stroudsburg, Pa., Dowden, Hutchinson & Ross.

Preiser, W. F. E., Rabinowitz, H. Z., and White, E. T. (1988), *Post-Occupancy Evaluation*, New York, Van Nostrand Reinhold.

Preiser, W. F. E., (ed.) (1989), *Building Evaluation*, New York, Plenum Press.

Preiser, W. F. E., Vischer, J. C., and White, E. T. (eds.) (1991), *Design Intervention: Toward a More Humane Architecture*, New York, Van Nostrand Reinhold.

Preiser, W. F. E., and Postell, J. (1993), "Post-occupancy evaluation feedback: Making the office work," *Office Journal*, 7.

Preiser, W. F. E. (1994), "Built environment evaluation: Conceptual basis, benefits and uses," *Journal of Architectural and Planning Research*, 11(2): 91–107.

Preiser, W. F. E., and Postell, J. (1994), *Improving Office Design Through POE*, Tokyo, Japan Institute of Architecture.

Purcell, T., Metcalfe, J., Thorne, R., and Hall, R. (1972), *Office Environments: Comparison of Users Response to Two Clerical Office Spaces of Different Layout in the One Organisation and Building*, technical report, Sydney, Department of Architecture, University of Sydney.

Purcell, A. T., and Thorne, R. H. (1977), "An alternative method for assessing the psychological effects of noise in the field," *Journal of Sound and Vibration*, 55(4)533–544.

Purcell, T., and Heath, T. (1982) "The two communities: Is there a common focus for designer-researcher collaboration," in *Knowledge for Design: Proceedings of 13th Conference of the Environmental Design Research Association*, ed. by P. Bart, A. Chen, and G. Francescato, College Park, Md., EDRA 3–15.

Public Works Canada (PWC) (1988), *Building Performance Evaluation Series*, a series of over 30 documents on this topic, Ottawa, PWC.

Rabinowitz, H. Z. (1975), *Buildings in Use Study*, Milwaukee, Wisc., University of Wisconsin, School of Architecture and Urban Planning.

Royal Australian Institute (RAIA) *The Building Maintenance Manual* (1983), Practice Note PN82, Sydney: Royal Australian Institute of Architects Practice Division.

Real Estate Norm Netherlands Foundation, (1992), *Real Estate Norm*, Second edition, November 1992, Neiuwegein.

Reed, D., Keller, E., and Shaw, J. (1981), *VUW Urban Simulator: User Manual*, Wellington, N.Z., School of Architecture, Victoria University of Wellington.

Rubin, A. (1987), *Office Design Measurements for Productivity: A Research Overview*, Gaithersburg, Md., National Bureau of Standards.

Runeson, G., and Tippett, H. (1985), *Quality Evaluation of Residential Buildings: A Pilot Study to Develop a Method of Assessing Changes in Housing Quality in Relation to Changes in Public Housing Policy*, research paper 85/1, Wellington, N.Z., National Housing Commission.

Rutter, M. (1979), *Fifteen Thousand Hours: Secondary Schools and Their Effects on Children*, Cambridge, Mass., Harvard University Press.

Sanoff, H. (1984), *Design Games*, Los Altos, Calif., Kauffman.

Sanoff, H. (1994), *School Design*, New York, Van Nostrand Reinhold.

Standards Association of New Zealand (SANZ) (1982), *Energy Conservation in Non-Residential Buildings*, NZS4220:1982, Wellington, N.Z., SANZ.

Standards Association of New Zealand (SANZ) (1984), *Code of Practice for Interior Lighting and Design*, NZS 6703:1984, Wellington, N.Z., SANZ.

Schneekloth, L., and Keable, E. (1991), *Evaluation of Library Facilities: A Tool for Managing Change*, occasional papers, Champaign, Illinois: University of Illinois, Graduate School of Library and Information Science.

Schneekloth, L., and Shibley, R. (1990), "Dialogic practice," in *Coming of Age*, ed. by K. Anthony, J. Choi, B. Orland, and R. Selby, Oklahoma City, Environmental Design Research Association.

Schneekloth, L., and Shibley, R. (1995), *Placemaking: The Art and Practice of Building Community*, New York, Wiley Interscience.

Schodek, D. L. (1973), "Evaluating the performance of buildings," *Industrialisation Forum*, 4(5).

Scott, D. (1984), *The Application of Alternative Economic Evaluation Techniques*, NRB project AD23C, Christchurch, University of Canterbury, Department of Civil Engineering.

Scottish Home and Health Department (SHHD) (1977), *In-Patient Accommodation*, Vol. 1: *Hospital Planning Note Series*, Edinburgh, Her Majesty's Stationery Office.

School of Estate Management (SEM) (1989), *Property Management Performance Monitoring*, Oxford, U.K., Oxford Brooks University.

Shibley, R. (1974), "Towards a military construction model of quality in architectural design," *Journal of Architectural Education*, 26(4).

Shibley, R., and Weaver, D. (1982), *A Monograph on Passive and Low Energy Alternatives in the United States: Passive and Low Energy Alternatives 1*, ed. by A. Bowen, New York, Praeger Press.

Shibley, R. G. (January 1985), "Building evaluation in the mainstream," *Environment and Behaviour*, 17(7):24.

Shibley, R. (1990), "Five building evaluation programs," in *Ameliorer l'Architecture et la vie Quotidienne dans les Batiments Publics*, ed. by M. Conan, Paris, Centre Scientifique et Technique du Batiment.

Shibley, R. (1995), "Commercial building activity," in *Solar Heat Technology*, ed. by R. Larson, Cambridge Mass., MIT Press.

Sims, W. R., and Becker, F. D. (1990), "Matching building performance to organisational needs," in *Performance of Buildings and Serviceability of Facilities*, ed. by G. Davis and F. T. Ventre, Philadelphia, ASTM, STP 1029.

Smith, C. B. (1981), *Energy Management Principles*, New York, Pergamon Press.

Sommer, R. (1974), *Tight Spaces: Hard Architecture and How to Humanize It*, Englewood Cliffs, N.J., Prentice-Hall.

Steele, F. (1973), *Physical Settings and Organisational Developement*, Reading, Mass., Addison-Wesley.

Steele, F. (1981), *The Sense of Place*, Boston, CBI Publishing.

Steele, F. (1986), *Making and Managing High-Quality Workplaces*, New York, Teacher College Press, Columbia University.

Stokols, D., et al. (1988), "Evaluating links between facilities design, employee productivity and organizational effectiveness," *IFMA Journal*, 18.

Tetlow, K. (1994), "Virtually brave new world" *Architectural Record*, September, pp. 88–97.

Thorne, R. (1981/84), "The inappropriateness of user and satisfaction studies for the designer, as demonstrated through problems of noise [and other distractions] in office environments," in *Design Research Interactions: Proceedings of 12th Conference of the Environmental Design Research Association*, ed. by R. A. Findlay, A. E Osterberg, and C. P. Tiernan, Ames, Iowa, EDRA, pp. 326–337; revised, extended version, Sydney, Department of Architecture, University of Sydney.

Thorne, R., and Turnbull, J. A. B. (1991), *Post-Occupancy Evaluation Case Study: Technical Report: A Fine Tuning Device for New Offices and Pre-Design Research Tool for a Redesign of Old Offices Occupied by the One Company*, Sydney, Department of Architecture, University of Sydney.

Thorne, R. (1992), *Another Side to Being a Clever Country: Working and Housing Environment for University Students*, Sydney, Department of Architecture, University of Sydney.

Tippett, H., and Sterios, P. D. (1987a), *Life Cost of Buildings: A Study of New Zealand Government Buildings to Incorporate Life Costing in Project Evaluation*, CRP 87-43, Vols. 1 and 2, Victoria University of Wellington, N.Z., Centre for Building Performance Research.

Tippett, H. and Sterios, P. D. (1987b), *Life Cost of Buildings: A Study of New Zealand Government Buildings to Incorporate Life Costing in Project Evaluation*, Vol. 3, *Appendices and Sample Cases*, Victoria University of Wellington, N.Z., Centre for Building Performance Research.

Turner, D. P. (ed.) (1969), *Windows and Environment,* Sec. 12, London, Pilkington Brothers.

Twitchell, A. A. (1966), "An appraisal method for measuring the quality of housing," in *Urban Housing,* ed. by L. C. Wheaton, New York, Free Press, pp. 394–402.

Vischer, J. C. (1989), *Environmental Quality in Buildings,* New York, Van Nostrand Reinhold.

Wade, C., Baird, G., and Donn, M. (1987), *Wind Tunnel User Manual,* School of Architecture, Victoria University of Wellington, New Zealand.

Wade, C., Baird, G., and Donn., M. (1987), *A Guide to carrying out Wellington City Council pre-design wind tunnel tests at the Victoria University School of Architecture.* School of Architecture, Victoria University of Wellington, New Zealand.

Watson, C. G. (1985), "Participating in placemaking: Design development meetings for Hokio," presented to the *People and Physical Environment Research (PAPER) Association Conference,* Melbourne.

Weidemann, S., and Anderson, J. R. (1985), "A conceptual framework for residential satisfaction," in *Home Environments,* ed. by I. Altman, and C. M. Werner, New York, Plenum Press, pp. 153–182.

Whiddon Associates, Inc., WI/Ostgren Associates, Inc. (1989), *Office Productivity and Workstation Environment Control Research Planning Workshop,* October 11–12, 1988. Palo Alto, Calif., Electric Power Research Institute.

Whitelegg, J. (1993), *Transport for a Sustainable Future: The Case for Europe,* chapters on time pollution and the cost of transport, London, Belhaven Press.

Wineman, J. D. (ed.) (1986), *Behavioral Issues in Office Design,* New York, Van Nostrand Reinhold.

Wyon, D. P. (1987), "Buildings fit for people to live and work in," in *Det Sunda Huset,* ed. by N. Dawidowicz, T. Lindwall, and J. Sundell, Stockholm, BFR, pp. 195–201.

Yuill, D. (1985), "Understanding electricity costs," in *Energy Manager's Workbook,* Vol. 2, Sec. 4, Newmarket, U.K., Energy Publications, pp. 27–36.

Zeisel, J. (1984), *Inquiry by Design: Tools for Environmental-Behaviour Research,* Cambridge, U.K., Cambridge University Press.

Zeisel, J. (1989), *Towards a POE Paradigm in Building Evaluation,* ed. by W. Preiser, New York, Plenum Press, pp. 167–180.

Zimring, C., Wineman, J., and Kantrowitz, M. (1986), "P/A POE: Energy past and future," *Progressive Architecture,* April, pp. 114–123.

Index